SPIRIT DIVE

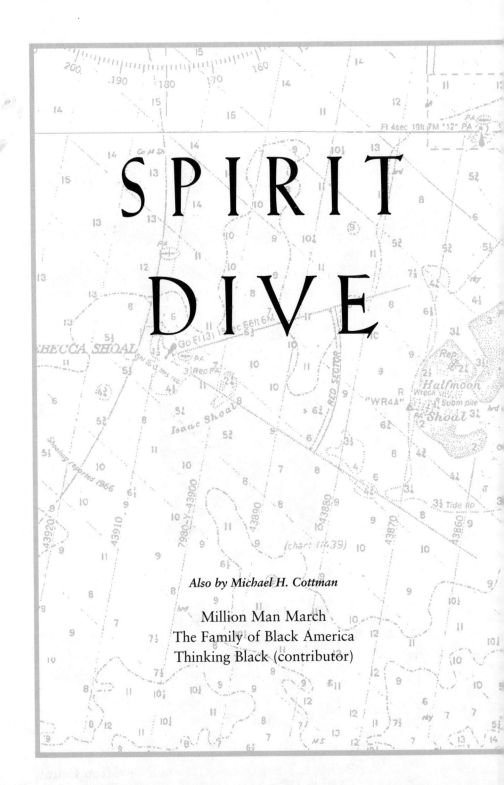

SPIRIT

DIVE

Also by Michael H. Cottman

Million Man March
The Family of Black America
Thinking Black (contributor)

AN AFRICAN-AMERICAN'S
JOURNEY TO UNCOVER
A SUNKEN SLAVE SHIP'S PAST

MICHAEL H. COTTMAN

Previously published as

THE WRECK OF THE HENRIETTA MARIE

THREE RIVERS PRESS

NEW YORK

Published by Three Rivers Press, 201 East 50th Street, New York, New York 10022. Member of the Crown Publishing Group.

Random House, Inc. New York, Toronto, London, Sydney, Auckland

www.randomhouse.com

THREE RIVERS PRESS is a registered trademark of Random House, Inc.

Previously published as *The Wreck of the Henrietta Marie* in hardcover by Harmony Books in 1999.

Printed in the United States of America

Design by Lenny Henderson

Library of Congress Cataloging-in-Publication Data

Cottman, Michael H.

Spirit Dive: an African-American's journey to uncover a sunken slave ship's past / by Michael H. Cottman

Includes index.

1. Key West Region (Fla.)—Antiquities. 2. Henrietta Marie (Ship). 3. Excavations (Archaeology)—Florida—Key West Region. 4. Underwater archaeology—Florida— Key West Region. 5. Afro-Americans—Florida—Key West Region—Antiquities. 6. Slave-trade—History. 7. Cottman, Michael H.—Journeys. I. Title.

F319.K4C68   1999

975.9'41—dc21   98-29574

ISBN 0-609-80552-5

10 9 8 7 6 5 4 3 2 1

First Paperback Edition

For my lovely wife, Mireille, my wonderful daughter, Ariane, my mother, Roberta, and my father, Howard, who have all been so patient and supportive through my four-year journey above and beneath the sea. Thank you for your love and constant reminders that I was on the right course.

For the African ancestors I will never know, who inspired me to travel the West Coast of Africa, to explore the underwater world on the continent of my forefathers, and to tell the stories of proud people, stories they could not tell themselves.

WITH SINCERE THANKS

My sincere thanks to the Mel Fisher Maritime Heritage Society and, in particular, Madeleine Burnside, executive director; David Moore; Corey Malcolm; Angus Konstram; Nigel Tattersfield; and Moe Molinar for offering the research and insight about the *Henrietta Marie* that helped make this book possible.

ACKNOWLEDGMENTS

To my darling daughter, Ariane: I wrote this book in my office thinking about you, watching you grow up, keeping an eye on you as you climbed steps for the first time; looking forward to seeing you run into the room, your bare feet slapping the hardwood floor; listening to you saying "Da-Da" and pointing to me. Read about your cultural history in these pages and know that I will always love you and be here for you, just as my parents have always been there for me.

To my lovely wife, Mireille: For the past four years you listened to every detail about the *Henrietta Marie,* from bow to stern, day after day, without so much as a frown, and thank you for your love and support, your insight, and your feedback. Thanks for proofing pages late at night in between changing diapers, wiping up spills, reviewing spreadsheets, and feeding the baby. Thank you for talking through every idea from early morning until late in the evening for four long years, no matter how time-consuming or how mundane; thank you for giving me your periodic pep talks to keep me focused when things turned chaotic; and most important, thank you for giving us our little jewel: Ariane Michaela Cottman.

To my mother, Roberta, and my father, Howard: Thank you for raising me with a purpose, a passion for history and African-American culture, and reminding me of my obligation to tell the stories of our rich past; thank you for all of your loving support through this four-year journey, through its peaks and valleys; thank you for being there to answer the phone each time I called from Africa or London or Key West or the West Indies to say I'd stumbled across a discovery or was feeling the stress to produce. Thank you for being there on the other end of the phone—and throughout my life.

To my aunts, Jean and Pat Favors, and my uncle, Eddie: Thank you all for your steadfast support and love. Jean, thank you for helping me sort through the tough times, for listening, providing comfort like a warm hug, and reminding me that the role of family is to offer a solid foundation during times of need; thank you for never allowing me to think the worst, but always encouraging me to press forward, knowing there would be better days ahead. You have helped shape my life personally and professionally and for that, I am eternally grateful. I love you dearly. You are a wise woman—even for a Redskins fan.

To Marie Brown, my literary agent, friend, confidant, and touchstone: Someone once asked me how they should select a literary agent, and my answer was simple: It depends on what you're looking for in an agent. If you are looking for someone to ink the deal, I said, go to the Yellow Pages. But if you're looking for someone with depth and intellect, someone who cares about the written word as well as stories about African-American people, someone who will take calls no matter what time of the night, someone who can help shape thoughts and guide a writer through the long process of crafting a wise and poignant product, offering solid advice at all times, that person is Marie Brown. I quickly added that she's spoken for and sent him back to the phone book. Thank you, Marie. I couldn't have written—or crafted—this book without you.

To my friends at Crown Publishers: Shaye Areheart, my editor and partner in publishing: You came into this project in the midst of chaos, when we were hanging in publishing limbo and unsure about our options. You embraced this story of the *Henrietta Marie* from the time you got involved, with compassion, thoughtfulness, sensitivity, and a connection to the purpose of this work. You understood why this book is important for people black and white, and you offered an extraordinary and wonderful editing touch—as well as insight—that enhanced the story of a slave ship that many never knew existed. In you I have found not only a new editor but also a new friend.

Dina Siciliano, associate editor: Thanks, Dina, for being patient with my constant—and sometimes rambling—calls, constant additions and revisions, faxes and Fed-Ex packages, and my long scribblings in the margins. Thanks for being responsive to my weekly questions about the publishing process. You were a delight to work with and one of the most thoughtful, organized—and diplomatic—people I know. There's a place for you in public service.

Lenny Henderson: Thanks for your assistance, your creativity, and your hard work in helping to illustrate the story of the *Henrietta Marie* in the most compelling way possible, and thanks for understanding the importance of it all.

To Larry Bivins, Neil Foote, Clem Richardson, Steven Bacon, Hank Jennings, and Eugene Niles: Thank you for being the brothers I never had; you are true friends for life.

To Yolanda Woodlee: Thank you for being a good friend for many years (we won't say how many!), and now my deskmate at the *Washington Post,* my confidant and political-beat buddy. Thanks for helping me settle in at the

Post and in D.C., and thanks so much for facilitating the paper-shredding mission—I'm truly glad you're on my side!

To Jeanne Fox-Alston: Thanks for all of your long-term support, generosity, and friendship, and for being a true sister in spirit.

To Dr. Jose Jones: Thanks for your time, patience, friendship, and sense of humor, and for spending late evenings sharing the stories of our history. Most important, thank you for your profound contribution to this book; thanks for your tips on scuba diving and for forming the National Association of Black Scuba Divers; I remain a proud member of the organization because of your vision of bringing African-American divers together above and beneath the sea.

To Josanne Lopez: Thank you for so much: your tireless interviews for the book, your compassion, wisdom, and advice; helping me organize thoughts and words. Thank you for four years of patience, caring, and understanding; thank you for your photography and thoughtful words of inspiration at all the right times.

To Adrienne Ingrum: Thank you so much for having the vision and foresight to recognize that the story of the *Henrietta Marie* needed to be told and this book needed to be written. Thanks so much for starting this process five years ago and turning a two-hour conversation on a snowy evening into a hardcover reality.

To Pamela Newkirk: Thank you for simply listening to my stories when you were trying to get your two lovely daughters off to school, grading papers, or putting finishing touches on your own manuscript. Thanks for offering advice and wisdom, thank you for your wonderful sense of humor, and thanks for caring about me through this entire process.

To Sandra Gunner: Thank you for several years' worth of outstanding advice and feedback. Thanks for all of your thoughtful suggestions, caring conversations, and your true friendship.

Quincy and Margaret Troupe: In the spirit of friendship, you opened to me your lovely home with a view of the Pacific at a time when I needed to get away and write. Through your generous hospitality and your help in talking me through the crafting of my words and my thoughts, I was able to write a substantial portion of the book. When I read the words I wrote in California, I will always think of you.

To Lee May: Thank you for years of guidance, friendship, and wise advice that I have never forgotten, words that I keep with me to this day as I go about writing and reporting. Thank you for all of your support and for talking me through tough times as well as good times. You are a true brother, and I appreciate all of your support.

To Jackie Jones: Thanks for your warmth, insight, and advice—day and night; thanks for listening and bearing with my many moods and chaotic times during the writing of the book. Thanks for being there for me at *Newsday,* and before, thanks for your editing on the manuscript, and my freelance stories and for talking me through story ideas over the years. You have meant so much to me; you are a very giving person with so much talent to share; thanks for sharing some of that with me.

To Lisa Baird: We've come a long way since *Neighbors NW,* where you edited my stories—the ones under steel-gray skies; you know what I mean. Your talent for knowing what I'm trying to say and finding the perfect way to help say it has always amazed me. Your assistance in editing this manuscript made all the difference; thank you for taking time from your beautiful daughters—and my goddaughter—to travel to the suburbs to edit my words, at least once, as I recall, until 1 A.M.; thank you for your inspiration throughout this entire process, and most important, thanks for your brain power and crazy sense of humor.

To Manie Barron: Thank you for being an understanding sounding board, someone I could turn to for the "real deal," thanks for making sense out of a fast-moving and unpredictable business; thanks for helping me through a process that I knew little about, learning the publishing world from the inside out. And mostly, thanks for your continued support. And yes, I still owe you a drink!

To Yanick Rice and Ingrid Sturgis: Thanks so much for bringing me aboard the BET Weekend. My experience has been wonderful and I look forward to working with you both in the future; you really provided me with a wonderful opportunity while working on the book.

To Dr. Alison LaVigne: Thanks for being a wonderful friend; your stories about your family and of life growing up in D.C. were heartwarming tales and came at the right time—on many days when I needed a break after hours at the computer screen. Your stories were a constant reminder that there was life outside the windows of my home office, where paperwork was piled high and my work, at times, seemed overwhelming. Your humor was— and will always be—a joy. Thanks for a series of wonderful and much needed distractions—and for simply being there to listen.

Hank Jennings: My brother, dive buddy, Million Man March partner, and soul mate of the *Henrietta Marie.* This has been an extraordinary journey and you've been with me every step of the way, above and beneath the sea. Thanks for all of your ideas and insights. I based the book's opening on your idea and on discussions we've had so many times in Key West, on dive boats, and at the site of the *Henrietta Marie.* Because of our shared underwater experiences, you are as much a part of this story as the *Henrietta Marie* itself.

Harold Cook: Thank you for sharing your depth of knowledge about the history and the people of Africa; thank you for your wonderful sense of humor, your rich stories, and your tips on bartering; and, mostly, thank you for the ability to make me feel like family.

Special thanks and throughts: To Donna Britt: Thank you for your constant encouragement to "go deep" with the manuscript, your true friendship, your wonderful contribution to these pages, and your ability to make me think about issues in ways I might have overlooked. Most of all, thank you for steering me to all that is significant. Indeed, your work is done—good luck in the next galaxy!

To David Moore: Thank you for your intelligent and methodical pursuit of the origin of the *Henrietta Marie*. Without your gift of detective work and passion for uncovering history, there would be no *Henrietta Marie*, no story to tell, no book. You are a rare individual who understands, through this sunken slave ship, the complexities of the past and the challenges of the future. I could not have completed this project without your assistance, research, guidance, and perspective. Thanks for all of your time, talent, proofreading, and countless unselfish efforts.

To Moe Molinar: Thank you for finding the shackles from the *Henrietta Marie* on the ocean floor. It was you who truly brought the *Henrietta Marie* to the forefront of the archaeology community and to the world. Without your phenomenal discovery, this slave ship would still be buried beneath sand and clay, quite possibly for another three hundred years. Your contribution was invaluable and, for this, there are so many—historians, educators, students, children, divers, archaeologists, writers, and artists—who, like me, will be forever grateful.

My debt of gratitude for your profound contributions: John Hope Franklin, Cornel West, Randall Robinson, and Michael Eric Dyson.

Thank you to my brothers and sisters of the National Association of Black Scuba Divers: Jose Jones, president; Oswald Sykes, Hank Jennings, Eugene Niles, Jim Morgan, Dr. Shelia Walker, Ric Powell, Howard Moss, Eugene Tinnie, Lowaunz Koger, Paula Jones, Terry Sneed, Marion Sykes, Roslyn Woolfolk, Gary Sullivan, Andrew Rhoden, Pete Taylor, Sonny (007) Hill, and David Harrison.

To my friends in Key West: The Mel Fisher Maritime Heritage Society, Dr. Madeleine Burnside, executive director; Corey Malcolm, director of archaeology; Angus Konstram, curator; Dylan Kibler, photographer; Pat Klein, photographer; Sub Tropics Dive Shop; Dr. Robin Lockwood; Ken Schultz; John Brandon; and Cristian Swanson

To my friends and colleagues who offered a listening ear: Audrey Edwards, Adrienne Ingrum, Felicia Lee, Clem Richardson, Larry Bivins, Neil Foote, Steve Bacon, Cheryl Bacon, Wilbert Bacon, Octavia Bacon, Yolanda Woodlee, Jennifer Preston, Jan and Doug Heppe, Jeanne Fox-Alston, Kevin Merida, Jay and Christine Harris, Renee and Alison LaVigne, Lamar and Diane Gatewood, Geri and Michael Tucker, Bill and Corinne Douglas, Sandra Gunner, Elizabeth Johnson, Bob Slade, Bob Pickett, Ann Tripp, Charles Ethridge, Fatiyn Muhammad, Kate Phillips, Roseann Fochi, Richie Esposito, Miriam Pawel, Mike Muskal, Jane Fox, Rich Galant, Patrick Nana-Adjei, Rick Firstman, George Curry, Flo Purnell, Rev. Calvin Butts, Gaynelle Henderson, Jake Henderson, Harold Cook, Rev. Curtis Jones, Rev. Enoch Perry, Michael Days, Angela Dobson, Howard Manly, David Dinkins, Lonnie Soury, Marsha McGee, Keith Harriston, Ed Blake, Larry Alston, Michael Days, Angela Dodson, Paul Brock, Morris Thompson, and Deborah Heard.

To my friends in Africa and supporters of Africa: Ibrahima Top, guide, historian, and friend; Joseph Ndiaye, curator, the Slave House, Goree Island; Henderson Travel; Theo Komaclo, Air Afrique; David Lazik, Air Afrique; Hadair El-Ali, Oceanarium Dive Center; Ambassador Mamadou Monsour Seck; Air Afrique.

To my friends in Jamaica: National Library of Jamaica, Mr. Patrick Bennett, Jamaica Heritage Trust, Gary Casson, Buccaneer Scuba Club, the Department of Archives, Spanish Town, Christine Mair, Air Jamaica, The Jamaica Tourist Board, Lloyd and Joyce Mair, Judith Clarke.

To my friends in Barbados: Wayne and Wendy Yearwood, the Barbados Museum and Historical Society Library, the Barbados Department of Archives, the National Library Service, Underwater Barbados.

To my friends in London: Guildhall Library; National Maritime Museum; Angus Konstram; Tower of London; The Ambrozniak's, Chittingly, England; Nigel Tattersfield.

To the *Henrietta Marie* scholars and consultants: Russell Adams, Ph.D, chairman, Department of Afro-American Studies, Howard University; Linda Heywood, Ph.D., associate professor of history, Howard University; John Thornton, Ph.D., associate professor of history, Millersville University; James Rawley, Ph.D., University of Nebraska.

A special message: To the Henderson family, Gaynelle, Jake, Shirley, Freddye, and Carole: Thank you for embracing me and making me truly feel like a member of your wonderful and loving family. You have offered me numerous opportunities to travel to Africa to visit the people of the villages of the Gambia; to climb the peaks and paddle the lakes of Burkina Faso; to camel caravan over the sands of Timbuktu; to see the babies of Jenne; and to cruise the rivers of Senegal and wipe away tears inside the Slave House of Goree Island. For those who do not know, the Henderson family—Freddye and Jake Sr., two visionary pioneers—started Henderson Travel in 1955 and became the first black-owned travel agency in the country and the first travel agency to take black groups to Africa. That history and passion for Africa was passed along to their daughter, Gaynelle, my big sister, who is not only one of the brightest people I have met but also someone who shares a rare sense of adventure and passion for African-American history, one who relishes visiting those unexplored places most people only read about. Thank you, Gaynelle, for adopting me and thanks to your entire family for making my spiritual journey and my personal pilgrimage to Africa an experience I will never forget.

And, of course, to Howard and Evelyn House.

CONTENTS

PROLOGUE

On most snowy evenings in Detroit, after I had finished my homework, I would sit on the hardwood floor in the living room of my family's two-story home watching adventure programs on our grainy black-and-white Zenith television.

Without leaving the room, I would visit worlds I could hardly fathom, a young, inner-city kid who dreamed of taking voyages on ships and journeys into the unexplored worlds of swashbucklers and heroes on horseback.

After dinner, I would watch one of my favorite programs, *Sea Hunt,* an underwater adventure series, perhaps the first underwater program of its kind.

I was a ten-year-old ocean enthusiast, intrigued with underwater action. I watched anxiously while Lloyd Bridges squeezed into his thick black rubber wet suit, strapped on a double set of oxygen tanks, and plunged into an ocean filled with more mystery than marine life.

I would sit so close to the television that my mother would often remind me to move back and sit on the couch. I still remember feeling that the closer I was to the TV set, the greater my chances of experiencing an underwater sensation.

It was an adventure that was far removed from reality for a young black boy from Detroit who grew up in a predominantly black middle-class community a block or two from a series of housing projects. I was raised in a place where dreams of exploring the ocean were sometimes muddied by the harsh realities of street life in urban America.

Little black boys in Detroit played basketball, baseball, and football in the park near home and tried hard to stay out of trouble. I can't recall too many black youngsters rushing to the public pool for a swim. I do remember black people getting hurt, sometimes by the police; some getting arrested for crimes they had committed and others led away in handcuffs just for standing on the corner or drinking in public.

Scuba diving was the last thing on the minds of young black boys in Detroit. Black boys played hard and talked of driving fast cars, throwing touchdowns in the NFL and shooting baskets at the buzzer in the NBA. But scuba diving rarely came up in conversation; my buddies would snicker at the mention of underwater exploration.

There was something appealing about a man swimming among sea animals and exploring a portion of the world that was remote and unpredictable.

And of course, even at ten years of age, I was keenly aware that this particular underwater explorer was white.

I remember calling my mother into the living room on those weeknights around eight o'clock, pointing at the television screen, and asking her to sit with me and watch men swim with dolphins.

My mother had already taught me to swim from the time I was very young. On "Family Night," she would take my hand and lead me to the shallow end of the pool at the YWCA, not far from our home. With my feet locked in place at the edge of the pool, I would wait for my mother to make her flawless platform dives into the water and swim over to me. She would gently guide me through the pool and send me off to slap water until I reached the deep end, then dog-paddle back to the safety of her arms.

By the time I was seven, I was swimming the length of the YWCA pool—underwater.

"Mom," I announced proudly one evening, "one day I'm going to swim underwater in the ocean."

My mother nodded warmly, giving me plenty of encouragement. As she rubbed my head, she told me that I could do anything I set my mind to, although I have always wondered if she didn't think I had an overactive imagination.

Thirty years ago, I could not have known that I would be a scuba diver, that I would turn my passions for the sea, adventure, and African-American history into a journey to uncover a slave ship's past.

After leaving home years ago and facing the challenges of raising my wonderful two-year-old daughter today, I can now understand why my parents prepared me to pursue a purpose in life, to follow a calling, to follow my heart.

I now understand that my parents were not only making it possible for me to chase my dreams but they were also teaching me to recognize my purpose when it presented itself.

Everyone needs a passion in life. We all need that special endeavor that makes us feel whole, something that drives us day in and day out—an intense fire inside that cannot be extinguished—a passion some may not understand, yet a passion that we cannot imagine living without.

For me, *Sea Hunt* was an escape of sorts. For one hour, I wrapped myself in a watery fantasy, leaving behind the sirens in the streets, the occasional fights after school, the pressure from friends to smoke cigarettes, and my father's constant reminders to study hard and make something of myself.

There was something tranquil about watching a man float in the depths of the ocean, and I was mesmerized, perhaps because it was such a foreign idea to a black youngster growing up in the middle of the country, far from the Atlantic and the Pacific Oceans.

Perhaps part of the attraction of *Sea Hunt* was what the ocean came to symbolize for me then, and still represents for me today—a personal retreat from the concrete and chaos.

On warm Sundays after church, my dad would drive my mom and me to the mouth of Lake Huron or Lake Michigan, several hours away. Those beautiful lakes had a calming effect on my mind as well as my soul. It was the one drive I looked forward to on Sundays, getting away from the city and staring out over a vast blue lake with no end in sight. I'd sit on the shore, wondering what it would be like to swim underwater, and then I'd conjure up a menagerie of marine animals that I would encounter along the way.

I knew even then, thirty years ago, that I would somehow find a way to swim deep beneath the ocean, that black people would explore the sea, and that I would be among them.

I've always been a daydreamer. During class in elementary school, I would stare at the world map hanging from the wall and tell my classmates which remote parts of the world I planned to visit. I found Africa to be the most alluring and complex, this enormous continent with so many countries, languages, and dialects; it was so far away, and yet a place where everyone looked like me.

The depiction of Africa on television in the 1960s was limited, one-sided, and racist. Tarzan, the smart white man, swung from vine to vine, calling the jungle's obedient wildlife to his aid. On the other hand, Africans, who had lived in this land for centuries, were portrayed as fearing these same animals and depending on Tarzan for help, safety, and, sometimes, even directions.

Shirtless African men were hauling huge trunks on their backs for British hunters, known as bwana—Swahili for "master" or "boss"—and African men were getting the whip for walking too slowly or for being too scared to enter an area that was considered sacred.

It was Hollywood at its worst. Africans were presented as demoralized and humiliated tribesmen who were often physically abused. Tarzan, a white hero in a loincloth, whose vocabulary consisted of "Me Tarzan, you Jane," for reasons that are still unclear—after all, why wouldn't he be fluent in one of the many African dialects—was the savior of Africans who were oppressed by British hunters looking for big game and African treasure.

It was Africa from a white perspective and, unfortunately, the only perspective I knew until my mother and father found books that introduced me to the rich history and culture of Africa and the wonders of a faraway continent where my ancestors were born.

I began to read about Africa in encyclopedias and learned about its many countries with separate languages and dialects. As a boy, I pledged not only to experience the mysteries of the sea but to gaze upon the beauty of Africa's coastal countries as well as the interior lands with their wide and mighty rivers.

I'd think about Africa's rivers while walking along the Detroit River, a working waterway where freighters from Canada would glide past the city skyline at night. I'd think about the ocean's secrets each time my parents took me through one of the aquariums we visited in every city within driving distance.

My parents and I would look through tempered glass and study the marine life—mammals and fish. We'd learn about their habits and the oceans where they could be found.

As a man, I am still dreaming, but I dream as I explore the sea and the land of my ancestors. I have combined my passions for history and adventure and along the way I have gained a greater understanding of myself.

Whether connected with pain or pleasure, it seems that African-American people have a natural association with water: the oceans we were forced to cross; the harbors where African women were sent to dive for pearls at dangerous depths; and the rivers and lakes where we fished, swam, bathed, and were baptized.

As I write this passage, I'm forty-two and my beautiful two-year-old daughter, Ariane, is walking around the neighborhood with her mother.

What a tremendous responsibility parenthood is: This little person expects so much of me—to keep her warm in the winter, to cuddle her after a bad dream, to feed her when she's hungry, to protect her from any number of dangers, to heal her when she's sick, to love her unconditionally—forever.

Her eyes brighten even my darkest days and her smile reminds me that family always comes before anything else.

A friend of mine believes that children somehow select their parents as they search for the perfect home. If this is true, I thank my daughter for choosing us. I can't imagine life without her.

I'm looking forward to a lifetime of fathering, to family vacations, and, perhaps, scuba diving someday with my daughter.

But for the moment, I am content to drive to the lake near our house where the water is still and I can sit in the sun and tell my daughter about her family—her aunts, uncles, cousins, and grandparents—and about her African ancestors who lived along the marshy banks of rivers that I have seen and rivers that I will never find.

   Someday I will tell her about the importance of the ocean in our lives and walk along the beaches where she can listen to the sounds of the sea. Somehow I know it will be a fine place for fathers and daughters to talk; a place where I can release my child to all life has to offer and she can dream, too.

TIME LINE

Significant Dates During the
Henrietta Marie's Period of Operation

5 May 1696	*St. John of Dunkirk* proceeded against and condemned by Admiralty as prize and sold a few weeks later. This vessel fits the profile of the *Henrietta Marie,* ie., 120 tons burden and eight guns.
September 1697	Signing of Treaty of Ryswick, effectively ending King William's War.
18 October 1697	Will of John Scorch written, indicating an upcoming voyage from London.
10 November 1697	Will of Edward Humble written and signed at Gravesend.
10 June 1698	Will of Peter Christopherson dictated nuncupitive during Middle Passage.
17 June 1698	Will of Peter Christopherson indicates his death during Middle Passage.
9 July 1698	Barbados shipping records indicate the *Henrietta Maria,* ". . . foreign built, 9 men, 114 tons, 8 guns . . . ," delivered "250 Negro slaves and 105 Elephants Teeth."
11 July 1698	Nicholas Prideaux writes to superiors in London from Barbados reporting the arrival of "Deacon, an interloper from the Bite with 220 Negroes."
12 July 1698	Log of HMS *Bonaventure:* James Childerness, master, noted "A Ship from Guinnea anchored here [Carlisle Bay, Barbados]."

28 July 1698	List of separate traders in Barbados indicates *Henrietta Maria* under William Deacon delivers 188 slaves to William Shuller, Esq. at £19:1:3 per slave.
23 September 1698	Log of HMS *Speedwell*, William Force, master states ". . . this day sailed for London . . . Capt Deckons . . ." from "Carlile" (Carlisle) Bay, Barbados.
26 December 1698	Will of Peter Christopherson indicates a possible execution of such and subsequent presence of *Henrietta Marie* back in London.
January 1699	Records indicate that London merchant Christopher Astley purchased some ivory from *Henrietta Maria*.
THE HENRIETTA MARIE 1699	Inscription on the ship's watch bell.
15 July 1699	Royal African Company records indicate that Thomas Starke loaded ". . . 282 lbs Great Bugles [beads] . . ." worth £18:15:6 onto the *Henrietta Maria*.
16 August 1699	Royal African Company records indicate that Anthony Tournay loaded ". . . 33 tonns of Iron . . ." worth £449:12:6 onto the *Henrietta Maria*.
18 August 1699	Royal African Company records indicate that Daniel Jamineau loaded for William Deacon, ". . . 1792 lbs Great Bugles 60 Short Gurrahs 3 1/2 cwt Shot Linnen 2 1/2 cwt Broad Germany . . ." worth £192 onto the *Henrietta Maria*. This shipment was signed off by James Barbot.

30 August 1699	Royal African Company records indicate that Thomas Winchcombe loaded ". . . 6 cwt of pewter . . ." worth £34:4:6 onto the *Henrietta Maria*.
1 September 1699	Royal African Company records indicate that Robert Wilson loaded ". . . 1200 Copper Barrs 7 1/2 cwt Pewter 4 Doz felts 70 halfe Cases Spirritts . . ." onto the *Henrietta Maria*.
5 September 1699	Jamaican shipping records indicate that the *Henrietta Maria* held clearance certificate from London on this date.
13 September 1699	Will of John Taylor written indicating an upcoming voyage from London.
c.15 September 1699	Probable sailing date of *Henrietta Marie*.
21–23 September 1699	London's *The Post Man* mentioned "the *Henrietta Maria* of and from London bound for Guinea, is arrived at Cowes [Isle of Wight]," due to contrary weather.
30 September–3 October 1699	*The Flying Post* indicated that all vessels [and undoubtedly the *Henrietta Marie*] had sailed from the Isle of Wight vicinity.
18 May 1700	Log of HMS *Saudados Prize*, John Wheeler, master, states "A Ship Cam in from Gunny . . ." to Port Royal, Jamaica, on this date.
18 May 1700	List of slavers [probably separate traders] in Jamaica indicates the *Henaretta* under Thomas Chamberlaine delivers 190 slaves.
25 June 1700	Jamaican shipping records indicate the *Henrietta Maria* (120 tons, 8 guns, foreign-built, square-

sterned, and under Thomas Chamberlaine) was loaded with 81 hogsheads of sugar, 11 barrels of indigo, 14 bags of cotton, and 21 tons of logwood.

November 1700

The estate of Thomas Chamberlaine of the *Henrietta Maria* settled in London, suggesting a knowledge of the loss of the ship.

SPIRIT DIVE

1

The talking drums echo through the village of stalks and thickets as fireflies sprinkle the darkness shortly before sunrise.

On the swampy banks along the West African coast, where the shoreline is often swollen by heavy rains, young women, in the early-morning sun, wade through a marsh thick with mosquitoes to bathe their babies.

Teenagers with bare feet walk slowly down dirt roads with stacks of firewood on their heads as old women with wrinkled hands sit in the shade weaving mats from large palm leaves.

The men, mostly fishermen with heavy silver bracelets adorning their upper arms, walk across soggy soil to the coast, where they climb into slender wooden canoes to fish the waters of West Africa.

Life was the same in most of the coastal villages throughout West Africa in the early decades of the fifteenth century. There, quiet settlements of African families prospered among the rows of thin bamboo shoots that towered over low thatched-roofed houses. Then, as now, children tossed twigs onto hot stones to hear the crackling of wood.

The villages of West Africa were peaceful, structured societies of tightly knit, stable families who all worked to provide for the village where they lived. This was a hardworking, resourceful civilization, and it remains so today.

There are communities of craftsmen and artists, masters of gold, copper, and bronze, painters and sculptors of detailed hand carvings; educators and thinkers; fishermen and blacksmiths; weavers and potters; priests who perform religious services, including weddings and funerals; dancers and musicians who pluck the soothing strings of the kora; poets who sit on log benches and tell mesmerizing stories; and men who heal the sick with pouches fat with herbs and words of faith.

Elegant women wear hand-dyed robes of vivid reds and vibrant oranges. Everyone helps to educate and raise all of the children. This is a society where the senior members share their wisdom and are revered and cherished like royalty until their last breath.

There are systems of government, hierarchies of power; village elders and community councils preside over meetings and help to settle differences. There are judges and senators and chiefs, each marked with a distinguishing scar of leadership above his eyebrows. Such scars are the result of a hot knife cutting into the flesh.

It is these leaders who help prepare the boys for their rites of passage, help them to become men, and, in some cases, warriors. The boys are taught to shoot bow and arrows, to fight with double-edged swords, and to master the art of throwing a javelin.

The wise men assemble the people of the village for weekly religious services and preach to them of decency to neighbors, cleanliness in the village, and honor among men and women. This is a community built on trust.

ʊʊ

For as long as anyone could remember, life in the villages along the shores of West Africa was simple and safe. Then one day, without warning, the wind brought violence to the villages, and no one slept in peace anymore.

In 1441, according to historians, two Portuguese ships sailed the coastline of West Africa looking for opportunities to exploit the fishing banks and to steal gold from the African people.

When the ships dropped anchor, the African villagers, their curiosity aroused, approached the pale men with stringy hair who had rowed ashore. The seamen quickly overpowered at least a dozen people, loaded them into longboats, and sailed away.

These strong-arm raids didn't last long. They ultimately evolved into the more routine capturing and trading for Africans, as Europeans were fast to establish a formal system by persuading some African kings and chiefs to capture their own people and sell them into slavery.

For long periods after the abductions, some of the children from the villages would climb the tallest trees to watch for the return of the great Portuguese ships that had snaked their way along the Rio Real—ships with long guns aimed at the shore; ships with tall sails that snapped in the breeze; dark ships that creaked in the tide; ships that brought chaos and fear and always left death in their wake.

Calm would become only a memory for the people of the West African villages. Lives would be lost in this steady state of terror called slavery.

A life of peace had been stolen from these African families. Those taken were stripped of their titles and even their names, snatched away from everything familiar. No one was safe from slavery—not the smallest child, not the mightiest warrior.

And so, the people of these villages along the west coast of Africa could only embrace their children, comfort each other, pray, and wait for the ships to come.

2

Suddenly, rain was falling like lead pellets on the wooden deck of the *Virgalona.* A storm was blowing in from the coast of Cuba and Capt. Moe Molinar was at the helm of his fifty-one-foot salvage boat, riding the swells and wiping seawater from a face browned by years of sun.

Directly ahead was a fury of rain and clouds, a dark wall that seemed to advance by the second, nature's none-too-subtle way of testing the limits of man's determination at sea. Moe's throat was dry, despite the pelting rain. There was nothing but ocean in all directions. His navigational heading was 120 degrees northwest; his speed 10 knots; his destination the sunken Spanish galleon *Nuestra Señora de Atocha* and its fortune of precious stones.

But the goals for this particular workday would have to wait for favorable weather: July 19, 1973, was not a good day to challenge the power of the sea.

"It's a great big ocean out there and the bottom seems to change regularly," Moe would often tell his crew. "It's as if the sea decides when you've worked hard enough or paid enough of a price to be rewarded with what you're looking for."

With the rusty fifty-pound anchor rumbling over the side of the *Virgalona,* Moe had signaled to his six-man crew that he was poised to ride out a series of six-foot waves that were splashing hard against his weatherworn vessel in the Gulf of Mexico.

It was a day that brought stiff winds and mounting swells to a watery stretch of nowhere. Moe was thirty-seven miles west of Key West, Florida, and ninety miles north of Havana, where turbulent waters are no surprise to seasoned seamen.

But for Moe Molinar and his crew, it was also a day filled with anticipation, and, as usual in his line of work, there was always a sense of experiencing the unknown.

The winds picked up and Moe's forty-five-year-old *Virgalona* rocked wildy in the tide. The wooden V-hull vessel with peeling paint had been with Moe longer than some of his friends.

It was given to him by Mel Fisher, the man who hired Moe and taught him everything he knows about the rigorous and unpredictable business of underwater treasure hunting. It was a boat that was made for hard work, a sturdy craft designed to withstand the roughest of seas.

As the captain of the *Virgalona* for more than a quarter of a century—the only captain of African descent hired by Fisher—Moe was accustomed to riding out storms. Living on the sea was a way of life for this sixty-two-year-old Panama native, a man who prefers a stormy day at sea to a sunny day on land. Unflappable and intensely focused, he has a gift for communing with the sea and an ability to navigate the nuances of the ocean that leaves even veteran seaman confounded. He seems to understand the ocean's rhythms, to interpret its patterns, and he has certainly learned to respect its power. He knows when to surrender, retreat, and start again the next day. He doesn't fight the sea. All of this has made Moe a legend among those whose livelihood depends on the sea.

Drenched from the downpour, Moe and his crewmen set about securing the gear on board as they prepared to head to calmer seas in the Marquesas, a thin stretch of tiny, lush uninhabited islands halfway between Key West and where they were being battered by this sudden storm.

They took turns filling each of the twelve scuba tanks from an onboard compressor. Moe locked down the galley and took a swig of cold water from a jug resting in the ice-stuffed cooler. The deck was slippery. Moe called out a warning to his longtime crewman John Brandon.

A stout, red-bearded man in an old baseball cap, he has a handshake that would shame a vise.

People listen to Moe. He doesn't say much, and what he does say, he says softly. But he has too much experience to be ignored, too many trips to sea to be second-guessed.

Moe and the crewmen walked carefully from one side of the deck to the other, repositioning their dredging equipment and checking their navigational headings. They would reach the Marquesas soon and find shelter from the wind and the rain. As the boat plowed through the sea, they sipped beer and plotted their course back to this site once the weather cleared.

⊍⊍

Although Moe had checked the weather before leaving the dock, no one had anticipated the storm. Weather changes without warning in the Florida Straits. So once they dropped anchor in the Marquesas, Moe climbed into his bunk, got as comfortable as possible on the worn-out mattress, and tried to fall asleep to the off-beat pounding of rain and the uneasy swaying of the *Virgalona* as she rocked in the sea.

The night passed quickly.

This venture—temporarily ill-fated—had its origins on a humid afternoon the previous summer. Moe and his mentor, Mel Fisher—probably the most well-known treasure hunter in the world—had teamed up that day with a trim thirty-four-foot Chris-Craft dubbed *Holly's Folly*.

Her captain, Bob Holloway, had radioed for Mel and Moe to meet him, saying that he had registered a "strike" at New Ground Reef with the boat's magnetometer. The magnetometer is a cylindrical electronic instrument that registers fluctuations in the earth's magnetic field, allowing salvagers to locate large chunks of iron underwater.

On that August day, Holloway's all-woman crew tossed a buoy overboard to mark the spot of the strike, and then Holloway quickly slipped on a scuba tank and dropped fourteen feet to the bottom. He descended directly on top of a 750-pound iron cannon buried in the sand.

Knowing the *Virgalona* carried compressors for air fills and plenty of scuba tanks, Holloway made his way back to the surface to wait for Moe and Mel. In a matter of minutes, the *Virgalona* had arrived and Moe's divers had strapped on their gear and made their way to the site of the cannon.

Nearly a year later, they were back, in hopes of raising more artifacts from the seabed.

The next day, gray clouds were hanging overhead and the ocean near New Ground Reef was still rough, but Moe was planning to make a dive anyway. He had seen worse days—the day before, for example.

Brandon reached inside four mesh bags and pulled out the regulators. Each of the crew members connected the rubber hoses to the compressor and tossed the excess hose over the side of the boat.

Moe grabbed his scuba tank and attached the regulator to the top, then slowly turned on the air until his dive gauge indicated the tank was full. He placed the regulator to his mouth and took a hit of compressed air.

"If everybody has air, let's go to work," Moe said as he pulled a worn wet suit over his legs and zipped it to the neck.

Rolling backward over the edge of the *Virgalona*, Moe plunged into the Gulf of Mexico and bobbed on the ocean's surface, waiting for the rest of his crew to enter the water. He took a second glance at his gear while foamy swells of salt water slapped his 175-pound frame from side to side like a huge wet hand.

Five other divers were on board the *Virgalona,* preparing to roll over the side of a boat that had covered more miles over whitecaps than any boat on the horizon and was known as a genuine good-luck charm.

One by one, the divers followed Moe into the Gulf of Mexico's shifting currents, each wearing gloves and carrying mesh bags, a compass, and spearguns—five-inch-long knives, which were fastened to their legs.

They were tireless underwater hunters in black suits with worn elbows and torn knees. All were veterans of deep-water dives and were intimately acquainted with shifting currents and adept at recovering sunken treasure.

The divers had already spent two bumpy nights aboard the *Virgalona* since leaving dock in Fort Pierce for a planned three-week excursion working the site *Holly's Folly* had found twelve months earlier. Now they were resuming their underwater search after being turned back by bad weather the day before.

Rain began to pelt their bare heads as Moe waited for the divers to assemble in the water. He wanted to get off the bumpy surface as quickly as possible, knowing it would be easier underwater and that pulling himself along the ocean floor would be a lot less agonizing than trying to swim through choppy waves for even a few minutes. He also wanted to conserve as much air as possible for his underwater search.

Slowly, they slipped below the ocean's surface directly under the stern of the *Virgalona*. Moe waited for his crew of divers to reach twenty feet and then glanced at his compass. The tiny numbers inside the bezel gave Moe a heading west of 270 degrees. He kicked his way west into a mile-wide maze of silt and seaweed and made a steady descent through a school of shiny barracuda to the murky ocean floor.

Moe broke from the pack, drifted with the currents, and found himself swimming in thirty feet of water, surrounded by sandy haze and a blur of marine life. His crew was out of sight, but they were probably not more than a few feet behind him. Underwater, the thick-roped anchor line that was knotted tightly to the bow of the *Virgalona* appeared as a slender shadow floating in the sea.

When the *Virgalona*'s twin engines shut down on the surface, there was a deep quiet, broken only by the slow and easy rhythm of Moe's breathing and the crunch of a few fish nibbling on coral.

Visibility had reached only ten feet as Moe inched along, using his wide fins to kick hard against the current. The stalks of tall grass were beginning to resemble an underwater jungle in the shallows of the Gulf of Mexico, where the most feared predators are the saw-toothed reef sharks that zigzagged just beyond Moe's reach.

Moe was used to seeing sharks—sometimes big ones. He didn't like them, but he did respect them. His simple self-taught strategy for shark survival had never failed him, and today was no different: Ignore them, keep your hands out of sight, and most likely they'll go away.

Once after being harassed by a huge shark that followed his divers all day, Moe decided to call off the search for treasure temporarily. The next morning, he pulled on the anchor chain, but it was tight. Suddenly, the boat began to shift sideways, and there was an enormous shark halfway out of the water, chewing on the steel chain like a saw.

The shark slipped under the boat, but they could still see it through the clear ocean water. Moe slipped six rounds into the chamber of his .44 Magnum revolver, leaned over the side, and fired several shots, missing the shark each time he fired. He waited for a few hours before ordering his divers back into the water.

Now, the ocean was a warm eighty-two degrees and Moe was thirty feet down, relying more on years of intuition than on technology to search the sea. Sharks began to take shape in the distance, but they were of no real concern. Moe knew they just wanted a closer look at these people who would be taking control of their space for several days running.

More worrisome were half a dozen fat-faced grouper that yanked at Moe's regulator, confusing the coiled scuba hose with the four-foot-long black worms that make their home inside the forests of coral.

Drifting past sea fans and swaying seaweed, Moe slowed every few feet to explore under ledges and peer into crevices, his breathing rate cut in half to conserve air from his single scuba tank. Every so often, the current would change direction, spinning Moe around and forcing him to adjust his underwater path.

Finally, he took a deep breath, then exhaled hard, purging the air from his lungs and dropping facefirst to the ocean floor, where, on his belly, he could survey sand-covered ledges close-up, as if he were looking through a large magnifying glass.

Sea horses and snapper drifted with the reef current as Moe sifted through a thick blanket of sand. He had been underwater for about an hour and had covered nearly a mile. The day was yielding nothing; he was getting tired and was running low on air.

He knew it was time to head back to the *Virgalona* for an afternoon break and a full tank of air, but Moe Molinar hates to give up. He and his crew of divers were searching for glitter in the sand, treasure that had been buried by time and long forgotten by everyone.

"If it's down there, I'll find it," Moe always says.

He is almost always right.

"Moe" is a nickname. His given name is Demosthenes, after the ancient Greek naval commander who was a specialist in strategy during war at sea. For the past three decades, Moe has made a career of hunting sunken treasure. He met his wife, Mary, in a Florida hospital thirty years ago. She was a nurse's aide who cared for him while he was recovering from a minor boating accident.

Despite his aversion to using maps, his crew and colleagues insist that he possesses an extraordinary—even somewhat mystical—ability to navigate underwater and find gold and precious stones.

Moe is more comfortable speaking Spanish than English. He prefers his boat to his car, the ocean to the shore, and wet suits to dress suits. He'd rather fry up platters of fish with his crew aboard the *Virgalona* than wait to be served at a popular restaurant. On board ship, Moe never needs dinner reservations and the catch of the day is truly fresh and authentic. His salvage boat, loaded with equipment, has shadowed the route of a thousand ships before it.

Shortly after Christopher Columbus's first voyage to the New World in 1492, Spanish conquistadors explored and claimed lands ranging from present-day Argentina to California and Florida. Included in this vast new empire were Mexico, the Caribbean Islands, and all of South America except for Brazil, which went to Portugal by papal agreement.

Spanish kings soon learned, however, that claiming the land and holding on to it were separate achievements. In ensuing centuries, foreign interlopers overran the edges of the empire, including most of North America, Jamaica, parts of Hispaniola, and many smaller Caribbean islands. The bulk of the empire remained in Spanish hands until the revolutionary wars of the nineteenth century, when Spanish rule was overthrown and independent republics were established.

Trade between Spain and the new colonies, although heavily regulated by the Crown, initially proved profitable. By the early 1500s, however, richly laden merchant ships were falling prey to pirates. Many were fired on and inadvertently sunk in the waters around Florida and the Caribbean, where they remain to this day. However, most were lost in storms.

Soon, treasure fleets of merchant vessels sailing the Atlantic Ocean were protected by Spanish war galleons that served as a floating security escort against pirates, but they couldn't protect against natural disasters.

On September 4, 1622, in a ferocious hurricane, the Spanish treasure ship *Nuestra Señora de Atocha* smashed into a mound of coral reefs near the Marquesas, about twenty-five miles west of Key West.

With her hull savagely ripped open, the vessel quickly sank, drowning everyone aboard, with the exception of three crewmen and two enslaved Africans, and taking gold, silver, and $400 million worth of sparkling jewels to the ocean bottom, where they lay under the sand for nearly 360 years, until Moe Molinar discovered them.

Since 1972, Moe has recovered tens of millions of dollars' worth of gold and silver from more than a dozen ships, mostly the fractured Spanish galleons scattered along the ocean floor in South Florida waters.

Moe was reluctant to leave the site of the sunken *Atocha*. With nightfall only about an hour away, Moe decided to make one last sweep of the ocean floor before heading to the surface.

And then his hands, wrinkled from prolonged contact with salt water, hit against something rigid, unfamiliar, and cold in a way that had nothing to do with the eighty-degree water around him.

Lying flat on the bottom, his chest pressed hard against sand, Moe's eyes widened through the sting of salt water that was seeping into his mask. Seasoned divers know that over time the ocean always gives back what it takes, but this dive seemed especially cryptic, and Moe was noticeably disturbed by the objects that were coming into view as he lingered in thirty feet of water. Slowly, with rugged hands, he parted layers of the ocean floor and watched the sandy grains scatter with the current like leaves in a fall wind. He blinked twice, as if his eyes were deceiving him.

Directly in front of him, caked in rust and limestone, were two feet of encrusted iron; ancient weighty chunks were piled high in the form of a pyramid, as if someone had deliberately—and efficiently—stacked them.

What is this? he thought to himself. What have I stumbled onto?

Reluctantly, as if the pile would bite, Moe tapped his fingers gently on the mound of rusty iron. It was solid and sinister. The heavy heap didn't have the texture of treasure that Moe was accustomed to touching; this was a part of the past he had never experienced, something that sent a sharp chill through his body.

He reached out again, this time lifting a large chunk of encrusted iron from the ocean floor and holding in his hands a pair of hardened, sea-soaked shackles.

No longer concerned about surfacing, Moe stared at the iron pile for what seemed like an hour. As if suddenly punched in the gut, he was struck by the painful realization that the heavy iron handcuffs he was holding were designed to fit tightly around black wrists much like his own. Moe cringed as he let the shackles drop to the ocean floor, and he furiously began to wipe the rust from his hands—along with the generations of pain and bondage associated with it.

His discoveries were usually met with joy and raucous celebration, but there would be no laughter this time, just a mixture of curiosity, sorrow, and pain. Thirty minutes later, the stacks of encrusted shackles were barely visible as Moe widened his search pattern underwater. The visibility was now less than five feet, the Gulf of Mexico transformed into a cloudy green maze.

Moe's mind was nearly as clouded as the waters around him. Where did the shackles come from? How did they get there? How long had they been buried in the sand? How many more shackles were there?

He knew only that the shackles weighed about six pounds each and had two holes the size of quarters to hold a thirteen-inch-long bolt that locked into place, which had brought constant viselike pain to black wrists.

It was an unsetting day for Moe Molinar. The usual things he found in the sea were silver coins and jewels, the cache of wealthy aristocrats traveling from Spain. But these mysterious relics, pieces of a puzzle that would reveal stories of degradation, torment, and captivity, were something else entirely.

With each pair of shackles uncovered from the ocean floor, Moe was shaken by the firsthand discovery of man's inhumanity to man. His hands were jittery and his body was numb.

He swam farther into the silt. He wanted to be careful not to lose sight of his crew, but something was pulling him toward more iron shapes in the distance—more shackles, nearly hidden from view. These were smaller, thinner, and lighter in weight than the six-pound encrusted handcuffs he had just recovered. They were almost flimsy but designed to slide over wrists that were not as thick as those of adult men. These fit in the palm of his hand—shackles that he knew were made specifically for women and children.

He could barely hold the tiny cuffs without crying out underwater. So he stayed down a while longer, checking his pressure gauge every now and then, and offered a prayer for these African people he had never known.

By sunset, Moe had hoisted dozens of rusted, soaked shackles onto the *Virgalona,* bulky ones as well as tiny ones—painful reminders of a time when sons and daughters like his own were not spared from chains and whips.

Like a videotape player, Moe's mind replayed every image he had ever seen of the African holocaust and freeze-framed them: men, women, and children with ebony skin who were snatched away from everything familiar, placed in chains, and stacked in the bellies of reeking ships like planks of lumber, their backs crisscrossed with scars.

The irony of the moment was undeniable: The last black men to touch these shackles had been bound by them and forced on a three-month voyage, packed in the lower decks of a sweltering ship with little food and water. Centuries later, the first person to touch those same shackles was another black man—a freeman, Moe Molinar.

Moe had somersaulted off the side of his boat that morning on a routine dive. He emerged hours later from a devastating past, a visit to the ocean bottom that would change his life forever.

At sixty-four, Moe is perhaps the only successful *black* treasure hunter in the world, but in his search for gold and emeralds, he had stumbled onto something much more important, an underwater site that contained the only shackles he had ever seen during his thirty years of searching for underwater treasure. After all, it was treasure that Moe had been hired to find, not the historical evidence of his heritage.

Moe kept his thoughts to himself as he handed the first few shackles up to his crew, who placed them on the deck of the *Virgalona.* And for a few minutes, even though he was surrounded by a dozen men he considered friends, men he had shared the seas with for a decade, he was not sure they would understand his connection to these relics, or understand his torment.

No other artifact, silver coin, or shiny stone had possessed the same kind of power for Moe as these shackles.

Aboard the *Virgalona*, he had no one to share his feelings with, no one who could truly understand his past. So he spoke only about the archaeological and historical value of the shackles and the underwater site that had no name.

For a moment, a rusted pair of shackles had brought him close to a multitude of black souls. Later, after he docked and arrived home, after the sun had buried itself into the sea, he whispered to his wife, Mary, that he had found tools of the slave trade.

"There was a stack of shackles in the sand," he told her. "I knew right away what they were and what they were used for. I knew the shackles were from a slave ship. It hit me, like someone hitting me in the head. I was holding shackles that had bound the wrists and legs of black people who had been brought here as slaves by white men."

⊽⊽

They dropped anchor again later in the summer of 1973. It was hot and humid. The seas were fairly calm, but the crew members were anxious to begin their search patterns. Using compasses and laying out one-hundred-foot sections of yellow line, it took less than thirty minutes for them to relocate the wreck.

Underwater, Moe returned to the pile of shackles resting near the coral. He seemed distracted underwater, staring at the shackles and wondering about the vessel they had to have come from, a vessel that had hauled a cargo of people who looked like him.

As the divers surveyed the ocean floor, they discovered more objects hidden in the sand: glass bottles, elephant tusks, pewter mugs, cannonballs, pewter spoons, pewter bowls, and an iron cannon that weighed nearly eight hundred pounds.

Word spread quickly among divers and treasure salvagers throughout the United States that Mel Fisher's divers had not only discovered unlimited treasure at the *Atocha* wreck site but had also stumbled onto something far more phenomenal. The artifacts were unloaded from the *Virgalona* and stored in a warehouse in Key West for safekeeping.

Months passed. Moe and his crew went back to hauling millions of dollars in gold, emeralds, and hundreds of silver coins from the *Atocha* onto the *Virgalona,* and the obscure artifacts that hinted at horrors from a brutal era sat and gathered dust.

At sea, a half-mile area in the dark Gulf of Mexico was known to divers only as the "English wreck"—its precious remains holding answers to three-hundred-year-old questions, like a tightly rolled message in a bottle, waiting to be opened.

3

Ten years passed before the "English Wreck" was mentioned again. Rusted artifacts had been sitting in a dusty building in Key West while divers guessed at their origin and how long they had been resting on the ocean floor.

On July 7 1983, on their third trip to the site, a salvage team lead by Henry Taylor, operating from the twenty-eight-foot dive boat *Trident,* began to work the site on New Ground Reef in search of more artifacts from the English wreck. Taylor traveled with a crew that included archaeologist David Moore, Jimmy Amoroso, and Duke Long, all expert underwater salvagers.

The crew anchored on the reef some thirty-five miles west of Key West in a shallow site where currents whip up without warning.

David Moore, a North Carolinian who had logged hundreds of hours on underwater wrecks, had spent much of his life waiting for an opportunity to explore historical treasure. He couldn't have cared less about precious stones, diamonds, and emeralds; he was only interested in assembling the puzzle from the past through artifacts discovered on his watch.

He had answered an ad in *Skin Diver* magazine placed by Duncan Mathewson, a Mel Fisher archaeologist looking for six graduate students—three to work on the *Atocha/Margarita* site and three to work on the 1715 fleet off the east coast of Florida. David, in graduate school at East Carolina University, took the $150-a-week job.

While Henry Taylor and David Moore were busy setting the anchor in place to keep the *Trident* steady over the site, Duke Long put on his gear and plunged over the side.

"Duke had a habit of always jumping into the water first to see what the visibility was like," Moore recalled later.

The visibility was murky and somewhat silty from an earlier rain, but the divers were determined to work the site for much of the day. Moore had spent most of his field experience diving off the Outer Banks in North Carolina, where visibility was usually about five to six feet.

The divers split the site into two areas, a north sector and a south sector.

Moore and the other divers were on the ocean bottom now, spreading the sand with their hands, in search of anything they could find. It was tedious work that didn't always pay off. After several hours in the water, Moore had seen mostly coral and sand, and the divers were getting chilly.

The longer they were underwater, the more body heat they would lose, forcing them to end their search until they could warm themselves on deck under the Carribean sun. They would search for hours at a time, digging in the sand, marking off areas to place grids, hoping to recover a clue about the mysterious vessel. They searched through a world as constant and changing as a desert—white sand as far as the eye could see—where one piece of coral looked like many others and where having enough air to breathe was always a concern.

Around noon, most of the divers were climbing aboard for a break. Even David, known among his friends as someone who could conserve air better than most, was reluctantly pulling himself on deck after an hour underwater. The sun had peeked behind the clouds and many of the divers were peeling off their wet suits when they heard Long shout from the sea.

"Hey, you're not going to believe this!"

Everyone ran to the side, energized by the excitement in Long's voice.

"I think we found something big!" he called up to them, motioning for them to come and help.

Pulling their wet suits back over their wrinkled legs, the divers jumped overboard, not knowing exactly what Long had stumbled upon. At twenty-five feet, they began to unearth a limestone-encrusted bell-shaped object from its sandy crypt. It took several divers to pull it free. Slowly and carefully, they hoisted it onto the boat and moved it gently to the middle of the deck.

In a puddle of water on the deck sat what would be the most significant artifact discovered from the wreckage. The bell was thirteen to fourteen inches high, two-thirds of it thickly coated with marine growth and limestone, but the remaining third apparently had been protected from the salt water by the sand and clay in which it had been buried. For the divers, this was a rare find, a genuine starting point for research.

For about ten minutes, the four men just stood and admired the bell, stunned by their discovery and weary from their dive.

David was bouncing his two-hundred-plus-pound frame on the balls of his feet like a kid who had just opened a Christmas present. "I'm not sure what we have yet, but maybe this bell has a date," he said.

The bell was a fascinating find. Shipboard tasks had always been divided among regular watches of four hours each, as is still the custom aboard military and merchant ships. This bell, thought to be a watch bell, sounded every half hour to signal crew changes on board a vessel. Time was kept with an hourglass that was turned every half hour. The bell was sounded when the glass was turned, beginning with one stroke half an hour after midnight, with an extra stroke being added every half hour after that. Watches on deck were changed every eight bells.

This bell would be the clue that would lead researchers to a horrible past of pain and unconscionable acts inflicted on men, women, and children in unprecedented numbers. These crimes were so brutal that strong men, their chests tight from fear, would prefer to jump over the sides of slave ships to a certain death rather than endure another day on board.

These people were chained by the hands and neck and hauled into the hull of stinking ships with no light, no fresh air, and no sanitation. Conditions were so intolerable that people would methodically plan suicides simply to escape.

Imagine seeing sharks devouring live bodies and still hoping you'd have a chance to swing both of your legs over the rail. Imagine watching your wife raped, flogged, and raped again. Imagine seeing your uncle strung up by his feet and split open like an animal, an example for oth-

ers who might consider revolt. Imagine being chained in the hold of a
slave ship.

ᴗᴗ

Before long, divers were beginning to emerge from the Gulf of Mexico
after a hard day of searching for more artifacts, precious relics that when
pieced together would tell the three-hundred-year-old story of the slave
trade.

David pulled off his wet suit and paused for a moment, staring at the
bell. As an archaeologist, underwater sleuth, and a historian, this was the
sort of find he lived for. After centuries underwater, this bell could give a
name to the wrecked ship and identify the port from which she had
sailed. He was already doing detective work, piecing together clues to
recreate a picture of events that had occurred centuries ago aboard this
doomed ship. The bell would become the key that would unlock many
secrets and answer many questions.

After he had cleaned up and gotten something to drink, Moore began
to pry away the marine growth with his hand. Realizing this could take
hours, he reached for a screwdriver and gently picked away at the green
crust that covered the surface of the bronze bell. Numbers slowly began
to appear. First, a 9.

"We're onto something," Moore shouted. "Here we go!"

Within seconds, another 9 appeared, then a 6, and then a 1—1699.
The English wreck had a date.

Moore was mesmerized. He chipped faster and faster as letters
emerged: An *I*, then an *H*, followed by *A*'s, *E*'s, and *R*'s.

Like contestants on a midafternoon game show, the men recited what
was now clearly imprinted before them:

HENRIETTA MARIE, 1699.

"We've got a name!" Moore shouted. "We've got a date! We're in
business."

4

*T*he gold-studded ceiling inside the cathedral of white marble was fifty feet high and slits of sunlight crisscrossed the pine pews through diamond-shaped stained-glassed windows.

A black preacher wearing a flowing white robe was gently dipping my head into a wide porcelain basin filled with water and reading from a tattered leather-bound book of Scripture.

I felt what I thought was thunder shaking the wooden floor beneath my feet, but I later learned it was the rumbling of an organ with tarnished ivory keys piping gospel music from balcony to basement.

The minister closed his Bible and dabbed my face with a double-folded cotton towel before turning to the congregation:

"Let the church say AMEN!" he proclaimed.

"AMEN!" the congregation bellowed back.

Those images from my childhood echoed in my head as a ten-foot wave crashed through the arched windows of the church, flooding the pulpit and snatching me from the minister's grasp, my fingers slipping from the palms of his drenched hands.

A ferocious undertow tossed me into a series of somersaults, propelling me past long planks of wood and slamming me into the side of a strongbox loaded with iron chains.

I was sucking water and gasping for breath. I couldn't tell up from *down. I could, however, see something sparkling from inside the metal box. I reached in and grabbed something thin and hot. I dropped it immediately, but it was too late. My hand was scalded by a gold necklace that was smoldering from fire. My hand was throbbing, swollen, and red with pain. There was someone swimming in the distance, but it was murky and I couldn't tell who it was, nor could I let the person know that I was injured.*

I peered back into the box. The necklace was now charred and appeared to be quite old. A large word dangled from the chain. SLAVE.

BUZZ-BUZZ!

BUZZ-BUZZ!

I sprang to my feet as if I had been hurled from an ejection seat. My heart was beating so hard, it felt like it would bore a hole through my chest. My forehead was clammy. The doorbell was being pushed insistently.

It was about 2:00 P.M. and I had fallen asleep on the couch. It was one of those strange sleeps; I had heard the buzzing from far away, but, for whatever reason, I couldn't get up to answer the door.

By the time I got there, a deliveryman from Federal Express was driving off, but the package he had for me was leaning against the front door. Inside were airline tickets for a flight to London. More than a decade after David Moore discovered the *Henrietta Marie*'s bell at the bottom of the Gulf of Mexico, I was planning a trip to England to research the origins of the *Henrietta Marie* and her slave-trading voyages across the Atlantic.

I was compelled—if not destined—to retrace the route of this slave ship since learning about the sunken vessel from a group of African-American scuba divers.

As each day passed, I felt as if I needed to know more about the *Henrietta Marie*—more about her history, her owners, and their terrible business. I needed to know about the man who had captained the *Henrietta Marie*; the ironmongers who had manufactured the shackles for the ship; the crewmen who had set the sails and helped navigate the 120-ton vessel from London to Africa; the deckhands who had enslaved Africans as part of their daily duties, men who had shown no remorse in senselessly slaughtering rebellious human beings in the time it takes to blink.

I was preoccupied with learning about the places where the *Henrietta Marie* had anchored—London, the coast of West Africa, Jamaica, Barbados. I wanted to learn about the fear and fascination so many black people around the world have with water—the ocean.

I had a seemingly innate desire to know more about how so many black people could have been enslaved for so long, how these atrocities could have happened, and what lessons we could learn—as blacks and whites—from the *Henrietta Marie* since her discovery.

But I was also beginning to understand more about myself: that what was leading me to England was a need to locate the evil aboard the *Henrietta Marie* and call it by name. I wanted to learn more about the oppressors and the oppressed; I wanted to learn more about the resolve of the African people who were my ancestors.

I was feeling haunted by a ship that sailed more than three hundred years ago and yet seemed a part of my daily life.

This experience of retracing the history of a slave ship would be a kind of therapy. It would get me away from the issues that were disturbing me, rechannel my negative energy, and give me a chance to learn more about the history of slavery, and the history of the African people.

David Moore had called me twice from Greenwich, England, a suburb of London, where he was researching seventeenth-century slave ships and the pirate Blackbeard. Blackbeard was the most notorious pirate in the history of seafaring. With a beard that almost covered his face, he would strike terror into the hearts of his victims, according to some early accounts, by weaving wicks laced with gunpowder into his hair and lighting them during battle. A big man, he added to his menacing appearance by wearing a crimson coat, two swords at his waist, and bandoliers stuffed with numerous pistols and knives across his chest.

The sight of Blackbeard was enough to make most of his victims surrender without a fight. If they gave up peacefully, he would usually take their valuables, navigational instruments, weapons, and rum before allowing them to sail away. If they resisted, he would often maroon the crews and burn their ship. Blackbeard worked hard at establishing his devilish image, but there is no archival evidence to indicate that he ever killed anyone who was not trying to kill him. Blackbeard's lawless career lasted only a few years, but his fearsome reputation has long outlived him.

It is believed that one of Blackbeard's ship's, the *Queen Anne's*

Revenge, which wrecked at Beaufort Inlet, North Carolina, in the mid-1700s flying his dreaded black flag, may have been used as a slave ship. Historians and archaeologists, including David Moore, believe that Blackbeard may have been involved in the slave trade by pirating slave ships, selling off the cargo of African people, and forcing some of the enslaved African men to join his murderous crew. For many Africans, however, serving with Blackbeard was better than living a life in chains.

David Moore was working out of the National Maritime Museum, a sprawling structure of white pillars and shiny tile on rolling hills and manicured grounds that overlook the winding River Thames. A student of underwater archaeology, he is the foremost authority on the *Henrietta Marie.* I decided that if I wanted to learn more about this ship, I should become the foremost authority on David Moore.

I arrived in London at 6:00 A.M. after a nine-hour flight. There were a dozen flights landing at Heathrow Airport between 6:00 and 8:00 A.M. from all over the world. The line for customs and immigration seemed to snake around every corner of the airport. Families were lounging on luggage, looking more like fans camping out to buy tickets for a rock concert than travelers. The light brown faces of some of the Middle Eastern and Indian women were hidden behind dark veils, while other women were wrapped in colorful silk dresses. Babies were wiggling and crying in strollers. It took nearly three hours to reach immigration, the first checkpoint. I was hungry and exhausted. After a few questions about why I had come to Britain, I was allowed to pass and continue on to customs, where the line was even longer, although moving at a tolerable pace.

I noticed that most travelers were questioned briefly and sent on their way, except half a dozen African businessmen who were being interrogated off to the side. Their luggage had been opened and turned upside down; their clothes were stacked in piles on a table and papers from their briefcases spilled out onto the floor.

They were the only black people on line other than me. They were the only African people in sight. They were the only people being harassed.

Perhaps they had broken the law. Perhaps they were wanted for crimes. Perhaps they were innocent of any wrongdoing and were simply catching hell for being black. I never found out. I was ushered along by an official who asked me not to tie up the process by rubbernecking.

It was ironic, I thought, visiting England to research the atrocities inflicted on African people by the British (and other European powers), and my first encounter with British law enforcement was witnessing the harassment of African people. I have become hypersensitive to situations such as these because I've seen black people harassed so many times before—and it's happened to me. Overreaction? Perhaps. And perhaps not. But three hundred years after slavery became big business, the British were still humiliating black people.

On Monday morning I met David Moore at the National Maritime Museum. The library, which would become the base for my research work, was a magnificent room with tall ceilings and cherry-wood shelves filled with rare books by British historians and scholars about the Middle Passage and slave-ship captains who kept detailed journals of their voyages.

It was a room where visitors were required to check their belongings with a security guard and where the librarian, an able woman with a pink wool sweater draped across her shoulders, would look up over her wire-rimmed glasses if conversation rose above a whisper.

The books on the shelves were from the seventeenth and eighteenth centuries and could not be removed from the museum. Not suprisingly, the books were all written from a British perspective, and so I received the standard interpretation of the slave trade by arrogant "educated" white men. And still their rationale for beating and murdering and enslaving a generation of people shocked me. These books, volumes filled with repulsive and inhumane characterizations of African people, were stacked on shelves by the hundreds.

The first day that I walked into the library, David was hunched over a long wooden table in a far corner of the room, with a mess of papers scattered around him. He was seated between two towering stacks of books, some of them written in French.

"Well it's about time," he said, wearing his usual grin and extending his hand. "How was your flight?"

"Long," I said.

"If you're hungry, we can get something to eat, but you may want to look around first," he said. "There's plenty of valuable material in here that's going to be of use to you. We can always talk about a game plan for the next two weeks over a beer later."

"Sounds good," I said, walking to a shelf and pulling out a book. "I'll eat later."

We spent the rest of the day researching material and scanning the pages of books that we would never have found in the United States, books that had been out of print for decades.

I sat in the middle of the library, surrounded by tall wooden shelves, the silence broken only by the turning of pages, and looked at dozens of books in which enslaved black people were pictured naked in chains and packed into ships.

I pored through volume after volume, scribbling names, authors, publishers, dates, and page numbers to photocopy later. The subject matter was troubling. I had never been confronted by so many books about slavery, books written by authors whose interpretations and views were painful for me. Slavery was, for captains and crewmen, simply business.

In one particular book, *Slave Ships and Slaving,* George Francis Dow wrote:

A very important part of the coast, in old slaving days, was Calabar, Old and New, and the Bonny River. Ships of considerable burden could anchor on the hard, sandy ground in eight fathoms, in the river at New Calabar...and as these towns tapped an extensive back-country, they traded slaves in large numbers....

The blacks living there, through frequent contact with Europeans, were of a more civilized sort than elsewhere along the coast, and a half dozen vessels would sometimes lie at anchor in the river at one time.

From 12,000 to 15,000 slaves were exported annually from this locality, during long periods of years, the English, French and Dutch participating in the trade. These slaves were brought down the rivers from market towns, a hundred and more miles away, having originally come from a considerable distance in the interior.

Some were undoubtedly prisoners of war but many were kidnapped by raiding parties.... The arms of some of men would be tied with grass rope and a man who happened to be stronger than common might also be pinioned above the knee....

...They were ironed, or chained, two together, and when they

were hung, a rope was put around their necks and they were drawn
up to the yardarm clear of the sail. This did not kill them but only
choked or strangled them....

They were then shot in the breast, and the bodies thrown over-
board. If one only of the two that were ironed together was to be
hung, the rope was put around his neck and he was drawn up clear
of the deck and his leg laid across the rail, and chopped off to save
the irons and release him from his companion, who at the same time
lifted up his leg until the other was chopped off, as aforesaid, and he
released.

It became more difficult with the turn of each page.

To read some of this material, you would never know that the cargo
being discussed were *people,* flesh and blood. Africans were never
referred to as people in these books. They were called "slaves," and "sav-
ages," "pickaninnies" and "beasts," "creatures" and "merchandise."
The word *human,* to characterize black people, never surfaced once.
While I shouldn't have been surprised, it was an observation that came
painfully close to home, as I was a black person and I knew the relentless
nature of racism.

The entire business of the slave trade was vile and lucrative, and the
details I read in the library made me cringe: The British not only participated in the trade; they sanctioned the business and charged a tax from
the captains of slave ships so the government could also benefit mone-
tarily. They called their slave-trading enterprise the Royal African Company.

Reading about the murders and atrocities aboard slave ships made me
more determined than ever to chart the path of the *Henrietta Marie.* It
wasn't the first time I had read this kind of material, but it was the first
time that I had been associated so closely with a slave ship. Realizing the
possibility that my ancestors—members of my family—could have sailed
aboard the *Henrietta Marie* was numbing.

What have we as a people endured? How many black people died?
Ten thousand? One hundred thousand? A million? This, I thought, was
the world's forgotten holocaust.

The next several days in London were illuminating, if torturous. I
spent each day in the library compiling material on the slave trade in the

late 1600s, the era in which the *Henrietta Marie* sailed from London. David Moore had already done a great deal of research on the *Henrietta Marie* and I had come to London to supplement his investigation, uncover fresh facts, and experience the research myself.

"We'll be closing in fifteen minutes," the librarian whispered that first day. The museum's staff were sticklers for leaving on time. The library closed at 5:00 P.M. The preparation to close began at 4:45. I took a few last notes to remind myself where I had left off, so that I wouldn't lose any time getting started the next day.

"You 'bout ready for a beer?" David asked, putting his arm around my shoulder.

As we headed out of the library, I noticed we were part of a group of about twelve people who were all walking down the steps, across the parking lot, and down a narrow street about fifty yards from the museum to the same place: a pub named the Plume of Feathers.

We walked past a bronze plaque bolted onto a cast-iron gate designating the prime meridian. It divided the eastern hemisphere from the western hemisphere. The museum was in the east, the pub in the west.

It was dark and smoky inside the Plume of Feathers. A row of pinball machines lined the back. One by one, staff members from the museum walked into the pub, loosened their ties, and, without asking, were handed foamy pints of beer from behind the bar.

The Plume of Feathers is a favorite watering hole for the folks at the National Maritime Museum. About a dozen of them who had stopped by the pub came over to welcome me to London.

"What are ya drinking, mate?" asked one researcher, wearing a short-sleeved white shirt and a pencil-thin black tie. "It's on us, of course."

"Well, thank you," I said, surveying the taps of beer.

"I'll have a pint of Foster's," I shouted to the bartender.

Silence.

Cigarettes burned in the ashtrays. No one bothered to play another selection on the jukebox. For a moment, I thought everyone had stopped breathing.

"We couldn't buy you *that* beer in good faith, mate," the researcher said, without using the brand name. "It's *Australian* beer, you know."

I had been in London less than twenty-four hours and I was already on the brink of an international scandal because of my poor barroom etiquette.

"I'll have what everyone else is drinking," I told the bartender.

"Wise choice, mate!" he shouted over laughter throughout the pub.

David and I took our beers off to a corner table to discuss the week's agenda. We were planning to team up with his friend Angus Konstram, who was the curator of weaponry for the Tower of London.

In the mid-1980s, David had come across two of the *Henrietta Marie's* eight large cannons on the site of the slave ship's wreckage. He had immediately contacted Angus. This Scotsman is an expert on weapons, particular large and small guns and ironwork. He did some preliminary research on the *Henrietta Marie* and thought he might have located the foundry where her guns were manufactured in the late 1600s. I would speak with Angus in a day or two, but now I wanted to spend some time with David going over the details of his research. I was anxious to start piecing together this transatlantic puzzle.

David worked with a number of historians and scholars who specialized in the history of the seventeenth- and eighteenth-century slave trade, some from Howard University and others from Millersville University of Pennsylvania, the University of North Carolina, Vanderbilt University, and the University of Liverpool.

More than ten years after he made his first dive to the *Henrietta Marie,* Moore talked about the ship as if he were still diving the wreck site. He was still gripped by the extraordinary discovery and its relationship to a period that is without parallel in the annals of African and American history.

Among the seven thousand artifacts recovered from the *Henrietta Marie* were the largest collection of slave-ship shackles and English-made pewterware ever found on one site. Experts now consider the *Henrietta Marie* the world's largest source of tangible objects representing the early period of the slave trade, providing us with greater insight into the African diaspora.

Under the silt and sand off Key West, divers discovered a collection of cannonballs of varying sizes, grenades, lead shot, cookstoves, and a compass. Knives and cutlasses were recovered, as well as washbasins and a wealth of pewterware, spoons, tankards, and bottles. Divers also brought up copper coins, several ax heads, a grindstone, and a surgeon's saw—commonly used for amputations at that time.

The *Henrietta Marie* also carried thousands of glass beads. Some of them were large striped varieties called "gooseberries." Most were the tiny type known as "seed" beads. Everywhere the divers stirred up silt, they unloosed these tiny beads—small balls of bright yellow or green or white, dark blue or brilliant turquoise.

The beads were made in Venice, a center of the fine art of glassblowing. The little beads, easy enough to make, were used as mere decorations and considered worthless trinkets by the Europeans. Until the slave trade, that is.

In Africa, the beads took on a new importance. African artisans used their most delicate craftsmanship to work these beads into assorted finery, while medicine men incorporated them into their healing rituals. They became a token of social status, political importance. The West African kings of Ghana, Mali, Songhai, and Nigeria were known to have worn beaded regalia so heavy that they had to be supported by attendants to rise from their thrones.

The Africans appreciated the tiny beads not because they mistook them as precious stones but because they were the product of an exotic technology, the equivalent of which was unknown in their homelands at that time. The beads became precious in their own right and were soon linked to whatever was valued in the cultures of the people who owned them and incorporated them into their customs.

The *Henrietta Marie* would have carried thousands of these little beads anytime she set out from London on a slave-trading voyage. On a voyage in 1699 Thomas Starke, one of the *Henrietta Marie*'s chief investors, consigned more than forty-eight pounds of bugle beads to the ship. Starke was an attorney and a wealthy man—in large measure as a result of the slave trade.

Nearly one hundred sets of shackles of varying sizes with bolts and loops have been recovered from the wreck—the largest slave-ship collection of shackles ever found on one site. The wrist and leg irons were used to confine as many as 325 African people in her dank hold.

"The men were all put in irons, two and two shackled together, to prevent their mutiny, or swimming ashore," Capt. Thomas Phillips of the

London slaver *Hannibal* wrote in 1694 in an account contemporary with
the *Henrietta Marie*.

David and I sipped beer and talked about the slave trade and his early
involvement with the *Henrietta Marie*. He'd been researching the ship for
fifteen years at this point and always seemed to keep his files with him
wherever he went.

"The *Henrietta Marie* has always taken a backseat to the gold and
glitter of the wreck of the *Atocha*—the treasure that was found in that
wreck fired people's imaginations, but the artifacts from the *Henrietta
Marie* were just stuck in a corner of the museum," David said. "Of all of
the thousands of shipwrecks that have been located around the world, I
am familiar with fewer than a dozen that can be positively identified as
slave ships. And the *Henrietta Marie* is the only one that has had any sort
of archaelogical control placed on her excavation—at least that I know
of—so that certainly makes her significant and unique."

But it was the nearly one hundred pairs of shackles found in the wreck
of the *Henrietta Marie* that were so haunting for David, as well as for me.

"As an archaelogist," David said, "I attempted to view the site as
objectively and as scientifically as possible. But when you look at those
shackles, what that ship was doing—her objective—really hits home.
Those shackles haven't been handled by more than one or two people
since they were worn by slaves."

David and I couldn't be more different, on the surface at least. His
long graying hair contrasts with my short-cropped style; he chews
tobacco, while I chew gum. He's a morning grouch; I'm an eager early
riser. He's methodical and content to pore over research in the library for
months on end, while I hunger for contact with the real people and places
that will make our quest come alive.

David is a white man from North Carolina, and I am a black man
from Detroit. Where my voice tends to carry across a room, he speaks
softly—with the kind of deep southern accent that strikes a certain
awareness in a black man. Collective racial memory makes us wary
whenever we hear it.

Yet, we had this in common: a passion for history—in this case, the
history of a slave ship and the peculiar institution she helped to sustain.

5

A brisk wind was blowing along Thames Street as I made my way across town and rounded the corner onto a busy stretch of the street in the heart of London's prim financial district. I turned up my collar, stuffed my hands into the pockets of my leather jacket, and walked against the morning rush.

It was quite a contrast on a weekday morning in London's Stock Exchange: executives in gray suits with white faces carrying coffee and briefcases, all staring at me—an unmistakably underdressed stranger with black clothes and matching skin.

I passed the row of glass and steel towers, stopping every now and again to read the addresses. I was getting closer to my destination: a centuries-old one-story brick chapel.

I was looking for what I believed was the final resting place of Anthony Tournay. When the captain of the *Henrietta Marie* declared her cargo, one entry was recorded from Tournay, an ironmonger and shackle maker who provided the *Henrietta Marie* with her thirty-three tons of iron—450 pounds sterling's worth, equivalent to about $265,000 today.

Tournay, historians believe, was one of the merchants who supplied the *Henrietta Marie* with some of the hundreds of pairs of shackles and chains that were aboard the slave ship when she sailed the Middle Passage.

According to British historian Nigel Tattersfield, Tournay was a merchant in the slave trade and the son of a wealthy lawyer. He had served his apprenticeship with Edward Ball, a well-known merchant adventurer.

He had lived in an area of London that was traditionally the habitat of London ironmongers, among them Ambrose Crowley, the most prominent manufacturer and ironmonger of his day. Crowley had also provided the Royal African Company with many of the dreadful tools of the trade: chains, neck bands, and shackles, as well as iron bars, one of the staples of the business. The commercial and social relationship between Crowley and Tournay was close; they both lived in some style on Thames Street.

Portraits of family ancestors adorned the walls of Tournay's home, as did a likeness of Sir Francis Drake. Silverware graced the tables and silver candlesticks lit the house. Tournay paraded around town in a shiny "chariot machine" pulled by his own horses.

Tournay profited greatly from the business of selling Africans to the highest bidder, showing no apparent remorse for the thousands of people who suffered and sometimes died while cuffed in iron that he supplied. And yet he often gave generously to charities around London, particularly to organizations that helped feed and clothe poor children.

When he died in 1726, at age seventy-six, he left one hundred pounds sterling to St. Thomas Hospital in Southwark and smaller gifts for the education of poor children, including a sum to Skinner's School in Tunbridge Wells.

Tournay was typical of many slave merchants. He was wealthy and influential. He was generous with the servants in his employ—he arranged to have them paid for two full years after his death—and he was considerate of his family.

But Tournay's benevolence ended when it came to Africans. He thought of them as subhuman, unworthy of being treated in the manner of other underprivileged people. He profited from the misery of African people because it was a business—a lucrative business—nothing more.

Tournay may have been buried beneath the sixteenth-century chapel, where I now stood. Located in the heart of London, St. Mary

Abchurch is a small redbrick church with stained-glass windows and a dark little chapel crisscrossed with sunlight filtering in through wooden shutters.

I thought again of how Tournay had amassed great wealth by marketing his iron shackles to the *Henrietta Marie* and slave ships like her. I stood inside the old church and thought about the vast wealth made from the business of selling black people and how years ago, just steps away, a foundry had turned out shackles used to keep African people enslaved.

I wasn't sure I was in the right place. All around me, on the floors and walls, were long gray tombs, the names faded by time, many of them barely legible. As I leaned over the crypts, trying to make out the inscriptions, an old cleric with trembling hands and tattered collars approached me and asked my business. I told him that I was looking for a particular grave, not that of a friend.

He explained that many bodies had been buried in this church centuries ago and the crypts were stacked on top of one another. It would probably be impossible to know exactly how many are entombed there, he said.

The cleric left me alone after suggesting that I was looking more for answers within myself than in the inscriptions on old graves. He shook my hand and told me to take all the time I needed.

I stood alone in this dark chapel, feeling an inner rage, angry about the treatment of people I'd never known. The *Henrietta Marie* was offering me a rare opportunity: to visit the waterways where she had sailed, to give names and personal histories to faceless slave traders. African-Americans rarely get a chance to find a name, locate a person, or trace the history of those who can be held responsible for torturing generations of our ancestors.

I had found a place to direct my anger. I could finally shout; I could curse and scream for the Africans who had died without the chance to speak, curse, or scream for themselves.

At that moment, Anthony Tournay was the target of my rage. He was no longer able to hear my cries, no longer able to hurt my people, no longer able to peddle his wares. Still, I stomped the ground hoping he was under the thick layers of stone.

I had found someone real to blame—someone whose dust was likely within twenty or thirty feet of me, at the most.

It was silent inside the church. I stood and stared, thinking about the atrocities aboard the *Henrietta Marie* and about the complexities of slavery; about the people, black and white, who support discussions about the slave trade and race in America, and the people, black and white, who refuse to give slavery a second thought, arguing to keep this particular piece of history buried in the past, or, at least, in its place.

"Good luck in your travels, my son," the cleric said, reaching out to touch me, his hands as cold as the River Thames. "I hope you find what you are looking for."

I walked out in a daze of emotions.

I wasn't ready to absolve the racists of the past—or, for that matter, the bigots of today. But neither was I going to blame all white people for the atrocities of the past. I won't use race as a crutch to harbor hostility, but being black and male in America has its unique challenges and they can be arduous, humiliating, and, at times, deadly.

White women have clutched their purses and pulled their children close when I stepped onto elevators; I have been followed by store security guards for no reason; I've been mistaken for a liquor store thief in Detroit; I've been refused service at a gasoline station; I've been run off the road in Louisiana by white men screaming "nigger" from a pickup truck; I've had a man in Manhattan hand me his parking-lot ticket, assuming I was the garage attendant, as I waited for my own car to be delivered; and I've been asked to leave a restaurant in Georgia because the owner feared for my safety.

My mother and father always taught me to forgive and pray for those who have lost their way. But I wasn't in the mood to pray for a slave trader, and I knew full well that my feelings about racial injustice weren't going to be sorted out standing inside a musty old church.

But I left the chapel thinking, Perhaps this is not a time for anger; perhaps this is a time for healing.

I climbed into a taxi. The driver was listening to a speech by a black politician who was calling for the crown jewels to be returned to their rightful owners and demanding reparations for black people as a result of slavery.

"We just want respect," the taxi driver said. "Black people want respect. We are not respected in London or anywhere else in the world."

I didn't sleep much that night.

In the morning, I called David Moore. He and Angus had traced the history of the eight cannons that were stationed on the *Henrietta Marie*'s deck to a rural foundry, Stream Mill, outside London. It was there that they believed the weapons had been manufactured.

Over the telephone, David spoke of Angus, his accomplishments in the field of seventeenth- and eighteenth-century weaponry, and the fact that he was an easygoing guy who knew his way around the English countryside—as well as many of her great pubs.

The next day, I took a ferry from London to Greenwich, a pleasant forty-five-minute cruise along the Thames River past ports like Wapping and Rotherheith, where the *Henrietta Marie* had most likely docked in the 1690s.

It was not hard to visualize life along this muddy brown river three hundred years ago. It was a working river then, as it is today, a major transportation waterway to the English Channel and then to the open sea.

I was feeling anxious again as I thought about the *Henrietta Marie* and her cargo of innocent people. I was focused on the research, but, for the first time as a journalist, I had become part of my own story.

ᙀᙀ

When I arrived in Greenwich, Angus and David met me. Angus had a firm handshake and a quick smile. This stocky student of history had done plenty of research on the *Henrietta Marie*'s armament, including the two cannons that were recovered off the coast of Key West.

He had noticed early on that both big guns contained marks that could help lead us to the foundry. The top of the first gun had been eroded on the seabed, but the second cannon was clearly marked with the letter *S*, representing the mark of either the casting furnace or the founder. Both guns were six feet long and weighed about seven hundred pounds each.

Recent research by Nigel Tattersfield has produced evidence to suggest the *Henrietta Marie* was originally a French privateer captured and brought into Deal on the southeast coast of England in 1695. That vessel was registered as fitted with eight cannons.

When the *Henrietta Marie* called into Barbados, the local shipping agent described her as being armed with eight guns, each about six to eight feet long and weighing between 750 and 1,000 pounds.

The marks on the *Henrietta Marie*'s second gun suggested the cannons were produced in the Stream Mill foundry at Chiddingly in Sussex. This rural iron foundry produced almost 450 tons of iron guns under the direction of John Oxley, Sr., whose son took over the foundry in 1695.

These guns were produced for John Fuller, a local landowner and gun founder. Fuller's major foundry was at Heathfield in Sussex, but he had rented the Stream Mill facilities when the war with France had led to an increase in demand by the merchant marine.

All of the foundries were located within forty miles of Deal, where the *Henrietta Marie* was fitted out for her 1697 voyage. Ease of transport by river and sea meant that vessels in Deal could be easily and readily supplied from these foundries at minimal cost.

Indeed, it is possible that the *Henrietta Marie*'s guns were not even bought. The will of Thomas Westerner, Sr., bequeaths all of his iron guns to his son. This refers to the contemporary practice of some Wealden founders of leasing their guns to merchantmen for the duration of a voyage, either with a view to the merchantmen purchasing them from the proceeds of their hopefully lucrative voyage or with the understanding that they would be returned upon the completion of the vessel's voyage.

The *Henrietta Marie* was heavily armed for her size, but she was still no match for the marauding pirate ships that would commandeer slavers, killing the seamen aboard and taking the Africans belowdecks for their own profit.

"Hop in, mate. Let's go find a foundry," Angus said, the door of his four-wheel-drive Jeep swinging open. I climbed into the backseat.

We didn't know exactly where we were going, but we did know that we were heading toward Sussex, some seventy miles southeast of London. We also had a general idea of the place we were looking for. We were simply hoping that it might still resemble a drawing in a very old book that Angus had found at the library.

Angus had a map of Sussex, but what we needed were smaller county maps to pinpoint the location of Stream Mill, which we weren't sure existed on any present-day road maps. We stopped at a gas station, topped off the tank, and headed onto the highway to Sussex.

It was a rainy afternoon, October 2, 1994, the wind ripping through the canvas top of the Jeep. Angus, wearing a short-sleeved T-shirt, was comfortable with the window rolled halfway down so he could flick the ashes from his cigarette into the country air. I quickly pulled my jacket over my head.

The countryside along the road to Sussex was like a painting: Wooden farmhouses straddled hundreds of rolling green acres and horses grazed in the fields. The skies overhead were gray, but that did nothing to diminish the charm and unassuming freedom of this landscape.

We drove about thirty miles before we pulled into a small town for directions to Chiddingly. Angus bought a county map, which we each looked over. There was no Stream Mill or Stream listed.

"We'll keep driving," Angus said in his thick Scottish brogue, and stepped hard on the gas. "It's out here somewhere."

"Just try not to kill us getting there," David said, cranking up the radio so Angus could hear the soccer match.

Angus's driving was legendary, I had come to learn.

"Jeeps were made for hard driving," he said, racing into the next county.

I flipped through several pages of Angus's research material I had photocopied and brought along for the ride.

Depending on the winds, it may have taken the *Henrietta Marie* as long as three months to sail from West Africa to the West Indies, her hold crammed with as many slaves as the traders could wedge in—the more slaves, the greater the profit.

In addition to her heavy armament, the *Henrietta Marie* would have carried a substantial number of small arms. This is reflected in the customs records made when she left Deal in 1697 and in the artifacts recovered from the wreck itself. Slavers required small arms for crew protection off the West African coast, in the event of a boarding action at sea or, perhaps more important, in case of a slave revolt during the Middle Passage.

The expected armament of slavers as reported in customs returns included military muskets, fowling pieces, musketoons and blunderbusses, pistols, cutlasses and hangers, boarding pikes and grenades. While sentries guarding the slaves would have been armed while at sea, the remainder of these weapons would have been stored aft, for use in an emergency.

Shipboard slave revolts were an ever-present danger. James Barbot of the slaver *Albion Frigate* recorded one uprising: "We caused as many of our men as convenient to lie in the great cabin, where we kept all our small arms in readiness, with sentinels constantly at the door and avenues to it. Once the revolt began the crew moved out to line the low'r wale of the quarterdeck, where we stood in arms, firing on the revolted slaves."

The Jeep slowed down.

"We should pull into a store and buy another map," Angus said, making a sharp right turn with only a moment's warning. I folded my notes into my briefcase.

We had traveled into another county and the towns off the highway were getting smaller and more rural, offering fewer places to buy maps. We parked along the street to stretch our legs while Angus went into a general store.

When he returned, we helped him unfold the new map and searched quickly for anything starting with the letter *S*. But, again, there was nothing even close.

"We're not going back to London until we find Stream Mill," Angus announced, pounding the steering wheel with his fist. A light drizzle turned to steady rain. The hills seemed to be getting larger and the farmhouses were now much farther apart. We stopped at a pub for lunch and to plot our next course.

"Think we'll find it?" David asked Angus.

"Have a lit'l faith, will ya," Angus said.

Our concern was that because of the rain and gray skies, nightfall would come earlier than usual and we would almost certainly lose our way to Stream Mill in the dark. Even in the daylight, we weren't sure if we were headed in the right direction.

An hour later, we found our way onto the main street of another little town. They were all beginning to look alike. Angus bought yet another county map and spread it out across the front seat. We each scanned a portion of it.

It took only a few minutes for Angus to announce his find.

"Here it is!" he shouted. "It's here!"

In the middle of the map, in tiny, easily overlooked italic letters, were the words *Stream Mill.* They were situated near a speck on the map called Chiddingly, the village we had been vaguely headed toward all along.

We didn't know if Stream Mill was public land or private property, or if there was anything to see should we be lucky enough to get access to the grounds.

The squiggly map lines to Stream Mill pointed to a maze of tiny paths off the highway, forks in the road, winding lanes, and narrow roads near Chiddingly.

"We're very close," Angus said, pulling out the photocopied picture that showed Stream Mill in the 1800s. "We're looking for something that looks like this."

Angus was a wild driver, but he was an expert in his field and knew a little something about getting around rural England. We turned off the highway and onto a narrow paved road that we followed for about five miles.

Following the map carefully, we passed a dirt road off to the left, another to our right, one more to the left.

"That was our turn," Angus said, his foot pounding the brake pedal and throwing the Jeep into reverse.

The passage was just wide enough for the Jeep, nothing more. We took a right turn at a sharp fork, driving onto a road that seemed even narrower and rockier than the others. Wet, leafy branches brushed against the Jeep and dripped inside. The road zigzagged like a series of eights; it was hard to tell where it ended. Angus just kept driving, slowing occasionally to steer clear of holes in the road.

A gravel driveway intersected the end of the road. About thirty yards away sat a large two-story stone house with creamed-colored shutters and a thick, wooden front door. It looked as though it had a story to tell.

We pulled into the driveway, turned off the engine, and sat, gratefully stunned by what we saw. No one uttered a word. Alongside the house ran a stream nestled in a wooded thicket. It resembled the photograph that Angus had copied from *Wealden Iron* by Ernest Straker, published in 1931.

"This looks like the photo from the book," I said, staring at the photocopy.

"This is it!" Angus said. "We found it!"

"Now what do we do?" David asked.

"Well, let's tell them the truth: We're writers, scholars, and archaeologists," Angus said. "We're here doing research. We're likable guys."

We climbed out of the Jeep and walked along the gravel driveway. The yard seemed to stretch into Scotland. We could hear dogs in the distance; the winds seemed to carry their barking for miles. It was quiet and absolutely peaceful. There wasn't another home anywhere in sight.

Angus knocked on the door. A thin middle-aged woman in baggy beige shorts answered. She had fine wrinkles at the corners of her blue eyes, a mess of blond hair, and a sweet, scatterbrained expression. She was surprisingly pleasant for a woman suddenly confronted by three strangers on her doorstep.

"Hello," Angus said, sounding more Scottish than ever. "I'm Angus Konstram from the Tower of London. We're writers, scholars, and archaeologists. We're researching the history of a slave ship that was discovered in waters near the United States, and we have traced the maker of its fine cannons to your backyard. May we have a look around?"

At that instant, I thought about the block I lived on in Brooklyn. If three men from another country knocked on my door and asked to come in to conduct research, would I be accommodating? I was glad I didn't have to answer that question. In New York City, a home owner in the same situation would most certainly be dialing 911.

The woman was charming and extremely animated. She introduced herself as Marilyn Ambroziak and said she and her husband, George, had owned the house for several years and had converted it into a cozy bed-and-breakfast.

"We hope we're in the right place," Angus said. "We're looking for the old Stream Mill foundry."

"You're in the right place," Marilyn said. "This is where the foundry used to be in the late 1600s. How you found it, I don't know, but this entire area was a foundry for ironwork at one time. We own ten acres of property here."

Although Marilyn had not heard of the *Henrietta Marie,* she knew plenty about the history of their property: She knew the foundry had been used to manufacture guns—specifically cannons—and she recognized the name Fuller as that of one of the people associated with the foundry.

She disappeared upstairs for a few minutes and returned with a few old photos of Stream Mill taken in the mid-1800s.

"Take them if you'd like to photocopy them," she said. "But I need them back. C'mon outside; I'll show you around."

We walked around the side of the house and Marilyn pointed to a ten-by-ten-foot sealed area that was layered with brick. "This is where the foundry used to be," she said. "This was the site of the furnace. Our house was built over it."

This was once the site of a foundry where four-ton crescent-shaped hammers powered by water paddles pounded hot iron at 150 strokes a minute. Today, there are still ale bottles strewn across the yard under layers of grass and dirt, some broken, some not, tossed to the turf by Swedish laborers who constructed the cannons with sweat and muscle.

"We used to think it was fascinating from a historical perspective to find old ale bottles from the seventeenth century all over the yard, but now they're just a pain in the ass," Marilyn said, laughing. "These bottles are everywhere! Would you like to see the stream now?"

"Certainly," I said.

"Watch your step," she told us. "It may be a bit muddy."

The stream was about fifty yards from the back of the house. We made our own path through soggy shrubbery. The grass was wet and I could feel glass cracking under my feet. We walked through a maze of trees, swatting back branches until the stream came into view.

It was nearly hidden in the woods, but the little stream was still winding its way to London after all these years, its clear, cool water gently flowing over a dozen stone steps.

Angus explained that we were looking at what used to be a working waterway: once the cannons were manufactured, they were sent downstream where workers near town would drag the big guns from the water and haul the iron products onto ships or transport them to warehouses in London. During the casting process, they would mark their products—Stream Mill with the *S*—to protect their property from thieves.

With every turn down a dirt road and every step along a soggy path, I was coming closer to the *Henrietta Marie,* to knowing more about the slave trade and the enslaved African people who were forced to travel aboard a floating hell.

There was no question that we had located the foundry where the cannons were manufactured. John "Mad Jack" Fuller and his family, who were prominent citizens in London, had leased the land and the foundry.

The Fullers also owned several plantations in Jamaica and eventually moved from London to oversee their estates—and their enslaved African people—full-time.

It was the first solid connection to the *Henrietta Marie* that we had discovered. It felt strange. I was intrigued by the discovery, but I was also a bit unnerved about tracking down the manufacturers, learning the names of real people connected with the ship, and realizing and understanding that the Fuller family rose to prominence by exploiting and abusing black people who were forced to work their land.

"The Fullers were in a despicable business," I said. "I wonder if they're resting well."

George Ambroziak joined us downstairs and offered us a beer. We told George and Marilyn more stories about the *Henrietta Marie* and they shared more history about their property.

That I was sitting in the living room of a British couple, in a speck of a community in rural England, flanked by two white men—one from Scotland, the other from North Carolina—talking about slavery on property where tools of the slave trade were manufactured, said that these were unique times. African-Americans and whites can find common interests on which to build a relationship, even if the issue is unsettling to explore.

Finding ways for African-Americans and whites to communicate can be difficult enough. With the complexities, emotion, and pain associated with the subject of slavery, it becomes a challenge to believe that black people are not the only ones interested in learning about the history of the slave trade. It's the history of white people, as well.

George refused to allow us to leave the area without touring Chiddingly, a sleepy, tight-knit community of several hundred residents that sits far away from the noise of London. In *Wealden Iron,* William Straker mentioned "the iron hammer of Chiddingly," as people referred to it in 1548.

A pub and a small stone church sit fifty feet apart in the town square. Centuries ago, the commoners spent most of the year making thick layers of cheese to stack across the road, thus creating a cushioned platform for the village's self-appointed royal family, who did not want their feet to touch the ground while walking through the village. There are two eight-foot-high statues inside the church, a man and a woman wearing robes, rings, and crowns, each standing on a triangular block of cheese.

After the two-hour tour through the village, George and Marilyn filled us in on the unusual goings-on in the neighborhood.

It seems that late at night, in the quiet of the thickets around their house, Marilyn and George can still hear—and sometimes even see—the Swedish workmen laughing and drinking ale while the sound of a hammer pounding hot iron echoes in the night.

"Oh, yes, there are ghosts here," Marilyn said with a straight face. "We're used to them. They pop up from time to time. Nothing bad ever happens. But they are here. We've all seen and heard them."

"Real ghosts?" I asked.

"Yes," George insisted. "*Real* ghosts."

The sun was dropping fast behind the hills.

"Well, you know this is also a bed-and-breakfast, and since it's getting dark, you're welcome to stay the night."

"We appreciate the offer, but we'll be pushing on," I said. "Besides, it sounds like it's a bit crowded around here already with all the laborers in the yard."

We thanked George and Marilyn; they were pleasant people. As we pulled out, Marilyn stood at the edge of the driveway waving good-bye; George waved from a second-floor window.

I took one last look over Steam Mill as night began to blanket the hillside. As we drove away from the stone house, passing peaked silhouettes that had replaced the grassy knolls, I couldn't help feeling that my journey was predestined; that I was following an inner beacon, like a ship chasing a flicker from a lighthouse in fog.

I was being directed from continent to continent, from seaside to countryside, by a force that has guided more people over rough roads than Angus.

I was in good hands.

6

On a splintered wharf along the Thames River where pirates were left hanging by their necks long after they were dead, until high tides flooded their bodies, the Prospect of Whitby was a haven for slave traders and thieves.

London's oldest riverside pub was at one time a dark and dangerous tavern where the city's underside—muggers, pickpockets, and smugglers—would assemble, and where slave-ship captains and their crews sat amid swirls of smoke and swigged pints of ale as they waited for favorable winds to sail to the coast of West Africa.

The *Henrietta Marie* probably anchored along the Wapping pier in the spring of 1697, near the infamous old pub, first known as the Devil's Tavern when it was built in 1520.

Dockyard workers—some of them schoolchildren trying to earn a few pennies a day by scrubbing old ship ropes—would scrape the ship clean of barnacles, secure the riggings with rope, fasten wood together with iron spikes, and renovate the ship's galley to accommodate a large signal-burner cookstove that was made of copper and would have been surrounded by bricks to keep the fire from spreading throughout the ship, according to research by the Mel Fisher Maritime Heritage Society and *Spirits of the Passage* by Madeleine Burnside.

The first captain of the *Henrietta Marie*, William Deacon, may have taken a seat at the Prospect of Whitby's pewter-layered bar to sip ale as he tended to the business at hand—outfitting his ship and hiring her crew.

Preparing to sail from London, the *Henrietta Marie* would have stored a variety of anchors and been stocked with basic items: iron bars, glass beads, pewterware to trade for slaves in Africa; linen and calico cloth, indigo, and paint for the British inhabitants of the new colonies in the Caribbean; short-barreled blunderbusses and long-bladed cutlasses, short knives and pistols; freshwater, tobacco and rum, brandy and wine for the crew.

And of course the *Henrietta Marie* was rigged with the grisly tools of her trade: heavy chains, iron collars, and at least one hundred pairs of iron shackles for slaves' wrists and ankles, as well as sharp contraptions to pry open the mouths of African men and women who refused to eat.

Deacon would have walked the weathered docks of Wapping, rounding up a crew—carpenter, sailmaker, cook, ship's surgeon, ship's gunner. He needed eighteen men. He would have had to make his selections from among men of questionable backgrounds—outlaws and outcasts, drifters who lived from day to day doing odd jobs, legal or illegal. These men never knew more than a few dollars at a time, had more than a few brushes with the law, were more interested in their next shot of rye than their next bath, and had more expertise in beating, kidnapping, and rape than in navigating the sea.

They didn't have to be bright or necessarily healthy, just willing to accept one of the longest, harshest, and filthiest jobs available.

As he made his rounds of the wharf, Deacon may have stopped occasionally to watch the routine hangings at Execution Dock, where Captain Kidd was hanged in 1701.

Sipping a pint of beer myself inside the Prospect of Whitby, I thought about the Thames of long-ago autumns and how the muddy brown river would become so choked with slave ships, seamen could cross it by stepping from ship deck to ship deck.

I was reminded of stories about young men who were hit over the head and smuggled aboard slave ships, unwilling participants of the slave trade, forced to make the horrendous one-year-long voyages.

"This was a notorious place once," the bartender said as he served me a beer. "Bad people spent their time in here."

The pirates and slave-ship captains were long gone, but their pernicous intentions seemed to linger still in the smoky Prospect of Whitby.

Shortly after sunset on November 10, 1697, according to Tattersfield, the *Henrietta Marie* slipped her moorings and glided downriver to the English Channel.

At eighty feet long and weighing 120 tons, she would have been a small but impressive sight, flying the British Union Jack at her bow and stern and again atop her center mast—a good fifty feet above her deck.

She was fashioned of wood and fastened together by iron spikes. She moved fast under sail, propelled by the wind against her six canvas sails, attached with sturdy rigging in two square sails to the mainmast and foremost mast, a smaller triangular sail on the stern mast, and one stretched twenty feet before her bow from the bowsprit. She was designed with small cabins and low ceilings, low quarterdeck gunwhale, stepped decks, a galley, and air ports for ventilation belowdecks.

Her captain piloted her from just forward of the mizzenmast, aided by deckhands who stood near the railings to thwart any attempts the Africans, who would soon be loaded into her bottom decks, might make to jump overboard.

Research from the Mel Fisher Maritime Heritage Society tells us the following:

Deacon, at her helm, was no stranger to the sea, or to the slave trade. He had become proficient in the business, turning a tidy profit for himself from hauling his human cargo over thousands of miles of rough seas in the Atlantic Ocean destined to a life of slavery.

A young man for a ship captain at thirty years of age, Deacon had been handpicked by a consortium of investors who were attempting to minimize the amount they would have to pay in overhead.

He approached the slave trade as an international business, nothing more. He certainly didn't consider it personal. A professional merchant seaman from the village of Stepney on the north bank of the Thames, now an inner-city area of London, Deacon had captained at least two prior slave-trade voyages aboard the *Crown* of London—delivering some 305 African men and women to Barbados on April 22, 1695, and 211 in 1696.

During those slave-trading voyages, Deacon quickly earned a reputation as a fair captain, one who distributed wages equitably. Working a slaver was a business of arduous labor, fatal disease, and low morals on a ship where the stench of death was as familiar as the salty sting of seawater. Slave-ship crewmen had a stomach for misery; still, any crew needed a captain they could respect, trust, and count on for command.

Henrietta Maria was the daughter of Henry IV, king of France, and queen consort of England's King Charles I, who reigned from 1625 to 1649. But the ship was probably not named for her. It's more likely that the *Henrietta Marie* was named for the wife, sister, daughter, or even daughters of someone associated with the ownership of the vessel, the common practice of the day.

The earliest known date of operation for the *Henrietta Marie* as a slave ship is 1697, the year that saw the end of the War of the Grand Alliance, known as King William's War in North America.

The ship carried a first and second mate and, immediately below them in rank, a boatswain. One of these officers was John Scorch. Like Deacon, Scorch came from Stepney, and he had served as a Royal Navy boatswain, although he may well have held a higher position for this voyage.

The *Henrietta Marie* also carried the gunner and his mate, the cooper and his mate, one or two ship's carpenters, and some seamen, among whom were Edward Humble, Peter Christopherson, Claus Johansson, Christopher Trunifo, and James Kedd. Though slave ships were not required by law to carry a surgeon until 1788, the *Henrietta Marie* may well have done so. The ship carried an agent or accountant, whose job it was to record the goods exchanged for slaves.

Each of these men stood to profit from the voyage of the *Henrietta Marie*. At the end of their journey, they would receive a commission on the number of slaves delivered alive to the colonies.

Nigel Tattersfield wrote:

William Deacon's intention may have been to join the so-called New England fleet of merchant shipping, which had assembled off Cowes, on the Isle of Wight, during the last days of October and the

*beginning of November under the watchful eye of the Royal Navy.
This would have provided company and protection for the* Henrietta
Marie *until their ways parted in the Atlantic.*

Ironically, the headwinds the Henrietta Marie *struggled against
while working her way down the Thames to Gravesend were the
favorable winds for which the New England fleet had been waiting;
it had long departed by the time the* Henrietta Marie *reached the Isle
of Wight. She was on her own.*

Still, she did carry eight impressive cannons and she was built for
speed. Turnaround time was crucial to slave traders, as it could take as
long as one year to make the full circuit of the Triangular Trade—from
England to Africa to the New World and back to England.

And with a cargo as valuable and fragile as slaves—more than 50 percent would often die en route—the faster a ship could arrive in the West
Indies, the greater the chance of large profits for the traders.

Death wasn't simply anticipated; it was expected. Slave-ship captains
were encouraged to navigate the waters of the Atlantic efficiently to
ensure the swift delivery of their cargo—not to waste time and energy
caring for the sick, dying, and those who wished they were dead.

According to the Mel Fisher Maritime Heritage Society and *Spirits of
the Passage,* it took about three months for William Deacon to guide the
Henrietta Marie through the first leg of her voyage—from the English
Channel, through storms and swelled seas, to the Bight of Benin on the
West African coast—and then perhaps another month to sail through the
mouth of the Rio Real and to the shores of New Calabar.

The helm would have been sweltering as Deacon steered his vessel up
the Rio Real, and his crew overwhelmed by the heat and hordes of mosquitoes that brought disease with each bite.

Even so, Deacon probably still wore his felt hat and woolen coat
when he stepped ashore at New Calabar to meet the African leaders and
trade for black people with iron bars that were stored aboard the *Henrietta Marie.*

Once the trading was complete, Deacon sailed along the Calabar
River and Rio Real, repeating the process at other outposts. This activity
could last for several months in the oppressive heat, while some members

of his crew collapsed either from exhaustion or disease brought on by mosquito and other insect bites.

More than sixteen thousand slaves were taken from Calabar each year and forced aboard slave ships bound for the West Indies, but trading in New Calabar was a lengthy, wearisome, and deadly business. Captains would often double up on crewmen before sailing from London, knowing how heavy their losses might become.

As the *Henrietta Marie* glided along the Rio Real, her ship's carpenters busied themselves building half decks—really nothing more than shelves—from trees they found along the way, according to the Mel Fisher Maritime Heritage Society and *Spirits of the Passage*.

The half decks were installed in the *Henrietta Marie*'s hold to accomodate the nearly 300 Africans who would be hauled across the Atlantic to the West Indies.

Space per slave aboard the *Henrietta Marie* was usually about sixteen inches wide by five and a half feet long on the half decks, stacked two high and about three feet apart. There was no room for the Africans to stand and little room even to sit up straight. Sometimes they were forced to lie on their sides, in chains, for months.

"In the slave trade, as in every other, there were good years and lean. Sometimes the ships filled quickly, and the wooden shelves, which the carpenters had erected in the holds now empty of European merchandise, would be crammed with Negroes lying, as we have seen, like books upon a shelf," according to *A Study of the Atlantic Slave Trade, 1141–1807* by John Pope-Hennessy.

"In the worst ships," the author continues, "in which the slave-holds were not properly aired, nor the floors and shelves washed down with pailfuls of vinegar, in which the slaves were not properly fed and exercised; in which the crews were bestial and drunken, the market value of the valuable people declined day after day."

There was hardly any fresh air to breathe and even less room in which to die. It was not uncommon for an African man to wake, choking from the iron collar around his neck, to find a limp, lifeless body next to him, perhaps a friend or a brother, or a son.

Later, when the stench of the dead became too overwhelming, the crew would unchain the bodies and carry them topside, and throw them over the side.

In some cases—in the event of a pirate raid, for instance—the crew of a slave ship could easily dump its entire cargo. The slave deck on these ships was built on a tilt, with a trapdoor at the stern. The Africans were all shackled to the same chain, which ran the length of the ship on both sides and was attached to a heavy iron ball. To avoid the insult of watching pirates make off with their precious cargo, the crew could open the trapdoor and the iron weight would fall into the sea, dragging all with it.

There is no adequate way to count the number of Africans from the *Henrietta Marie* who were thrown into the sea, no way to count the number of families that were separated by slavery, no way to count the babies who died in their mothers' arms, no barometer to measure the loss of generations of innocent black people.

African people suffered unspeakable indignities in the overcrowded hulls of slave ships. They were branded with hot irons; they were packed so tightly they could not move or turn over; and they were not allowed to use latrine buckets. These were frequent atrocities that occurred aboard the *Henrietta Marie,* where screams and moans from the ship's hold were constantly overlooked by the half-drunk crewmen who walked the creaking wooden deck overhead, frequently peering through the inch-wide cracks in the deck to see if morning had brought any new dead cargo that needed to be tossed overboard.

A prisoner who refused to eat was met with many methods of force: They could be flogged repeatedly or their lips might be burned with a hot coal. The crew often dismissed these cries of pain because they did not want to slow the process of fattening the slaves for public auction.

At times on long voyages, the enslaved Africans who rebelled against being flailed, raped, and corralled like livestock would mutiny and try to overthrow the crew, who would often hide pistols in various sections of the ship to protect themselves from slave revolts.

In his paper "The World of the *Henrietta Marie:* Trading Routes and the Middle Passage," Dr. Russell L. Adams wrote:

> *The distances around the triangle trade route exceeded 10,000 miles. The core of the Middle Passage, of course, is the 1,800- to 3,000- mile distances between European holding pens in Africa and colonial auction blocks in the Caribbean or the Americas. Typical of the reac-*

tions of slave merchants to these great distances is the following quo-
tation from a letter to the Secretary of the Royal African Company
from an employee at Falmouth, England:

"*The 14th (of June, 1677) came in here the* Arthur *of London in*
nine weeks from Jamaica laden with sugar for London. She has been
twelve months out of England, for she went for Guinea to load
negroes, of which she made but an indifferent voyage, many of them
dying during their passage."

This statement is a succinct history of one triangular voyage of a
merchant slaver in the service of the Royal African Company: It
traveled from Falmouth, England, to Guinea, Africa, and from
Guinea to Jamaica and back to Falmouth. Many of its passengers
perished in the Middle Passage of what apparently was a money-
losing voyage. Falmouth was the last ship-provisioning and inspec-
tion port on the western tip of England. It also was one of the first
landings for ships returning from overseas.

Crewmen aboard the *Henrietta Marie* would have carried cutlasses
and pistols and patrolled the decks around the clock. "This police force
was armed whenever slaves were on deck, ready to subdue resistance by
any means necessary," Dr. Adams wrote. "One captain, Thomas Phillips,
in telling his story of a 1693–94 Middle Passage had this to say about
security aboard ship:

When our slaves are aboard we shackle them two and two, while we
lie in port, and in sight of their own country, for 'tis then they
attempt to make their escape to prevent which we always keep cen-
tinels upon the hatchways, and have a chest full of small arms, ready
loaden and prim'd...together with some granada shells, and two of
our quarter deck guns, pointing on the deck..."

Firing directly at slaves was viewed as a last resort because Deacon
would not have wanted to lose his precious merchandise unnecessarily.
The cargo that Deacon was carrying across the Atlantic, which slave-ship
captains referred to as "black gold," would bring him financial security.

If the slaves rebelled and managed to get out of the hold and onto the deck, the crew would barricade themselves in the stern, where the guns and ammunition were stored, until the uprising was brought under control, according to the Mel Fisher Maritime Heritage Society.

ʊʊ

There is one particular story that is extraordinary: *Equiano's Travels* is a powerful book by an enslaved African named Olaudah Equiano, who in 1789 published this account of his life—from being kidnapped in Nigeria, to slavery in the West Indies, and finally to freedom in England.

I learned that Equiano, who was born in 1745, was a member of the Ibo tribe. He was captured by slave traders from the interior of Nigeria—known as Calabar—when he was just ten years old.

Equiano wrote about the treatment of other slaves, the vile conditions on the ships, the African people who died from illness and the others who were thrown over the side for rebelling against inhumane conditions.

Historians believe that *olaudah* means "having a loud voice and being well spoken," and that *equiano* means "when they speak, others attend," implying a village spokesman. Equiano was given the name Gustavus Vassa by one of his slave owners after first being given the name Michael.

When he was released from slavery in 1766, he continued to use the name Gustavus Vassa, and he quickly became involved in the abolition of slavery movement, wrote other books, and traveled throughout England, speaking out against slavery.

In 1783, Vassa drew the attention of historian Granville Sharpe when he made Sharpe aware of the massacre of more than 130 slaves aboard the slave ship *Zong* off the West African coast.

Sharpe recorded this note on March 19 of that year: "Gustavus Vassa, a negro, called on me, with an account of 130 negroes being thrown alive into the sea...having been earnestly solicited and called upon by a poor negro for my assistance to avenge the blood of his slaughtered countrymen."

That *Zong* case led to many parliamentary battles over the slave trade, although it was years before abolition became law, and many years after Equiano's death.

To date, historians say, *Equiano's Travels* (it was originally entitled

The Interesting Narrative of the Life of Olaudah Equiano, the African)
is the only story that chronicles a voyage on a slave ship from Calabar to
the West Indies from the perspective of an African.

British writers used Equiano's book to help them retrace the movement of slave ships and re-create the history of slavery during the late
1600s and early 1700s. The ship on which Equiano sailed took the same
route as the *Henrietta Marie,* and the hell aboard the slave ship was nothing short of evil. Equiano wrote:

> *The stench of the hold while we were on the coast was so intolera-
> bly loathsome that it was dangerous to remain there for any time,
> and some of us had been permitted to stay on the deck for fresh air;
> but now that the whole ship's cargo were confined together it
> became absolutely pestilential.*
>
> *...The closeness of the place and the heat of the climate, added
> to the number in the ship, which was so crowded that each had
> scarcely room to turn himself, almost suffocated us.*
>
> *This produced copious perspiration, so that the air soon became
> unfit for respiration from a variety of loathsome smells, and brought
> on a sickness among the slaves, of which many died....*
>
> *The shrieks of the women and the groans of the dying rendered
> the whole a scene of horror almost inconceivable.*

Despite the floating hell that Equiano experienced, he was still able to
bring compassion to an otherwise ruthless business. He wrote about people as human beings, not as cargo. Having been separated from his sister,
he wrote:

> *Is it not enough that we are torn from our country and friends to toil
> for your luxury and lust of gain? Must every tender feeling be like-
> wise sacrificed to your avarice?*
>
> *Are the dearest friends and relations, now rendered more dear by
> their separation from their kindred?... Why are parents to lose their
> children, brothers their sisters, or husbands their wives? Surely, this
> is a new refinement in cruelty....*
>
> *I was soon put down under the decks, and there I received such*

a salutation in my nostrils as I had never experienced in my life: so that with the loathsomeness of the stench and crying together, I became so sick and low that I was not able to eat....I now wished for the last friend, death, to relieve me.

This wretched situation was again aggravated by the galling of the chains, now becoming unsupportable, and the filth of the necessary tubs, into which the children often fell and were almost suffocated.

...I feared I would be put to death, the white people looked and acted, as I thought, in so savage a manner; for I had never seen among my people such instances of brutal cruelty...."

7

Riding miles of whitecapped waves on her final approach to the island of Barbados, the *Henrietta Marie* anchored in Carlisle Bay on July 9, 1698—a three-month voyage.

Her rigging was tangled, her sails scorched, and she creaked in the tide like a worn-out rocking chair. Her crew numbered only nine—half of them having died, felled by malaria, dysentery, yellow fever, and sunstroke during the passage across the Atlantic.

Like their African prisoners who had died in the hold, they too had been thrown overboard, fresh food for the sharks that routinely trailed the ship.

As the survivors now understood, the ancient mariner's adage was more truth than myth: "Beware and take heed of the Bight of Benin, where few come out though many go in."

Barbados shipping records indicate this about the *Henrietta Marie:* "foreign built, 9 men, 114 tons, 8 guns." The records also state the ship delivered "250 negro slaves and 150 elephants' teeth."

The mission of selling slaves had taken a punishing toll on the *Henrietta Marie* and her crew, but nothing was as horrifying as the sight of her suffering and trembling mass of Africans chained in the decks below, crying out in agony.

The captain of the *Henrietta Marie,* William Deacon, was still at the helm, exhausted and possibly ill from his voyage, while the crewmen who had survived, some ridden now with scurvy, stumbled across the deck and down the gangway.

Below, in the stinking hull of the *Henrietta Marie,* Africans, some of them dead in their chains, were jammed in an oven-hot hold more than thick with polluted air.

They were limp from hunger, numb from abuse, their dark bodies bruised and branded.

℧℧

Nicholas Prideaux, a Royal African Company agent in Barbados, wrote promptly to Africa House on July eleventh, describing William Deacon as "an interloper from the Bight with 250 Negroes."

The hell for a cargo of African people aboard the *Henrietta Marie* had been transformed from floating death to a wind-whipped island in the West Indies just twenty-one miles long. Deacon, although tired, would have been anxious to unload his cargo and prepare to replenish his supplies and repeat his transatlantic voyage.

"At last we came in sight of the island of Barbados, at which the whites on board gave a great shout and made many signs of joy to us," Olaudah Equiano wrote of his voyage to the West Indies.

"We did not know what to think of this, but as the vessel drew nearer we plainly saw the harbor and other ships of different kinds and sizes, and we soon anchored amongst them off Bridgetown....They put us in separate parcels and examined us attentively. There was much dread and trembling among us, and nothing but bitter cries to be heard all the night...."

It was the *Henrietta Marie*'s first voyage to the lush tropical island where slaves were brought by the tens of thousands.

Perhaps just as many never made it. Disease was responsible for most of the deaths during the Middle Passage and was feared by the white crew as well as by the Africans. Overcrowding, spoiled food, depression from homesickness, and lack of fresh air and exercise encouraged the spread of diseases like scurvy, yellow jack, and dysentery, the three most common killers; they wiped out some of the toughest captains.

The Mel Fisher Maritime Heritage Society and *Spirits of the Passage* tell us that William Deacon was a man who carefully tended to his business interest. The Africans enslaved aboard the *Henrietta Marie* had to be sold at public auction, and the price fetched for each slave would determine his profit and the profit of the business investors who had hired him.

The *Henrietta Marie*'s voyage had been successful for Deacon. Most of the Africans arrived in Barbados alive, and the food and water had held out for the crew. While some of the black people had died, as well as half the crew, Deacon had factored in such losses. This was not a sentimental assignment.

Deacon would have walked the ship, inspecting the slaves and ordering his crew to give them extra food and then to have them shaved, washed, and given palm oil with which to coat their bodies. The captain was not trying to make it easy for the Africans; he was fattening them up and grooming them to improve their appearance. Deacon knew he could demand a better price if an African looked cleaner and stronger to potential buyers.

Africans destined for a life of bondage were led down the gangway of the *Henrietta Marie,* squinting and shielding their eyes with chained hands as they were forced into the harsh light of the tropical sun for the first time in months.

Captains would often arrange for slaves from local plantations to be brought to the ship to counsel the frightened captives. The African captives feared cannibalism, a terror that only increased when new white men began coming aboard to inspect them.

The plantation slaves would dutifully assure the newcomers that they would not be eaten, that they would merely be given work to do. For the slaves aboard the *Henrietta Marie,* arrangements had already been made.

The majority of them, 188 in total, were consigned to a slave merchant named William Shuller. A broker rather than a plantation owner, Shuller was a man of considerable importance in Barbados.

In the mid-1600s, he was a prominent citizen in the parish of St. Michael and served as a justice of the peace. But he made his lucrative living primarily from the brokering of black flesh. He died on May 9, 1715, after amassing a great deal of wealth.

Buying only those Africans who were in good health, Shuller paid an average of nineteen pounds for each slave, a total of £3,589. The price paid in Africa for a male slave was about three pounds, no more than an English peasant's annual wage.

According to the Mel Fisher Maritime Heritage Society, corrupt captains would sometimes try to sell as healthy those sick Africans who could still walk, for instance, packing the anuses of those afflicted with dysentery with oakum, a type of chalk used to keep ships watertight.

White newcomers to the islands might be fooled by the ploy, but in the long run, it only meant that buyers felt required to subject their African purchases to the most demeaning of examinations.

Sugar was scarce that year due to a slender crop, but Deacon managed to stow more than 118 hogsheads of brown sugar and 1 hogshead of refined white sugar belowdecks, along with 67 bags of ginger, which could turn a neat profit in London.

The 188 "healthy" Africans Shuller had purchased were taken to a nearby warehouse. No longer beset by the rolling of the ship, the slaves stumbled over the flat land as they marched along. They were pushed, poked, and beaten as they were herded down the streets. Shuller's warehouse was probably no more than an open corral: there, the slaves would spend the next few days huddled together, tied with ropes, while waiting to be taken to the auction block individually or in roped lots.

The African people aboard the *Henrietta Marie* in 1698 represented a mere fraction of the number of slaves who had been hauled to Barbados before them. The first English settlement of the island began in 1627. On February seventeenth of that year, eighty English settlers and ten black slaves who had been captured from trading vessels at sea set up camp on the west side of the island, according to writer Rachel Wilder, editor of *Insight Guides: Barbados*.

The black slaves introduced sporadically during Barbados's earliest years by Dutch and Portuguese traders were predominantly male. In fact, during the first fifty years or so of Barbadian English settlement, a severe imbalance of the sexes, black and white, tempered the population growth dramatically.

"Negroes imported to the sugar islands died much faster than they were born," wrote historian Richard S. Dunn. "West Indian slave masters soon gave up trying to keep Negroes alive long enough to breed up a new generation and instead routinely bought replacement slaves year in and year out."

In the early 1600s, Barbados became a stage for gamblers, fighters, and fortune hunters, for political refugees and outcasts, for kidnappers and their bounties. According to historian Hilary Beckles, the number of blacks on Barbados didn't exceed eight hundred throughout the 1630s. Even a decade later, the population numbered roughly 37,000 whites to only 6,000 blacks.

The 1640s were a pivotal decade for Barbados. These were the years in which the colonists "retooled" to manufacture sugar, making Barbados the first British possession to cultivate sugar on a large scale. The first man to bring sugarcane to the island was Peter Blower, in 1637. He had learned how to grow and process sugarcane in Brazil. At first, cane was used to produce rum, but by 1642, sugar would be producing sweet profits all by itself.

Historians say the population shift during Barbados's boom sugar years—roughly 1643 to 1660—was dramatic. The number of whites on the island decreased as small planters were squeezed out by the giants, who now owned hundreds of acres and hundreds of slaves. The black population increased quickly as slaves were brought in from the west coast of Africa, a practice that would continue for 150 years.

By the 1650s, Barbados's plantation system was intact. The island probably looked then, more than three hundred years ago, much as it does today: heavily cultivated, with very little forestland left standing.

Sugar meant great wealth for Europeans, and abject poverty for enslaved African people.

In 1645, according to historians, there were 5,680 blacks in Barbados; by 1684, that number had grown to 60,000. The slaves at that time—brought by the Portuguese and Dutch from areas that are now territories of Sierra Leone, Guinea, Ghana, the Ivory Coast, Nigeria, and the Cameroons—outnumbered whites four to one. It is quite obvious that without them, the plantations could not have existed.

By the time the *Henrietta Marie* docked in Barbados, there were about 42,000 enslaved Africans on the island, most of them laboring on the island's vast sugarcane plantations.

Sugar was more profitable than any other export from the British colonies; European planters raising sugar amassed profits very quickly. As their plantations grew, so did the numbers of their African laborers. Sugar was so lucrative and demanding a crop that European planters were willing to pay a higher price for Africans who were experienced farmers—the Ibo from the regions north of New Calabar were in particular demand.

Cutting sugarcane is perhaps the most demanding and difficult part of farming, according to *Spirits of the Passage*. It is still done by hand today with long, heavy-bladed machetes. Centuries ago, at harvest time, men and women worked side by side, naked, sweating and bleeding from the lashes of the overseers as they processed cane stalks into the brown *muscovado* sugar.

Sometimes the laborers—who were allowed only four hours of sleep a night and no extra food—died where they worked. The others would be forced to push the bodies of the dead aside and step over the corpses, stinking and covered with flies, to continue their work in the hot sun.

"I pity them greatly, but I must be mum/For how could we do without sugar and rum?" wrote the British writer William Cowper in the 1700s.

In Barbados, where planters had a reputation for providing for the slaves better than on other islands, according to historians, one adult African was given a pint of grain and half of a rotted herring for twenty-four hours. In a famous investigation of 1790–1791, no plantation was found where a slave received more than nine pints of corn or one pound of salt meat per week.

The mortality rate among newly arrived Africans was exceptionally high, with estimates of deaths running to 30 percent. Old and new diseases, change of climate and food, and suicide and excessive flogging were the main causes for the deaths.

Plantations throughout the West Indies were brutal and horrifying. The drill was the same: Enslaved Africans were sent to the plantations at daybreak and labored all day except for a thirty-minute period for breakfast and a two-hour period at the hottest portion of the day, which was frequently the time set aside for lighter chores.

The workday was long, sometimes eighteen hours. Plantation overseers did not distinguish between men and women in work requirements or in applying the lash. Investigators from the British Parliament reported in 1790–1791 that pregnant women were forced to work up to the time of childbirth and that one month was the maximum amount of time allowed to recover from childbearing.

Pregnant women were lashed severely when they were unable to keep pace with other workers, according to historians. Women who paused in the fields to care for their babies, whom they carried on their backs, were lashed with cowhide whips. Sometimes the wounds were so large that a finger could be inserted in them, according to *The Spirits of the Passage*.

This research tells us slave owners also discouraged African practices and rituals. The slaves were not permitted to attend religious services, speak to one another or sing the spiritual songs of Africa. If an African struck a white person, he would be severely whipped; for a second offense, he would be branded on the face with a hot iron. Another popular form of punishment was to suspend a black person from a tree by ropes and tie iron weights around his or her neck and waist.

Slave revolts were not so very frequent in Barbados, according to the Barbados Department of Archives. By an act of 1692, a slave who gave information that led to the uncovering of a planned conspiracy to revolt was entitled to be set free and "sent to such place where he or she desired."

During one attempted revolt, a group of slaves known as the Ashanti were to blow into conch shells at the appointed time to give the signal for their uprising. They were to kill all their masters and kidnap the most beautiful of the white women.

But the conspiracy was betrayed by a slave woman who told her master, Judge Hall, of the midnight plan. Hall informed Sir Jonathan Atkins, the governor, and immediate action was taken against the ringleaders, seventeen of whom were executed; six of them burned alive and eleven beheaded. Their bodies were dragged through the streets for hours as a warning to other conspirators, more of whom were later executed, as well. The slave woman who had betrayed them was eventually given her freedom.

A missionary named Father Labat documented his visit to Barbados, around the time the *Henrietta Marie* sailed to Carlisle Bay in 1698.

The English take very little care of their slaves and feed them very badly. The majority give their slaves Saturday to work on their own account, so as to satisfy their own needs and their families'. The overseers make them work beyond measure and beat them mercilessly for the least fault, and they seem to care less for the life of a Negro than that of a horse.

The clergy do not instruct and do not baptize them. They are regarded pretty nearly as beasts to whom every license is allowed, provided that they perform their work satisfactorily. They are permitted to have several wives and to leave them as they please, provided that they produce a large number of children, that they work well and do not become ill, their masters are satisfied and ask nothing more.

They are rigorously punished for the least disobedience and more so if they rebel, which does not prevent this happening very often. These wretches, seeing themselves provoked beyond endurance by their drunken, unreasonable and savage overseers, rather than by their masters, in the end lose patience.

And, although they are certain of being punished in a very cruel way, they think that they have achieved much when they are revenged on these ruthless tyrants. It is at such times that the English resort to arms and there are terrible massacres.

Those who are captured and sent to prison are condemned to be passed through the mill, burnt alive or exposed in iron cages in which they are packed and, in this predicament, are attached to the branch of a tree, or are left to die of hunger and thirst. This is termed putting a man to dry.

ᴜᴜ

I arrived in Barbados in mid-July 1995, not far from where William Shuller's warehouse of enslaved African people would have been located.

It was a spectacular day; gentle trade winds whispered across the island, cooling my skin against the afternoon sun. I watched a flock of black-bellied sheep cross the gravel road and old fishermen climb into hand-carved wooden boats and head out to sea.

It is an island off the beaten path, one hundred miles to the east of the Caribbean chain. The highest point of elevation is eleven hundred feet above sea level and 260,000 people live in a space just fourteen miles wide and twenty-one miles long.

Small children played near the ocean, splashing in and out of the foamy ankle-high waves that slowly rolled onto shore near Carlisle Bay in the parish of St. Michael, where the *Henrietta Marie* anchored some three centuries ago.

I was looking for more answers about the *Henrietta Marie* and the people associated with her. I was searching for some explanations as to how several generations of people were abused for so long and subjected to atrocities so heinous that knowing of them makes me feel a sense of sorrow and loss to this day.

What was the mentality of these European men? Was it greed? Power over passive people? Insanity? How can one group of people play God and indict several generations of others? What did they see at night when the demons came? If they came at all.

On my first day in Bridgetown, I took a cab to the main library and later to the Department of Archives to begin my research, but I couldn't stop staring at the ocean as we drove along the narrow streets.

The senior librarian placed a stack of books and documents in front of me and I began to flip through page after page of Barbadian history until, after hours of reading, I came across more personal information on William Shuller.

The books were old and weathered and the language was of the seventeenth century, with British spellings and Old English slang. But the word *slave* seemed to stand out and appeared often, sometimes as many as three times in one sentence.

In these writings, slaves were described with such malice and disregard for human life, that I realized the Europeans felt they had the privilege, the God-given right, to own another human being. Certainly the law did not argue against their assumptions.

A document from the early 1700s listed two African slaves, "John the Negro," who was baptized in 1713 at the age of forty, and "William the Negro," who was buried in the mid-1700s. Both men, the document said, were the "property" of William Shuller, and could have come directly from the *Henrietta Marie*.

Shuller belonged to the Gentlemen of the Vestry, a town council of St.

Michael's Parish, where wealthy slave owners like Shuller would lend their slaves to the parish for odd jobs such as road repairs.

He often attended meetings with the social and business elite of St. Michael's Parish, helping to set policy for the community and helping himself to better cash in on the slave trade.

The minutes for the meeting held on March 29, 1708, a gathering Shuller attended, read: "It was ordered that every person that possessed of any land within this parish shall for every ten acres, they are so possessed of send one able Negro one day to worke on the highways...."

As I walked the streets of Bridgetown, I was reminded of how Shuller herded African people into his warehouse to be scrubbed and shaved for the next day's auction. I passed old churches where years ago Catholics prayed and considered it their duty to force Christianity on "heathen" African people because they might eat one another or do themselves some other harm.

I smiled at the European tourists I encountered, some of whom preferred to stay behind the guarded gates of "all-inclusive" resorts in the late afternoon and evening, never mixing with the people of Barbados and experiencing its unique culture, character, and charm.

At 8:30 the next morning, I threw my mesh dive bag over my shoulder and headed down to the dock, where three young Bajan boys were filling aluminum scuba tanks and loading a peeling twenty-foot yellow fishing boat turned dive boat with extra weights, a cooler of water, and their personal gear.

"Hey, mon, you ready for some good diving this morning?" asked a stocky man named Dennis, my dive guide.

"I've been ready since I got here," I said, rinsing my mask and checking my dive computer.

"We got a good day planned for you," he said. "Lots of fish, some wrecks, and some special things."

We walked about three hundred feet down the beach, carrying tanks and equipment to the small boat, and loaded everything aboard. Dennis said it would take about fifteen minutes to reach the first site of the day, so I began to slip into my wet suit.

I sat on the edge of the boat as we motored across Carisle Bay. We dropped anchor a couple miles from shore. The sun was just beginning to show in the Eastern sky as the boat rocked gently in the steady breeze. I could see other boats pulling away from the shoreline, and as I looked over the bay and the ocean, I could see the different degrees of blue for miles—the deeper the blue, the deeper the water.

"Let me tell you a little about this dive," Dennis said. "The bottom here is about one hundred feet. You should see plenty of fish. Let's go."

Dennis was not long on words. His dive briefings were short, to the point.

With fins on my feet, I pulled my mask over my face, put my regulator in my mouth, and rolled over the side of the boat, splashing into a bay of warm waters that felt more like bathwater than seawater.

Dennis followed me, and within seconds we slipped below the surface and entered a clear blue world of tranquillity. As I descended from ten feet, I could see straight down to the sand ninety feet below, passing shiny barracuda and a shy reef shark as we headed down.

There was a slight current, just enough to move me along our dive path, past the large orange sea fans and soft beige anemones, long tube-shaped plants that look like pasta.

Underwater, on the sandy floor of Carlisle Bay, the high-swelled Barbadian port where the *Henrietta Marie* anchored in the late 1600s, I watched tiny, nearly transparent one-inch-long sea horses hide within thin strands of seaweed. In the distance and wedged in the sand, I saw rusty iron. I swam over to get a closer look. I was alone for ten minutes or more, searching among old ale bottles and chunks of broken anchors from long ago. It was hard to tell how old they were or how significant they would become.

I thought about generations of black children who were lost three hundred years ago. I was reminded of the many black children who are culturally lost today, in part because they have no link to their history, no link to their past, no understanding of how their ancestors suffered and how we as a people managed to survive.

Shifting with the currents where the *Henrietta Marie* anchored in the summer of 1698, I recalled how my mother and father took me to aquariums and taught me American history and black history in the evenings after school, and how my wife, Mireille, and I will do the same for our daughter one day.

When I was growing up in Detroit, my mother would read to me. She would read powerful stories of the black experience, of Frederick Douglass and Harriet Tubman, Mary McLeod Bethune and Sojourner Truth.

But she would also tell me about our family, and what we had accomplished through struggle. She was a natural storyteller, a teacher. Her stories were about achievements and survival.

My parents taught me to remember always the history of the slave trade, to never forget it, to use the issue of slavery for inspiration; to remind myself where I came from; to know that slavery is more about survival than death; to know that slavery should symbolize how we overcame adversity; that we are strong people, not weak; that we are determined people, not apathetic; that we are proud people, not ashamed.

8

With favorable trade winds and the northern current steering the *Henrietta Marie* toward England, William Deacon locked a pouch of sterling pounds inside his quarters, satisfied that he had completed the harsh three-month task he had been hired to do: sail to West Africa to trade for a cargo of slaves, auction them to the highest bidder in Barbados, and return to London with the profits.

Lifting anchor on September 23, 1698, the *Henrietta Marie* sailed out of Carlisle Bay after Deacon had purchased 118 hogshead of *muscovado* sugar and pocketed a handsome price for the sale of 250 African people. For Deacon, there was no remorse, no second thoughts. It was business.

Packed in the cargo hold of the *Henrietta Marie* were more of Deacon's possessions: sixty-seven bags of ginger and one hundred elephant tusks transported from Africa en route to England to be made into piano keys, ornate cane handles, forks and knives and combs.

It had been a lucrative voyage, and after the journey across the Atlantic back to London, Deacon retired as captain of the *Henrietta Marie,* deciding instead to become an investor in the ship's future slave-trade passages, according to historian Nigel Tattersfield.

Deacon's first order of business as an investor was to contribute a mixture of Venetian beads, bundles of linen, and rolls of imported cloth. His cargo was handled by James Barbot, who also traded for African people on the west coast of Africa during the sailing years of the *Henrietta Marie*. James Barbot was the nephew of John Barbot, an officer aboard at least two British slave ships between 1699 and 1704. The two published detailed, vivid journals of their experiences and observations of the slave trade and their voyages coincide precisely during the time the *Henrietta Marie* sailed to New Calabar.

John Barbot described in detail his voyage in "Abstract of a Voyage to New Calabar." It was through Barbot's journals that historians were able to reconstruct the voyage of the *Henrietta Marie* with greater accuracy.

With Deacon relinquishing his command, the *Henrietta Marie*'s group of investors, eager to continue their profitable slave-trading enterprise, hired John Taylor to captain the ship. Taylor had considerably less experience than Deacon and had to carefully plot his course to Calabar, a place he had never visited in a part of the world he knew little about.

For the first half of 1699, according to Tattersfield, Taylor would have supervised a refitting of the *Henrietta Marie:* carpenters, sailmakers, and riggers would have replaced her old ropes, cables, pulleys, and blocks. The planking on both hull and deck would have been packed tight with a mixture of oakum and tar.

On August 30, 1699, Thomas Winchcombe was responsible for loading pewter onto the *Henrietta Marie*. The pewter, valued at thirty-four pounds, was used to make tankards, bowls, basins, and plates and was a popular trade item in Guinea.

On September 1, six weeks after the *Henrietta Marie* had received her first consignment of cargo, Robert Wilson declared his freight. Along with twelve hundred bars of copper, four dozen felt hats, and seventy cases of alcohol, Wilson also contributed wrought pewter. Wilson was a London merchant and the executor of John Taylor's will, which Taylor wrote and dated on September 13, 1699.

Taylor, who was feeling ill in the weeks before the *Henrietta Marie* sailed for New Calabar, may have had a premonition that all would not go well. Wrote historian Nigel Tattersfield:

On September 15, 1699, the Henrietta Marie, *a genuine slave ship, sailed from the Thames River on its second voyage to the west coast of Africa.*

John Taylor was on a tight schedule.

The ship probably reached Madeira about the middle of October 1699; the Cape Verde Islands around October twentieth; Cape Mesurado, just south of Sierra Leone, about November second; and the river of Sestros about November fifth.

She would have sighted the Cape Coast Castle, the Royal African Company's stronghold on the Guinea Coast, about December eighth, and finally arrived at Cape Formosa and the Bight of Guinea in the middle of December.

The Henrietta Marie *was about to be transformed into the most dreadful of ships: half prison, half floating crypt.*

Along the main stretch of the Guinea Coast—from what is now Sierra Leone to Lagos in Nigeria—the usual practice was to anchor the ship six or seven miles offshore and carry goods for trading to the shore, using the ship's longboat and hired African canoes.

The main trading locations were Old Calabar River, New Calabar, Bandy, and Foko. On the Old Calabar River, Barbot wrote: "The air is very malignant and occasions a great mortality among our sailors that make any long stay."

Between twelve and fifteen thousand African people were taken from Calabar each year during the 1600s and 1700s, making it one of the busiest slave ports in Africa.

The Henrietta Marie *sailed to Calabar loaded with the usual trade goods: brandy, rum, guns, hats and waistcoats, Indian and Manchester cottons, multicolored china beads, iron bars, and copper rods.*

Captain John Taylor, like William Deacon before him, had a particular mission in Calabar: to find good healthy slaves, strong young men and women. No old people.

The Henrietta Marie, *like other slavers, probably anchored off Calabar for no more than four weeks, as many crew members were falling ill and food and supplies were dwindling.*

Toward the end of January, Taylor loaded about 250 Africans aboard the Henrietta Marie—*men, women, boys, and girls—all shackled together in the tight, rat-infested, sweltering lower decks.*

The smaller children, whose wrists were too slender to be held by shackles, were taken to a separate deck where they were piled on top of one another next to a few latrine buckets.

"After taking on fresh water from the Foko, which had a reputation for staying sweet for long periods of time, the *Henrietta Marie*, now a full-fledged slave trade ship, nosed her way out to sea," Tattersfield wrote.

"Taking advantage of the strong Guinean current, which set to the south, the *Henrietta Marie* would have made for the tropical island of São Tomé, which straddles the equator. Offering a sheltered anchorage, freshwater, and provisioning in abundance, São Tomé functioned as a springboard for the Middle Passage to the West Indies.

"The bulk of the food would have been yams, and the *Henrietta Marie* would have needed some fifty thousand for a cargo of 250 slaves. Provisioning the ship would have required about one week, occuring in early February 1700.

"The *Henrietta Marie* was no longer the sleek, freshly varnished ship that had cruised the waters of the English Channel so effortlessly a year earlier. She was now a dogged survivor whose sun-parched decks, scorched canvas, peeling paintwork and faded pennants were the consequences of the harsh business of slave trading along the Guinea Coast," Tattersfield wrote.

The last passage had taken its toll on crew and cargo. John Taylor, who suffered for weeks on deck, was dead, and the new captain of the *Henrietta Marie*, the ship's third commander, was a senior seaman named Thomas Chamberlaine.

On May 6, 1700, according to Tattersfield, "The tedious voyage across the Middle Passage was broken by the sighting of a long, low smudge of land off the starboard bow." Straight ahead was the island of Jamaica, lush and green, with tall rolling hills.

The *Henrietta Marie* was on a course for the harbor of Port Royal, which had been rebuilt brick by brick after an earthquake leveled the city shortly before noon on June 7, 1692, shattering the city's opulence, sinking much of the town, and, within seconds, killing two thousand people.

Thirteen acres of land slid into the sea. Nearly forty acres were covered by shoal water, and the land that remained was submerged by tidal waves.

With Jamaica in sight on May seventeenth, Chamberlaine called his crew on deck and prepared to groom his cargo. Sixty African people had died during the passage.

Research by Tattersfield tells us that male slaves were shaved with straight razors and small groups of men and women, no more than five or ten at a time, were allowed onto the decks for fresh air. Their skin was oiled and the ship's surgeon dressed their sores. They would be fed larger portions of food for the remainder of the voyage.

There were 190 enslaved African people aboard the *Henrietta Marie*—ninety men, sixty women, thirty boys, and ten girls—by the time she weighed anchor in windy seas and gusts of rain at Port Royal, Jamaica, on May 17, 1700.

Staggering down the gangway in the storm, the Africans who had traveled some fourteen weeks in the hold, chained together, were delivered to Jamaica nude, branded with the initials H-M, squinting from the bright sunlight, to which they were unaccustomed, their muscles tight and sore from three months of lying on their sides.

On May nineteenth, the slaves were rounded up like cattle in the square at Port Royal, where they were auctioned in groups "by inch of the candle." The potential European buyers who owned plantations in Jamaica would light a candle and mark sets of inches along its length. The bidder whose offer was the highest when the first inch had melted took the first group.

Chamberlaine collected the sterling pounds after he sold his cargo. The Africans from the *Henrietta Marie* were sold for £3,144. The men brought eighteen pounds each, the women sixteen pounds, the boys fourteen pounds, and the girls twelve pounds.

At the end of June in 1700, Chamberlaine set a course for England, sailing out of Port Royal harbor on a northwestward course that would take the *Henrietta Marie* past the Cayman Islands, around Cuba's Cape St. Antonio, though the Yucatán Channel, and into the treacherous stretch of water between the Tortugas and Marquesa Keys off the coast of Florida, according to Tattersfield.

It was in the Florida Straits that the *Henrietta Marie* was blindsided by powerful winds that battered the ship without warning; a fierce hurricane collided with the ship as she dropped all of her anchors trying hard to ride out the weather.

The storm ripped wood from the decks of the *Henrietta Marie,* leaving behind huge splinters in the sea, and snapped the massive mainmast like a twig as swells of salt water toppled the 120 tons of ship.

Captain Chamberlaine and his crew, about a dozen frantic men in all, wholly unprepared for such a sudden storm, were washed over the side of the ship, fighting against a wall of waves and grasping at broken planks of wood before they were swallowed by the raging force of nature.

It was a reckoning of sorts: the captain and crew of the *Henrietta Marie* dying a violent death, buried in the same seas where they had sent so many African men and women to their deaths; clinging to life in the form of fractured wood and struggling to stay above the surface before surrendering to a ferocious pounding surf. They were snatched underwater, victims of an unforgiving ocean, surrounded by the chains and shackles, manacles and leg irons that were their stock in trade.

There were no Africans aboard the *Henrietta Marie* when she sank thirty-seven miles west of Key West, Florida, on a sandy patch known as New Ground Reef. The Africans had been unloaded in Jamaica, where they faced a future of violence but not necessarily immediate death.

ᵕᵕ

I landed in Jamaica in the summer of 1995. The history of the Henrietta Marie had brought me to the island for research, above as well as beneath the sea.

Kingston was sweltering, as usual. The airport was packed, but at least my bags made it onto the carousel in short order. I loaded my garment bag and dive gear onto a cart and pushed my way through immigration and customs, then went straight to a rent-a-car dealer.

After taking a road map and listening to some quick directions, I drove to the hotel. It was a drive that should have taken about thirty minutes, but it took an hour negotiating Kingston's roundabouts—traffic circles with no street signs or speed limits, where goats almost outnumber the men who hang out there.

My shirt was soaked by the time I arrived at the hotel and my lungs were contaminated from the thick diesel fuel in the air. David Moore had arrived ahead of me. It was his first trip to Jamaica and he looked somewhat overwhelmed.

"You okay?" I asked, smiling. "This is a bit different from London, huh?"

We unpacked, made some phone calls to line up our business appointments, had a few beers, and outlined our week over dinner.

The next morning, we drove to the offices of the National Heritage Trust, a government-run agency that is responsible for overseeing the underwater archaeology and preserving the development of Port Royal's Sunken City, the portion of Port Royal that was reduced to rubble by the earthquake three centuries ago.

The meetings were lengthy and most of the people were accommodating, although I had to remind David that in Jamaica, and throughout the Caribbean, time moves a bit slower and nobody cares if Americans and Europeans are in a hurry.

After several meetings with archaeologists and the director, Patrick Bennett, we signed papers, handed over a processing fee, and were cleared to dive ancient Port Royal, which is protected by the National Heritage Trust and reserved for those conducting archeological and historical research.

The regulations were explained to us several times: We were to remove nothing from the ocean floor.

"We'll be sending someone from our Coast Guard to monitor your work," one official told us.

Three centuries after the *Henrietta Marie* anchored in the harbor of Port Royal, I was about to explore the place once referred to as "the wickedest city in the world," a haven for thieves, muggers, pirates, and whores who roamed the streets and owned rooming houses.

As a pirate, then lieutenant governor of Jamaica, the infamous Henry Morgan made his fortune in Port Royal in the late seventeenth century. Prostitution was legal and liquor poured like water day and night. During one month, July 1661, forty new licenses were issued for taverns and whorehouses. The citizens complained that nearly every establishment in town sold liquor.

Port Royal was a bustling town with well-heeled merchants who lived among the four-story buildings of brick walls and clay tile. One Port Royal merchant reported the following after the earthquake:

> Yet [the quake] had so little effect upon some people here, that the very same night they were at their old trade—drinking, swearing and stealing from their neighbors, even while the earthquake lasted and several of them were destroyed in the very act, and indeed this place has been one of the lewdest in the Christian world, a sink of all filthiness and a mere sodom.

It was 5:00 A.M., still dark, by the time I pulled my gear out of the car and walked down the dock to the Buccaneer Scuba Shop.

We were greeted by Englishman Gary Casson, his stringy blond hair hanging over the gold studs in one ear, who was busy filling tanks under the low archway of bricks that had once been a storage shed.

Casson, who had bounced around Bermuda and the Mediterranean doing odd jobs before landing in Jamaica, was our guide for the day. We showed him a letter from the National Heritage Trust.

"Bring the letter with you," he said in a thick British accent. "The Jamaican government takes this site very seriously."

It was quiet at Port Royal, now a quaint place of seaside hotels, bars, and restaurants. We walked to the end of the dock and climbed into a small rubber Zodiac that could fit no more than four people. He revved up the outboard and we motored across the harbor in the dark, the sound from the outboard motor the only noise for miles.

It took us only about ten minutes to reach the dive site. The sun was just coming into view.

"This is it," the dive shop's owner said. "There is a lot to see, I hope the viz is good. You'll be seeing the remains of some of the city of Port Royal; it's now underwater."

As I slipped into my fins and rinsed my mask, a Coast Guard boat filled with scuba gear pulled up alongside. Two young black men in blue uniforms were asking for our paperwork. Our papers in order, the clouds

giving way to sun, we rolled over the side of the boat and into the warm
waters of Port Royal.

ᙁᙁ

Buried in fifteen to fifty feet of water was a museum of crumbling brick
and rubble, the remains of Lime Street, where, centuries ago, a few
shillings could buy whiskey and women all night long.

Around me underwater, and wedged into the sand, was handcrafted
pottery that has survived, embedded for three hundred years among
rocks where a catastrophe has been frozen in time. Thirty feet below me,
in the silt and sediment, was a fractured fort where British soldiers had
fired on the Spanish.

Twenty feet beneath the surface, I swam along the cobblestone streets,
pieces of plaster, brick walls, and a staircase of concrete steps where
drunken pirates had once stumbled.

A reported nine hundred shipwrecks rest nearby, sunk by wars or
storms, each with tales to tell of violence and mutiny. The *Henrietta
Marie* has its own story to tell, a story of mystery and misery, a story of
slavery, a story of a proud people whose spirits were stronger than the
chains that bound them.

I swam silently underwater in the harbor where the slaver had
anchored in the tide and where her crew had hustled African men and
women down the gangway to the auction blocks.

How horrifying it must have been for Africans to arrive in Port
Royal—naked, chained, sore from whippings, in an unfamiliar country,
listening to an unfamiliar language spoken by pale people with whips
who poked with filthy hands at the mouths of these people. Suicide was
on the minds of many who for months had had to listen to the daily
clanging of chains around their bodies.

The waters seemed to warm up during our forty-five-minute exploration. I could see David nearby, peeking into corners and crevices. The
Coast Guard divers were casually swimming with us, pointing out
ancient artifacts to me along the way.

I was suddenly reminded of my young days in Detroit watching the
adventure television series *Sea Hunt*. Thirty years later, I was scuba diving, just as I'd told my mother I would one day.

What we couldn't have anticipated was that I would be diving the route of a slave ship, visiting the ports where my ancestors had been auctioned. It didn't matter that I didn't know the names of the enslaved African people aboard the *Henrietta Marie,* nor that I could not see their faces.

It was an intangible connection that I felt underwater in the harbor of Port Royal: a feeling of sadness at the thought of the atrocities that African people suffered, a feeling of privilege to retrace their passage, and a feeling of being humbled by the sea.

9

I was tracking the footsteps of John "Mad Jack" Fuller, the man who ordered the iron cannons for the *Henrietta Marie,* a seventeenth-century arms dealer who made a lucrative living trading in guns and slaves.

I had a place to start: Fuller had owned a plantation west of Kingston, near Spanish Town, in the late 1600s and early 1700s, and he was heavily invested in the slave trade. Fuller's trail started at the Institute of Jamaica, which houses most of the country's public records and is the clearinghouse for old maps, archival information, and books that listed property owners as far back as the 1500s.

We walked through the doors of the Institute of Jamaica and we were armed: pens, pads, and plenty of time.

"Hello. May I help you?" asked a soft-spoken middle-aged woman who introduced herself as Ms. Francis, the director of the library and public records.

"I'm Michael Cottman. I spoke with you on the telephone last week," I said.

"Yes, you're the writer from New York," she said. "We're all ready for you. Please, right this way."

Ms. Francis, a friendly woman, slightly built and motherly, like someone you've known all your life, led David and me upstairs to a second-

floor research room where a young man named Robert Wilson was waiting to assist us. He was very resourceful and friendly, and he knew his
business.

He directed us to the card file and gave us forms to fill out for the
research material we needed. We flipped through the file and went
straight to the *F*'s to find anything we could on John Fuller, who turned
up almost immediately, as did Rose Fuller, who we later learned was
his son, not a daughter or wife. Several other Fullers began to surface
and we filled out forms for all the material, figuring we should read
everything they had. Robert took the mound of small, square forms
from us.

"I'll get right on this," he said. "Have a seat."

Twenty minutes later, Robert was back with a stack of old books that
were in excellent condition. The books contained listings of property
owners from the late 1600s and early 1700s.

We were looking specifically for any property that John "Mad Jack"
Fuller may have owned during the time the *Henrietta Marie* sailed to
Jamaica in 1700. Based on our research, David and I believed that some
of the enslaved Africans who worked on Fuller's Jamaican plantation
may have traveled aboard the *Henrietta Marie*.

We split up the books and began pouring through the listings of property owners until John Fuller's name started turning up.

Hours passed. We stopped for a lunch of chicken curry, peas and rice,
and plantains, then returned to the Institute.

Robert brought out more books. In one I found the listing, "Fuller,
John, sugar plantation." The material said that John "Mad Jack" Fuller
owned a plantation known as Knollis Estate, located in the parish of St.
Thomas of the Vale, which today is St. Catherine.

"We've got a breakthrough here!" I said to David.

"Looks that way," he said, not looking up from the book. Fuller himself would have had to walk into the Institute of Jamaica and slap the
tobacco out of David's mouth for David to admit he was thrilled.

We took notes on each of the properties Fuller had owned. It seemed
that he had owned several plantations, but the largest estate, and the one
that was listed far more often than any of the others, was the fifteen-
hundred-acre sugar plantation Knollis Estate. We now needed to know

exactly where the property was located and, more important, who owned it today. We presumed that the fifteen-hundred-acre property was no longer intact, that it had probably been parceled out and broken up throughout the years.

We asked Robert to gather as many maps from the 1700s as the library had available.

"We close in thirty minutes," he said, looking a bit weary but still pleasant.

We had been sitting at the table for six hours straight. It seemed more like six minutes.

Before I left the library, I pulled a stack of research materials over to the side and took notes from several books that detailed the brutal history of life on Jamaica's slave plantations.

Sugar was the most lucrative commodity in Jamaica, as it was in Barbados. By the late 1600s, when the *Henrietta Marie* sailed to the West Indies, there were about sixty plantations. More than sixty years later, Jamaica had more than four hundred sugar plantations and was the world's largest single producer of sugar.

The largest Jamaican sugar plantations were villages in themselves. They consisted of the overseer's house and offices; the sugar works and mill; the boiling house, curing houses, and still house; the stables that housed the cattle used for grinding; the lodgings for the bookkeepers; the workshops for the blacksmiths, carpenters, and coopers; and the rows of houses for the enslaved African workers.

The people from Africa were forced to work, carving out a civilization with their hands, plowing the fields, and planting crops.

Punishment, of course, was a routine part of plantation life in Jamaica, which was no different from most plantation societies in the West Indies. Slave owners did what they wanted with African people; beatings and murder were constant occurrences, and slave owners often took African mistresses, by force if necessary.

One reason for such severity was the fear slave owners had of being killed in uprisings because they were so outnumbered.

Africans in Jamaica had few opportunities for recreation. In the evenings, some of them would gather outside their homes and sing and dance and tell stories of Africa, stories of hope.

After long days laboring in the fields, tired, sore, and sometimes plotting to escape to freedom, it was prayer—and faith—that sustained African men and women from one day to the next.

Prayer was something personal, part of their African heritage, something that couldn't be taken away.

"O Lord, bless my master," one old woman prayed. "When he calls upon thee to damn his soul, do not hear him, do not hear him, but hear me—save him—make him know he is wicked and he will pray to thee. I'm afraid, O Lord, I have wished him bad wishes in my heart—keep me from wishing him bad—though he whips me and beats me sore, tell me of my sins, and make me pray more to thee—make me more glad for what thou hast done for me, a poor Negro."

In Jamaica, historians wrote, there was prayer, but there was also outright resistance to slavery at every turn. Revolts were breaking out all across the island, but in 1760 the most serious revolt occurred. Known as Tacky's Rebellion, it began in the parish of St. Mary but spread throughout most of the country. Tacky, its leader, was a slave in Jamaica, but he had been a chief in Africa.

He gathered a small group of trusted followers before daybreak on Easter Monday and stole a supply of muskets, powder, and shot. By dawn the next day, hundreds of Africans had joined Tacky, overrunning plantations and killing white settlers. An uprising in Westmoreland proved almost as serious as Tacky's Rebellion.

Runaway slaves in Jamaica were known as "maroons" and were forces of power during the days of slavery on the island. According to historians, the word *maroon* comes from *cimarron,* a Spanish word first applied to stray cattle that roamed undomesticated in the wild. The meaning was soon modified to describe escaped Indian slaves, and later it was applied to Africans who escaped the plantations and formed their own communities. As early as 1546, more than seven thousand maroons were living on the island of Santo Domingo.

The maroons founded the longest-existing free communities of African rebels and runaways in Jamaica. When the English seized Jamaica from Spain in 1655, the retreating Spanish left behind fifteen hundred African slaves. These African people took to the hills after dividing themselves among three leaders. They lived for years in isolation, until they agreed to assist the Spanish, their former oppressors, in raids against the British.

By the 1720s, the maroons had amassed considerable power and influence and were split into two main groups, the Windward maroons and the Leeward maroons. A man named Cudjoe, of Akan ancestry, was elected leader of the Leeward group. He was a clever strategist, a general, and won many skirmishes against the British.

The leader of the Windward rebels was a former slave named Nanny, a warrior and sorceress who was able to command complete loyalty from her followers. Her contempt for her enemies is best described by the legend that she was able to catch the bullets of the English soldiers in her buttocks and hurl them back at them.

In the mid-1700s the maroons fought for years evading British troops. In the Second Maroon War, three hundred maroons, determined mountain men, held out against fifteen hundred European troops for five months.

ᙀᙀ

"I guess we should let you go home," I said to Robert. "What time do you start tomorrow?"

"Nine," he answered.

"We'll see you then," I said.

I left the library with mixed feelings: As enthusiastic as I was about tracing the history of the *Henrietta Marie* and locating the European people who had played major roles in the ship's history and economy, there was still a small part of me that was cautious about moving ahead, not sure what I would find. There were many forks in the road, each path leading to a multitude of stories about the *Henrietta Marie*—stories about life and death, faith and survival.

I was getting closer to sorting out my feelings about the slave trade through my research of the *Henrietta Marie*. I was beginning to understand what faith was all about. This ship had a way of pulling me in; it had a way of guiding me through different doors, where people—living and dead—associated with the *Henrietta Marie* were waiting.

That night, as I read over my notes from the day, I thought about my conversation in London with Tattersfield and his theory that slavery had nothing to do with race. It was, in his opinion, strictly an issue of economics, nothing more.

But the British never enslaved the Portuguese; the Portuguese never enslaved the Spanish; the Spanish never enslaved the French; and the French never enslaved the Dutch. Rather, they all conspired to establish an international commerce in the selling and trading of African people.

According to Dr. James Rawley, a history professor at the University of Nebraska, slavery in the late 1600s was not new.

"Mentioned in the Bible," he wrote, "practiced by ancient Greeks and Romans, functioning in the Mediterranean basin as well as in Africa," slavery had a long history. Slavery in the Americas, however, differed from earlier forms of slavery: It was derived from a single source—Africa; it was racial, exclusively black, and it was more harsh than the institution known by most earlier unfree people.

"But why was it that laborers had to be transplanted across a wide ocean to work in America?" Rawley asked. The answer usually advanced, he suggested, is that black slave labor was cheaper than white labor, even that of indentured servants, which were available for a term of years in return for ocean passage. African slave labor was indeed cheap.

At the end of the seventeenth century, British planters could buy a slave for six hundred pounds of raw sugar on the London market. British slave merchants could buy an African for the worth of sixteen guns.

"But another factor must also be considered," Rawley wrote, "—white racism." By the seventeenth century, Englishmen had come to believe Africans were inferior. An ethnocentrism emphasizing skin color—black standing for evil and the powers of darkness—set Africans apart not only from Englishmen but from red-skinned Native Americans as well, according to Rawley.

An English observer said Africans "in colour, so in condition, are little other than Devils incarnate." An early impression of blacks asserted that they were "a people of beastly living, without a God, lawe, religion, or common wealth."

But there was also a much larger issue, a more heinous scheme that would impact Africans for centuries to come.

One question that haunted me in London while I read the graphic and disturbing characterizations of African people by European slave traders was this: Why were black people systematically selected for slavery? Why were Africans intentionally and methodically targeted as slaves?

Perhaps, as some have suggested, their dark skin was so visibly distinguishable from white skin that it was easy to separate the white ruling class from their black captives.

If they ran away, dark-skinned people could not get lost in a crowd, they could not blend in with the white population, so to select black people as slaves would put to rest any confusion about who were the workers and who were the rulers.

So as a result of the Europeans' ruthless greed, slavery has become synonymous with generations and generations of black people because of one distinct characteristic: black skin.

How insidious, this business of slavery, which allowed those Europeans to concoct a global system that labeled black people as inferior, ignorant second-class citizens whose only purpose was to serve the wishes of whites.

How monstrous, to condemn hundreds of thousands of babies to a life of slavery and identify them as slaves from the time they left the womb simply because they were black.

This methodical decision to target black people and isolate them because of their skin color was racist by design, despite some historians' claims that slavery was more about business and profit than race.

There is no question that slavery was an extremely profitable business for some, but it was a business that was calculated and enforced based on the exploitation of one race of easily identifiable people—Africans.

ᙀᙀ

We were back at the library the next day at 9:00 A.M.

We were trying to pinpoint the precise location of Knollis Estate, the former Fuller property. Robert brought out stacks of maps and we flipped through the three-foot-wide charts for hours before the name of this plantation appeared on one of the maps dated 1697. The map was faded and the name Knollis Estate was written in tiny letters in its center. The problem, however, was that Knollis stood out on the map because it was not surrounded by any other towns that we recognized. After all, it was a map of the area in 1697; there wasn't much else around back then.

"Robert, do you have a road map?" I asked.

He returned with a 1995 road map of Jamaica. I circled the parish of St. Catherine with my finger and traced the area slowly. North of Spanish Town, near a town called Bog Walk, was the name Knollis.

"This has to be the same as Knollis Estate from the 1697 map," I said to David. "I think we found it."

"How do we find more information about the Knollis Estate?" I asked Robert. "How do we determine who owns the property today? How do we get more information on the Fullers—death certificates, deeds? And how do we get to what's left of the Knollis Estate?"

"You have to go to Spanish Town," Robert said. "That's where all the public records and archives are kept for St. Catherine's Parish."

"How far is it from here?" I asked.

"It's about a two-hour drive. I'll call ahead and let the staff of the archives department know you're coming. When do you want to go?"

"First thing in the morning," I said.

I flipped through a reference book about Jamaica that was filled with color photos of Spanish Town. It showed a picture of the town square—quaint, with a southern-style charm: flower-covered gazebos and park benches on well-manicured lawns surrounding a two-story white-domed building with detailed hand-carved designs.

I woke up early the next morning, 5:30 A.M., an hour before the alarm was set to ring. The sun was just rising over the mountains. I stood by the window leading to a small balcony and watched the night sky give way to day.

We left the hotel around 8:00 A.M. I wanted to get to Spanish Town early. We inched along in the diesel-heavy air of Kingston's rush-hour traffic for an hour until we finally left the city limits and began hugging the coastline before turning into the interior and driving, straight into the heart of Spanish Town's market area.

What I noticed immediately about Spanish Town was that it had changed radically since that photo was taken for the Jamaica reference book.

It was a town that had died some years ago. The town square was a maze of weeds, broken bottles, and dirt where grass had once grown.

There were no flowers, no gazebo, and the white-domed building was a crumbling mess of peeling paint and shattered windows, a decaying haven for drifters, drinkers, and small-time dealers.

Slavery had left an ugly scar on Spanish Town. After years of oppression on nearby plantations where they were forced to harvest fields of sugarcane and tobacco, the African men and women had left behind a bitter legacy that now haunted the black men in Spanish Town, who, stripped of hope, filled their days with liquor, their eyes as hollow as their bellies.

A narrow street was packed with shirtless men. They hung out smoking and sipping beer, some wandering with no clear destination in mind.

It was 11:00 A.M. Spanish Town was small, busy, and extremely dusty. There was bumper-to-bumper traffic from the time we crossed the city limits. After taking a wrong turn and getting tied up in fish-market traffic for twenty minutes, I hung a sharp right and came upon the street where the public records office was located.

As I pulled up to the building, I was greeted by a young man. "Hey, mon," he whispered as I climbed out of the car. "I'll watch your car while you're inside; you take care of me when you leave."

"I don't think so," I said. "Which one of these buildings is the archives department?"

"To the left," he mumbled, turning his back on me and walking toward a knot of men who had gathered to watch us.

"C'mon," I said to David, the only white man for miles—who was looking like he realized this fact.

We walked through a wrought-iron gate and into the office. It was a spacious room, but dark and musty. The lighting was poor and there were few windows. A woman named Ms. Williams introduced herself and said she was expecting us. We told her that we were looking for information about the Fuller family and the Knollis Estate. She nodded and disappeared behind a large door.

We waited for about fifteen minutes before she returned with a stack of reference books.

After we located Fuller's name in several of the books, Ms. Williams pulled by catalog numbers the detailed listings of property dating back to the 1700s.

This was a long process. Young boys peeked through the window and stared through the gate, curious about these visitors who were asking about old European property.

After more than an hour, Ms. Williams walked out of a large vaultlike room and over to our table. She was carrying two large leather-bound books covered with a layer of dust an inch thick. The binders were tattered along the sides and the words on the front of the shriveled books— *Probate Records*—were barely visible. The volumes dated back to the early 1700s.

The pages were brittle; it was like turning crumpled leaves. I was uneasy about handling documents so old and withered. The handwritten entries were faded but surprisingly legible.

The Fuller family had been very prominent in Spanish Town. John Fuller had been an attorney and a powerful landowner. His son Rose Fuller had been a Spanish Town supreme court judge. The name Rose had thrown us off for days. We thought Rose was John's wife until we found old family letters that explained the relationship.

We located handwritten letters from John Fuller's sons, Stephen and Rose. One letter from Stephen Fuller alerted Jamaican officials that slaves on the island outnumbered whites—"a vast disproportion between Negroes and whites"—and appeared to be concerned that they would be slaughtered during a rebellion.

In reading these letters, I was struck by one overwhelming fact: That African men would attempt to free themselves of chains, rise up to resist oppression, and fight—and die, if necessary—to secure their freedom seemed more like an afterthought to Fuller.

Public records and personal Fuller family letters from Kingston and Spanish Town showed that Fuller owned the fifteen-hundred acre Knollis Estate, then a sugar plantation. The Knollis Estate in the 1700s was located outside Spanish Town, about thirty miles from Kingston.

Myrtle Williams, another librarian from Spanish Town, walked over to our table with several thick and tattered binders tied in a bow with faded pink string.

The date on one binder was 1745. It listed the properties owned by the Fuller family, the types of products produced on the land, and the quantities of sugar, rum, and bananas produced annually.

There wouldn't be much left of the plantations from the 1700s. The great houses, the large mansions where the plantation owners lived, are all gone, burned by Jamaicans, who believe that violent spirits must be destroyed.

There are those who believe the tortured and restless souls of those who died violently still walk the dusty roads of Jamaica. People still report sightings of ghosts wandering in the hills, screaming in the night.

ʊʊ

We hired another Robert, a young man from Kingston, to drive us to Knollis. He had never been there, but as we had discovered, the area of Knollis is still listed on Jamaican road maps today. We set out driving through the Jamaican countryside, with the towering Blue Mountains in the distance, past old men on donkey-drawn wagons and little boys in school uniforms wearing backpacks. They waved at us from the side of the road.

After forty minutes, we saw a sign for Knollis and turned down a bumpy dirt road. We slowed in front of a small church. I got out of the car and knocked on the door of a house behind the church.

An elderly gentleman answered the door. I told him I was looking for the Knollis Estate.

He pointed me down the road about two miles in the direction of the Tulloch Estate, which in the 1700s was most likely part of the Knollis Estate but which has been parceled out to private owners over the years.

Since her husband died in January 1995, Ann Turner owns the Tulloch Estate. She runs it with her son.

Two hundred and fifty Jamaican employees work the three-hundred-acre banana farm today. Many of them pack bananas inside a one-story wooden warehouse that was used in the 1700s as a barracks where slaves slept, packed together on the floor after working sixteen-hour days.

The workers today put in long hours, harvesting the field, loading trucks, and packing bananas in the sweltering sun.

Some of the workers live on the property, and it was unclear whether everyone had homes with indoor plumbing or whether their employer offered a long-term health plan. Some have worked on the estate for more than forty years.

Time seemed to stand still on the Tulloch land.

Watching the Jamaican workers in the fields, the women hauling large boxes and packing fruit with calloused hands, reminded me of the drawings of their ancestors, who worked the same land more than three hundred years before. The pictures looked the same; only the names have changed.

I arrived on the Tulloch farm and introduced myself as an author from the United States who was researching a book. I was caught by surprise when Turner, after shaking my hand and asking if I wanted tea, immediately began to criticize black Americans for dividing the country by calling ourselves "African-Americans" instead of simply blacks.

"You're causing problems," she said with indignation. "It's segregation. You're starting a kind of apartheid by separating yourselves. Why are you doing this? Why are you being so divisive?"

I explained that some black people want to identify more closely with our African ancestors and that, in that spirit, African-Americans were not divisive but, rather, were celebrating our heritage.

"It's divisive," she insisted. "It's only going to cause more trouble."

I changed the subject, as it appeared that Ms. Turner and I had gotten off on the wrong foot.

I asked her the size of her plantation.

Again, I received a lecture.

"This is not a plantation," she argued, raising her voice so others could hear. This is a *farm*. That was then; this is now."

Her property resembled a plantation. It did then; it does today. The workers looked as overworked and underpaid as their ancestors had been. They were still being used to work inhumanely long days and they were not being compensated for the true value of their work.

As she spoke in her thick British accent, I looked over her shoulder at the base of a three-thousand-foot mountain and watched older women walking slowly, one clearly with leg pain. I wondered how much profit would end up in the torn pockets of the workers who toiled in the fields all day long picking tons of bananas that would eventually be shipped to England.

I walked across her land and shook hands with some of the workers.

I watched them smile at me, some of the women too tired even to wave their hands. I watched the men work the field on foot and on tractors; I watched the women walk slowly across the field balancing baskets of bananas on their heads.

Women hummed softly as they worked. The sound of Jamaican spirituals, born from Africa, seemed to fill the air.

Slavery, and the slavery mentality, robs people of their dignity and crushes their dreams. It is a dehumanizing experience to look into the eyes of mothers, fathers, sons, and daughters and realize that every aspect of their lives is controlled through fear and intimidation.

I spoke to a man who said he was seventy years old and had worked on the Tulloch property for as long as he could remember.

He was frail, though still packing bananas; he was bald and had wrinkles around his eyes and neck. He looked down at the ground as he talked to me, not saying much, but speaking softly.

"It's been hard sometimes," he said. "But we make do."

My afternoon came to an abrupt end when Ms. Turner appeared on a nearby hillside that overlooked her farm and where I now stood.

"Do you need anything else?" she shouted. "I'd better be getting back to work."

I thanked her for her time and wandered off this property where I was no longer welcome, looking back to watch the Jamaican men and women sweating in the fields. I stopped long enough to see that some of the old women looked up from the dirt to wave good-bye.

The old man with the wrinkles spoke to me as I walked away. "There's an old Jamaican family that's been around here for years. There are a lot of them, a large family. They live down the road; their name is Fuller." He pulled himself onto a tractor and motored away.

ᕫᕤ

In the shadow of the Blue Mountains, where clumps of cottony clouds rest on the highest peaks, Colin Fuller sat on the peeling porch of his one-story home, watching a light rain sprinkle the front yard, and spoke of sweating in the fields cutting cane for European landowners nearly seventy-five years ago.

In the 1920s, when Fuller was eighteen years old, he was hired to harvest the land of the sprawling Tulloch Estate, planting and cutting sugarcane and loading bananas in wagons hauled by teams of cows.

It was arduous work under a blistering sun. Fuller often labored in the fields for twelve to fourteen hours a day. It was a job that demanded much and paid little: his wages totaled one six-pence in English currency—about ten cents per day.

But over the years, Fuller said, he managed to raise seven children on a few shillings a month paid to him by his British boss.

Today, Colin Fuller is ninety-three years old and lives within walking distance of the Tulloch Estate. His mop of curly white hair is a contrast to his smooth black face with deep lines etched across his forehead, his skin permanently darkened by years of Jamaican sun.

His smile is quick and his hazel-green eyes are still sharp, as is his mind. He remembers much about his life on the Tulloch Estate, working in the fields, using a slender machete to cut the cane, picking bananas, and burying his four brothers and four sisters in earth that had become as familiar as family.

Fuller doesn't move around as well as he used to; the years have brought pain to joints in his legs and hands. He turns slowly in his chair and with a shaky finger points to a section of land behind the house to a thicket of tall trees, wild flowers, and high grass that stretches for miles, a place he's known for years.

"I was born right out back," he said proudly, "ninety-three years ago."

Fuller and his family were born in Bog Walk, and for as long as anyone can remember, many of them worked at the Tulloch Estate. Some of them slept in barracks on the property decades ago when the estate was used to harvest sugarcane and tobacco.

Today, there are dozens of black Jamaican Fullers who have settled in the community of Bog Walk and throughout the parish of St. Catherine. It is a farming area of vast banana, citrus, and coffee estates and home to about six thousand people. It is a community where generations of Jamaican families have worked the estates for many decades, perhaps even centuries.

Larkland Fuller, Colin's nephew, lives across the road.

At sixty-five years old, he is still muscular and fit; his tight handshake and hard hands tell the story of a man who worked for more than thirty years picking coconuts and carrying bananas from the fields. He wasn't happy working on the Tulloch estate and says the owners often exploited black laborers. So he quit.

"I worked very hard and got little money for my hard work," Fuller said. He was paid only about fifty cents a day. "I left there. They didn't treat black people good."

Farming is what Jamaicans did years ago, and it's what they do in Bog Walk today. In the seventeenth century and until slavery in Jamaica was abolished in 1838, Africans were always given the plantation owner's last name. After they were freed, generations of families that worked on the plantations settled in communities near the estates.

The Tulloch Estate, for example, which some researchers and historians believe may have been part of the three- to five-thousand-acre Knollis Estate in the 1700s, could have been owned by the Fuller family of Sussex, England, who manufactured the cannons at Stream Foundry that were mounted on the decks of the *Henrietta Marie*.

Because the Knollis Estate and surrounding properties were so vast, it is believed that enslaved Africans from the *Henrietta Marie* may have worked the Fullers' plantations in Jamaica. In the 1700s, slaves were transported to a number of plantations throughout the island.

The Fuller family occupied an important place in the political and economic history of mid-eighteenth-century Sussex. They were a wealthy and influential family that amassed their fortune by becoming one of the major gun producers for the navy and the army. They later diversified their wealth into slave holdings in Jamaica and participation in the lucrative sugar trade.

It appears, according to records from *The Fuller Letters: Guns, Slaves, and Finance, 1728–1755,* that the family owned their estates in Jamaica as early as 1703, after John Fuller married Elizabeth Rose and inherited a large amount of property.

The part of the estate that came to the Fullers in the early 1700s had been purchased between 1666 and 1685, and amounted to just over three thousand acres that consisted of Knollis Plantation, which was comprised of 1,128 acres in St. Catherine's and St. John's parishes; 820 acres known as Bullers Savanna Pen land; 195 acres in the Lower Sop Garden Land in St. Catherine's parish, and a house and parcel of land in Spanish Town, according to the Fuller letters.

In 1703, John Fuller was listed as an absentee owner who was dependent upon a variety of distant relatives to oversee the property. Fuller received various accounts of income and expenditure. Details of slaves on the property were not always forthcoming, since agents and family rarely visited the estate, according to *The Fuller Letters: Guns, Slaves, and Finance, 1728–1755.*

Fuller once wrote that "the Negroes were never surveyed, nor had we ever any list of them." It was Rose Fuller, John's son, who was dispatched to Jamaica in 1732 to oversee the estate and put the family's business in order.

Although John Fuller did not acquire the Knollis property until 1703, and the *Henrietta Marie*'s captain sold his cargo of African people at a public auction in 1700, it is believed that some of the 190 slaves from the ship may have been taken to the Knollis Estate. So when Fuller purchased the property, one theory suggests that he could have also purchased the African men and women who were already working the property, enslaved Africans who had made the passage to Jamaica aboard the *Henrietta Marie.*

Rose Fuller came to Jamaica at the most difficult time for the planters since the earthquake of 1692 and the French invasion of 1694. The price of muscovado sugar had fallen on the London market and the planters were faced with a guerrilla war from the maroons.

Rose Fuller's response to the price fall was to expand, cultivate acreage, and purchase more slaves. He eventually increased the Knollis Estate by about five thousand acres. Today, Lloyd and Joyce Mair own a chicken farm on 18½ acres of what was once this grand parcel of land.

The Mairs, a black Jamaican couple, inherited the property from Joyce's father forty-six years ago. Joyce recalls growing up on the property and spending afternoons in the backyard playing inside large iron pots that were used to process sugar during the slave trade.

I knocked on the front door of the Mairs' charming home, surrounded by an array of dazzling flowers of all sizes and colors—hibiscus, azaleas, orchids, crotons, bleeding hearts, and roses—and had only to mention that I was researching the history of a slave ship and was trying to locate the Knollis Estate before Lloyd Mair, now seventy-one years old and quick with his wit and memory, opened the door and invited me inside.

"You've found part of the Knollis Estate," Mair said. "We own eighteen and a half acres of it."

He offered me an ice-cold glass of coconut water and told me a little about the history of the property and more about his family history.

My visit was riddled with coincidences: Joyce's father was named Howard, as is my father, and Howard is also my middle name. Lloyd's son is named Michael, like me, and their daughter's baby, who was born in Miami while I was visiting Jamaica, is named Michaela, my daughter's middle name. Jamaica is where Mireille and I married.

I felt an instant connection, like distant family.

"Something brought you here," Joyce Mair added. "There is no question in my mind."

"Let me tell you something," Lloyd Mair said, smiling. "You were supposed to come to this house. You were supposed to come to Jamaica. You are at home."

ᴜᴜ

I couldn't say with certainty that Colin Fuller and Larkland Fuller—or the dozens of other black Fullers in Bog Walk—were descendants of the African people who were brought to Jamaica aboard the *Henrietta Marie.*

But as I looked deep into the hazel eyes of Colin Fuller, I thought that after four years of researching the origin of the *Henrietta Marie,* traveling to London and Africa and Florida and Barbados, for the first time, I had been guided to *black* people who may have a direct connection to the slave ship that I have touched and explored underwater.

Imagine that after all the books I've flipped through, after all of the scholarly papers I have read, after all of the captain's logs from slave ships past that I have studied, what brought tears to my eyes and gave me one of the most visceral rewards was walking along a narrow rocky road to the home of this old black man who sat on his front porch and talked to me about his life laboring on nearby estates.

What I know for certain is this: the Fullers of Jamaica are proud, forthright black people whose entire family history is based on honor and plowing property, where men and women worked side by side in the fields and in the home, where children were raised on mangoes and love, where the power of prayer at night brought the Fullers through their most difficult days.

I know for certain that I found a family that helped shape the economy of Jamaica by harvesting crops that benefited Jamaicans and Europeans. I met a family that is not bitter, despite the physical and psychological abuse they have endured through the years. They are straightforward enough, after all this, to say that they gave an honest day's work for a dishonest day's pay.

They know racism was as much a part of daily life on the estates as the crops they harvested, but children needed to eat and families had to be clothed. With strong, tough hands they farmed the property in the relentless heat of the day while their British overseers took tea in the afternoon shade.

Were these Fullers of Bog Walk descendants of African people who came to Jamaica on the *Henrietta Marie*?

Perhaps.

I may have actually been fortunate enough to meet the descendents of the first black people associated with the slave ship *Henrietta Marie,* or I may have simply met a family of hardworking people who largely ignored racism to contribute to Jamaica's growing economy, a family that quietly, and without recognition, helped write the history of Jamaica's vast agricultural properties by putting their hands on the land.

After twenty years as a journalist, I have learned to rely on my intuition and feelings. It was my intuition that led me to Jamaica to find the Fullers. And while driving off over a dirt road with miles of green fields and spectacular mountains before me, I believed the Fullers of Bog Walk and the slave ship *Henrietta Marie* share a link that spans centuries and have more in common than any of us will ever know.

10

They emerged from the sea dripping salt water, their rubber suits squeaking, their tanned, dark features barely visible inside the round masks pressed against their faces.

A dozen men with bulky ribbed hoses dangling from their shoulders, steel tanks strapped to their backs, and knives fastened to their legs appeared from deep below the ocean's surface, their clumsy fins slapping sand as they trudged across the beach, leaving a trail of webbed imprints on the shores of Grand Cayman.

Children playing along the shore, who thought the divers in black rubber were deep-sea bogeymen, abandoned their sand castles and ran screaming across the beach to warn their parents of the masked monsters who had appeared from the ocean.

Their underwater exploration over for the day, the divers stacked their fins in the sand and waded into a foamy surf where soft swells splashed their ankles and tiny sea drops that could have been mistaken for tears rolled gently from their cheeks.

Standing shoulder to shoulder in front of a sliver of sun, Albert Jose Jones, Lorenzo Milner, Jimmy Thorne, Dan Maloney, and Ronnie Burrell stared out over the calm sea, watching a silhouette of sails disappear over the horizon and savoring their dive as if it were the last warm day before winter.

These underwater pioneers had experienced the immense power of the sea; they had descended into the depths, chasing wide-winged stingrays that glided by just out of reach; they had come face-to-face with sleek sharks that zigzagged out of the shadows and vanished as quickly as they appeared; they had seen a school of rainbow runners shifting silently with the rhythm of the sea, the most entertaining choreography they had ever witnessed.

They had plunged into nature's aquarium and been dwarfed by its magnitude, stunned by its beauty, intoxicated by the freedom of flight; they had experienced total weightlessness, the closest feeling to zero grav-ity—floating freely over mounds of sponge coral and hovering over jagged ledges that dropped to extraordinary depths.

And in the eerie silence of the sea, where hand signals replace speech, the measured thumping of their heartbeats had been amplified, sounding like the thunder of African drums in their heads.

They were a rare sight on Grand Cayman in 1968. Even in this most popular of diving destinations, there was something noticeably distinct about these scuba divers: They were black.

Fresh from months of intense training in the frigid rock quarries of Virginia, they were underwater frontiersmen, deep-sea explorers—black frogmen. They called themselves the Underwater Adventure Seekers.

In 1968, when I was only twelve years old, Jones, a former military diver, took the Underwater Adventure Seekers to Grand Cayman for their first underwater tour outside the United States.

The civil rights movement was becoming a defining moment in Amer-ican history. "Burn, baby, burn" was the black community's social refrain of the day. The Black Panthers were confronting racial injustice; Martin Luther King, Jr., had been assassinated; Hank Aaron was slamming base-balls out of ballparks and closing in on Babe Ruth's home-run record; and James Brown was sliding across the nation's stages, screaming, "Say it loud—I'm black and I'm proud."

I was growing up in Detroit. A year earlier, I had been a young wit-ness to a city still smoldering from a weeklong riot that today remains a prototype for urban rebellion. I remember standing on the steps of St. Mark's Community Church at Twelfth Street and Atkinson, holding my mother's hand, my eyes stinging from the smoke.

I had seen helicopters crisscrossing the neighborhood, police shouting through bullhorns, some of them brandishing nightsticks and guns. Buildings and houses were burning and mobs of angry young adults were racing through the streets.

Any questions I had were silenced by sirens.

History was unfolding before my eyes. Twelfth Street was reduced to charred buildings and mounds of ashes.

Several thousand miles away from the concrete and chaos of urban America, as I tried to sort out in my young mind why violence was happening around me, these black scuba divers had traveled to the Caribbean to make history of their own.

Life was slow and easy on the island of Grand Cayman in 1968.

Men who were between jobs watched sand crabs crawl out of holes the size of quarters. Young boys who had learned to swim as toddlers would jump off the green algae-layered jetties, free-dive into forty feet of water, and, holding their breath for a little over a minute, spear fish just in time for lunch. Old men repaired tattered fishing nets; women weaved straw baskets in the shade of their straw sheds.

Jones and the black divers became the talk of the island. They had formed the first all-black dive club anywhere in the United States. They not only wanted to experience a sport that had been reserved for whites but they also yearned to explore and record their underwater adventures for their children.

Fresh from their first Cayman Islands dive, the men made their way to a stack of stones they converted into seats and began the tedious task of peeling themselves out of the thick rubber that clung to their bodies like a second skin—a process that took two people and even more patience.

Jones recalled that the procedure for getting into and out of their suits had transformed into an art form. Many of the divers dusted themselves with baby powder. Some wore women's panty hose to make it easier to pull the suits over their legs.

"Because the men were large, they couldn't wear the regular hosiery, so they had to wear the Big Mama brand name," Jones recalled. Wearing the panty hose, Jones said, wasn't as embarrassing as standing in line to buy it.

Fit and confident, the divers packed away their gear and strolled past the docks where white divers from Britain, the United States, and Germany prepared to board spacious dive boats and spend an afternoon underwater.

European tourists would stare at the black divers as they walked past. The looks were somewhat curious, more patronizing than inquisitive—the kind of looks that royalty reserve for peasants, the kind of looks that Park Avenue residents reserve for people outside their social rank: expressions that are used like blunt instruments.

Prying themselves into the lily white sport of scuba diving wasn't easy. No one was aggressively trying to prevent them from diving, but no one was embracing them, either. It was much more subtle, the way some people from the office are invited to the club for golf, and subsequent promotions, while others from the office never know the game is being played.

The divers made a decision to spend time on the water with people like themselves and learn more about the people and the culture of Grand Cayman.

"We weren't trying to make history," Jones said. "We were just a group of folks who wanted to enjoy the sport of scuba diving. It just so happened that we were the only black people diving at the time. We just wanted to explore and have fun, and I believe we changed some attitudes in the process."

Jones believed that the people who knew the most about Grand Cayman's marine life and best dive sites were the fishermen of Grand Cayman, the men whose livelihood depended on the catch of the day.

Hours before sunrise, while the island was pitch-black, only sparkling fireflies and a fisherman's flashlight illuminated the darkness. Each morning, Jones would watch the fishermen make their way along the rickety pier, hauling plastic buckets filled with raw fish. Tossing their nets into the stern of their wooden boats, the fishermen would chart a course, weigh anchor, and head out to sea.

In the evening, when the fishermen returned from sea, Jones and the divers would walk along the dirt roads, drifting from bar to bar, introducing themselves to black fishermen, buying beers in haunts only fishermen would frequent, and offering to pay for boat rides to the best reefs.

On one quiet evening, over a plate of stewed chicken, plantains, and

peas and rice, Jones met a man named Solomon Ebanks, a local fisherman who made a modest living with his boat and who boasted about
coming from a long line of successful, enterprising fishermen. He was tall
and slender with thick white hair.

"What can I do for you?" Ebanks asked, shoving a forkful of peas and
rice into his mouth.

"I'd like you to take us diving," Jones said. "We'll pay you for your
time."

Ebanks gave them a slow once-over; he paused and took his time
chewing his food. He took a long sip of beer and mumbled a few words
without looking up from the table.

"I leave at five sharp," he said.

That evening, Ebanks introduced Jones and the divers around town,
put them up in black-owned rooming houses, and talked to them about
the history of black people on the island.

The next morning, Ebanks was on the pier at 5:00 A.M. His wooden
fishing boat—like all the boats at the pier converted from an old war
boat—was loaded with netting and raw fish. The divers crammed on
board, pushed off from shore, and bounced across the waves, their bodies bumping the buckets of smelly bait.

Lorenzo Milner remembers those old boats as being awkward. He
was thirty-four years old and had been a navy engineer and part of a navy
experimental diving unit by the time he joined the Underwater Adventure
Seekers in 1959.

"There weren't many black people scuba diving back then," Milner
said. "But then, there weren't too many white people scuba diving, either.
We were unique, but white people were unique, too. It was a time where
people were learning more about the sport, and we were right there with
them. Many people didn't even know that scuba diving existed."

Milner recalled that traveling individually—the way many black people do today—was never done in 1959, several years before Congress
enacted civil rights legislation.

"We formed the club and traveled together for protection," Milner
said. "Protection was our first priority; camaraderie came later. We
couldn't travel on a dive trip alone and expect to check into a hotel without trouble, so we traveled in groups.

"Back then, there were white organizations designed to make trouble for us and they did this deliberately whenever they had the chance, and we knew this," he said. "In lower Virginia, white folks would give us hostile looks and try to intimidate us, but it didn't work. We were lean and young—and they weren't. But through the club, we learned to appreciate the camaraderie and the leadership that Jose displayed."

In the fall of 1953, with the sun barely rising over the jagged Kentucky mountains, a company of young crew-cut soldiers stood quietly along the edge of the white tile overlooking an Olympic-sized swimming pool.

Standing shoulder to shoulder, their chests out, their arms pressed against their sides, they were dressed in green fatigues and camouflage caps, their spit-shined steel-toe boots laced up to their ankles, the pungent smell of chlorine forcing frowns.

Looking straight ahead in stony silence, they awaited orders from a raspy-voiced drill sergeant who barked his commands even though he was standing close enough for the soldiers to smell the chewing tobacco on his breath.

Jones was one of several new recruits at Fort Campbell to sign up for the army's elite combat swimming course.

Few questions were allowed about the criteria for this course and fewer answers were given about what they would learn over the next several weeks, what their mission would be at the conclusion of the class, and what was expected of them. Information was hard to come by. Details were shared on a need-to-know basis and high-level commanders a half a mile away decided that new recruits didn't need to know much.

Twenty minutes passed and the soldiers were left standing in silence at the edge of the pool, staring at the water and wondering why they had never stopped in the locker room to change into shorts or swim trunks. Then, just as a few men gave into nervous fidgeting and began to shift from side to side, the orders came like thunder:

"Everybody in the pool!" the drill sergeant shouted. *"On the double! Move, move!"*

At that moment, Jones thought he had misunderstood the orders, but as he glanced around the pool, twenty men were diving headfirst, one after the other, into the water, wearing every stitch of clothing the army had provided for them. Suddenly, a recreational swimming pool that seemed harmless enough twenty minutes earlier had been transformed into a crowded, frenzied survival course.

Their orders were clear: "Swim 'til you drop."

Jones quickly plunged into the chaos and began swimming the length of the pool. He had been a competitor since he was young. He didn't want to be the last one in the pool, just the way he never wanted to lose the sidewalk relay races as a kid growing up in Washington, D.C., where his first experience in the water was paddling facedown in a washbasin.

It wasn't more than a minute before his waterlogged boots began to feel as if they weighed more than his body. With each stroke, Jones propelled himself past the crowds of sinking young men who were waving their arms hysterically, gasping for air, and trying to grab anything—or anybody.

His first instinct was to stop and help them.

"*Keep swimming!*" the drill sergeant yelled.

Jones picked up his pace.

The object of the exercise was to weed out the weak swimmers. It worked. Within minutes, officers were fishing recruits out of the pool like lobsters.

Jones had blocked out the confusion around him and with his head buried in the water, his clothes wet and weighty, he just kept swimming and swimming and swimming.

There were fewer people in the pool after fifteen minutes. Many of the men who had dived in ahead of Jones were now either sitting or lying on the side, breathing hard or coughing water from their lungs.

Jones kept swimming.

He was one of only a few men left in the pool on that day, and the only black man around. He knew that black people were not considered strong swimmers, and in a sense, this was personal for him: He wanted to prove the critics wrong, and he would settle for simply walking away from the pool, instead of being carried out.

As he kicked off from the edge of the pool to swim another lap, he heard yelling. "*Everybody out!*" the sergeant screamed. "*Out! Move it!*"

Jones, his legs like noodles, stood dripping with half a dozen other men who were coughing and resting on their knees after completing the grueling forty-five-minute exercise, the army's version of a pop quiz.

"Congratulations soldiers, you've been accepted into a special unit," the drill sergeant said with a sly smile that looked more like that of a used-car salesman than a commanding officer's. "That was the easy part. The combat swimming course starts tomorrow morning at oh six hundred. Then we'll do some serious swimming."

Jones swam for hours every day with his combat team. He mastered swimming fully dressed and could hold his breath underwater longer than anyone in his unit. He stood out as an exceptional swimmer—and as the only black man in combat swim training.

Several months later, while leaving the locker room and heading to lunch, he was approached by one of his commanding officers, who asked if Jones was interested in taking his interest in water training a step further.

"Sure," Jones said, always looking for a challenge and an adventure. "What did you have in mind?"

"Scuba diving," the officer responded.

Scuba diving? The notion of being trained to scuba dive seemed so far-fetched, learning to swim underwater with gadgets and a rubbery breathing apparatus. But it also sounded too intriguing to pass up.

Jones was hooked.

The training for scuba diving in the army was not glamorous, despite his special status of handpicked soldier. He trained early in the morning and late at night, in freezing Kentucky lakes and muddy rock quarries, in deep water and zero visibility, where Jones couldn't see past his own hand.

The pressure gauge had not been invented in 1953, so there was no accurate measurement for how much air was in his tanks.

"When our breathing got difficult, we'd pull on our j-valve, and we knew it was time to surface," he said.

Six years later, after Jones earned the Purple Heart during the Korean War, he returned to a segregated Washington, D.C., and, in the summer of 1959, invited six of his buddies over to the house.

Burnell Irby was one of them.

"How would you guys like to learn to scuba dive?" Jones asked.

Silence.

"I did ask that question in English, didn't I?" he said.

Over the next several hours, Jones talked about the thrill of scuba diving and the feeling of isolation he felt as a black diver. He wanted company.

Irby remembers the men talking among themselves for a few minutes. Diving was beginning to sound appealing to the group.

"It was an enthusiastic meeting," Irby recalled. "We are all young, we thought scuba diving sounded fashionable, and besides, my lady friend liked the idea. I think it had to do with trying something totally different. You didn't find black people talking about scuba diving in 1959. Jose was convincing; he had a vision back then for getting black people involved in scuba diving, and we went right along with him. I'm glad I did."

Irby, who has more than one thousand dives in his logbook, designed the logo for the Underwater Adventure Seekers.

"I remember my first trip to Grand Cayman," Irby said. "I looked up underwater and I saw the biggest fish swim over me. It may have been a manta ray. It had wings. I was twenty-nine years old and I had never seen anything like it before. When I got home and told my friends what I had seen, they looked at me in awe and said, 'Can that be done?' and I said, 'Sure it can, and I did it.'"

Each evening after work, Jones would meet his friends at a nearby swimming pool in Washington where he would teach them the fundamentals of swimming. They started with basic kicking and getting comfortable in the water. It wasn't easy—the sessions would last several hours—but before they could become good divers, they would have to become good swimmers.

After a few weeks, the group was swimming about ten laps a day and Jones was starting to teach them to swim underwater from one end of the pool to the other. Soon, they were getting confident and joking about making their first dive.

Jones put his new students through a rigorous training process. The army way was the only way he knew how to train people. He was cursed on some days and praised on others.

There was a gradual sense of pride among the divers and a sense of purpose for Jones. He was not only exposing black people to a world they had never known existed; he was fulfilling a larger vision to bring black divers into a sport and an industry that was reserved for white men. It was a chance for Jones to even the playing field and an opportunity to dive with people he felt more comfortable with in the water.

In late summer of 1959, Jones and his students loaded large bottles of air and a pair of scuba tanks into the back of a station wagon and drove to a rock quarry in Virginia for morning training exercises.

There were only two sets of scuba equipment, so Jones could take only one person into the quarry at a time—a process that took all day and sometimes spilled over into the evening. While one diver was underwater, the others would study their training manuals and wait their turn.

The ride to the quarry took about an hour. The men were nervous; it was their first time out of the pool, where they could see bottom at ten feet. The quarry was one hundred feet deep yet surprisingly clear.

In the quarry, Jones ran his students through a series of underwater exercises: navigation, removing masks and retrieving them, and learning how to maneuver underwater in stiff currents.

There were no certification agencies in 1959 and there were few places to get trained as a scuba diver. Most men who learned to dive, like Jones, were taught in the military. Jones's Underwater Adventure Seekers were trained nearly ten years before the Professional Association of Diving Instructors and the National Association of Underwater Instructors—today's leading dive-training agencies—were established.

On the muddy banks on the quarry, Jones, dressed in his wet suit, would stand with his clipboard in hand, checking off the exercises the divers had done and noting the drills that some would do over while the students formed a semicircle around him.

"The quarry was once a construction site that filled up with water that flowed from underground," Milner recalled. "We would do our training dives to depths of one hundred feet or more, diving along roadways and down to steam shovels, all kinds of equipment, and construction shacks. It was fun stuff."

The drive home from the quarry was always rockin'. The men, pumped up from a successful day of dive training, would ride along the highway in a 1957 station wagon, singing hits from the Coasters and the Platters all the way back to Washington.

But being black, on the highway in the 1950s, did have its pitfalls. Once, at a West Virginia roadside diner in the late 1950s, Jones walked up to the lunch counter. Before he could place an order, he was abruptly cut off by the proprietor.

"We don't serve niggers here," he told Jones.

"Well, I wouldn't, either," Jones responded. "I'll have a hamburger."

"The guy laughed, almost as if he was disarmed," Jones said. "I got my hamburger."

Jones was a social pioneer—underwater and on land—and he was making history. He was tearing down racial barriers and touring undiscovered quarries and oceans in 1959.

Like other African-American educators and black musicians, businessmen, and athletes, Jones was forging ahead with milestones of his own. Few people outside the diving industry knew it at the time, but Jones was methodically preserving a place for black scuba divers in American history.

Jones had also become one of the few black Fulbright scholars, had earned a doctorate in marine science, and was chairman of the Environmental Science Department at the University of the District of Columbia, where he introduced marine science as a curriculum.

In 1966, Jones introduced another diver to the Underwater Adventure Seekers. Shirley Lee, a young lifeguard with a fondness for adventure and a passion for swimming, became the first woman member to join the all-male club.

Lee remembers swimming more laps to train for scuba diving than she ever did training to become a lifeguard. She says she was not coddled by the men, nor was she asked to do anything they wouldn't do.

"It wasn't easy," she said. "They treated me just like one of the guys. I don't know if that was good or bad. I showed up at the pool every day and Jose would teach me something different, something I needed to know."

Lee would routinely haul twenty-five pounds of lead for her weight belt, her steel scuba tank, and her other gear to the boat to start her day of diving.

"Nobody carried anything for me; I had to do for myself," said Lee, who has logged more than one thousand dives in waters from Maryland to Morocco.

In cold and dark waters off Maryland and Delaware, Lee spearfished and spent hours diving for oysters. "Sometimes it was so dark, I could barely see my hands, so I would just feel around the bottom until I felt an oyster and then scoop it into my bag."

Toward the end of one oyster-diving trip in the mid-1960s, Lee said the weather became rough in Chesapeake Bay; their boat took on water and capsized in the storm. She tried to hang on to the side of the boat in freezing waters, but she knew she couldn't hang on long.

"My hands were numb, they were so cold," she recalled. "So since we were able to see land, we decided to swim for it. It wasn't until we got to shore and knocked on someone's door that we learned out boat had been about two miles offshore. A white gentleman gave us a ride into town and was nice enough to stop off at a liquor store so we could get a pint of whiskey. Riding into town, I appreciated Jose making me swim all those laps in the pool back in Washington."

Lee said she had no reservations about joining an all-male scuba-diving club, but several members of the club were worried that her husband, Lavelle, her high school sweetheart, might be concerned.

"They didn't want any trouble from my husband," she said. "They thought Lavelle would be upset about me hanging around all those men. So they asked me to get a letter from my husband saying it was okay to join the club. He wrote a letter and that's how I was accepted into the Underwater Adventure Seekers."

Of diving, Lee said, "It's as close as you can get to nature."

Jones has taught swimming and diving to more than two thousand students. Although they are of all ethnic backgrounds, the majority are African-American, all of them superb swimmers.

"Water is part of our history and our heritage," says black diver and anthropologist Sheila Walker. "We have a long relationship with water, with oceans and rivers and streams.

"We were a people created on the water, because the Middle Passage—the transatlantic voyage from Africa to bondage in the New World—was the creation of a new people."

The ocean did create a new people who showed a new kind of determination and strength, and a renewed sense of faith. The ocean also created the Underwater Adventure Seekers, descendants of these African people, black scuba divers whose historical significance has become clear as the years progressed: These are the black divers who helped bring the *Henrietta Marie* to life.

From the day they formed the Underwater Adventure Seekers in the 1950s and took their first trip to Grand Cayman, these black divers led by Dr. Jones would become a pivotal part of one of the most significant historical and archeological finds ever—the discovery of the *Henrietta Marie*.

How fitting that a group of black people who simply wanted to explore the ocean nearly four decades ago would someday be part of exploring the remains of a sunken slave ship.

Over the years, Jones has guided students from the cocoon of Washington's swimming pools to the currents of Fiji and Africa, Belize and Australia. He has seen club members meet and fall in love; he has watched children grow up at club picnics and has trained young people to compete in scuba tournaments. He has attended the marriages of many students and, years later, has taught their children scuba diving.

Jones started the organization to build relationships. He never imagined it would build a bridge to his people's past.

He still refers to his former students as his children: an organization of black scuba divers that started forty years ago in the living room of Jones's home and beneath the ocean, where he first saw a Caribbean sea filled with dark faces behind round masks.

11

Tiny drops of cold water began to seep into the two-inch-thick rubber hood that covered my head as I descended sixty feet below the surface of Sheepshead Bay.

With visibility reduced to five feet, I could barely see the fins flapping in front of me. A few yards away, the scattered wreckage of the *Lizzy D* was slowly coming into view a piece at a time—just before my dive mask was snatched from my face.

I was temporarily blind in fifty-degree waters; nothing was in focus underwater as I ran my hands along the sand in search of my mask. After a few seconds of swimming in circles, I felt a rectangular plastic piece and guided my hands to the strap, then placed the mask tightly over my face.

My dive instructor, who had yanked the mask from my face during a series of underwater training exercises, was in clear view and giving me a hearty thumbs-up.

It was mid-June 1990 and I was off the shore of Brooklyn, completing my certification for scuba diving. I was feeling pretty good about myself, having gone through a somewhat-traumatic experience several months earlier.

Before I earned my scuba certification card, I took a detour through Lenox Hill Hospital, where I was treated for a series of stress-related problems that were unrelated to scuba diving.

I had completed my classroom work and my required pool sessions with my instructor and was waiting to get my schedule to start my four open-water dives in Sheepshead Bay, Brooklyn, which are mandatory for scuba certification.

It was a busy time for me: I was planning a wedding in Jamaica for seventy guests, and at the age of thirty-four, I was visibly nervous at the prospect of a radical lifestyle change. I was moving from one position at the newspaper to another; I was also moving from New York to Philadelphia. And in my spare time, I was trying to squeeze in scuba. All of these life changes, I later learned, conspired against me.

Several days before my certification, I began to experience chest pains and shortness of breath. I've always been in good shape, so this unusual development alarmed me. In fact, it scared the hell out of me, since I had never been hospitalized, except for a couple of dislocated fingers playing high school football.

I visited my physician, Marc Spero, a great doctor who specializes in pulmonary medicine and dive medicine. He performed a routine stress test. He didn't like the results and, just as a precaution to rule out the worst, he admitted me for observation.

I checked myself into the hospital, where I was listed as a heart patient.

The emergency room was filled with patients and nurses. I walked into the waiting room, gave the nurse at the counter my name, and started flipping through the newspaper. I wasn't looking at the words.

Finally, after forty-five-minutes, I heard my name called and I walked into a processing area for the sick. I was asked to stretch out on a bed and several nurses came over and attached me to a maze of wires connected to a monitor that beeped every few seconds.

Questions about my medical history were coming from everywhere. I spent the first few hours in the emergency room trying to convince a rather aggressive nurse that I wasn't a junkie.

Days earlier, I had given blood at my newspaper, *New York Newsday,* and in an attempt to find a good vein, I had been pricked several times in both arms.

"Do you use drugs?" the nurse asked me.

"No," I said, lying on my back.

"You sure?" she asked again.

"I think I'd know," I said.

"Why do you have needle marks in your arms?" she asked.

"I gave blood the other day," I said.

"We'll see," she said, clearly implying I was lying. "We'll take some blood tests."

Not only was I in an emergency room waiting to be treated for something—I wasn't sure what—but I was being interrogated by a nurse who thought I was a drug user. She was convinced that I was not using drugs only after the results of the blood test were presented to her.

I wondered, even then, if she was skeptical of everyone who entered the hospital with needle marks and a story of giving blood, or just me, because I was black. I determined that this was not the time to dwell on whether I was being singled out because of race, an instinct we often have to fight against.

Hours later, someone came to get me, announced that my room was ready, and wheeled me to a ward marked CARDIAC UNIT.

As I lay on a hospital bed for what seemed like a month, waiting to be probed by cardiologists and interns, I overheard two nurses talking just outside my room.

"Did you see the new patient in there?" one nurse asked, referring to me.

"Yeah, it's really sad," the other nurse said. "He's so young and he looked like he was in such good shape."

They were writing me off, or so it seemed. Clearly, these remarks were not intended for my ears. I was in a ward where everyone around me was fifty years my senior, where some patients were holding on just to see family one last time.

Apparently, death was a frequent visitor to this ward. I wanted out.

I clamped my teeth tight to keep from shedding a tear and pretended to be asleep when the nurse came into the room to take my temperature.

I wanted to cry, but I decided that if I was going out, then I would do so with dry eyes. One of life's most difficult tasks is for a man to pretend not to hurt. It's an emotional game we play with ourselves; we've done it for centuries, and we've gotten quite good at it.

After three days of tests, my doctors came to a unanimous conclusion: I was completely healthy and my body was not the problem.

"Your problem," my doctor said, gently touching my arm, "is all above your shoulders."

I blew a long sigh of relief, paused, and prayed to God.

"So what are you telling me?" I asked.

"I am saying that you have to learn how to cope with your stress, but in the meantime, would you please leave this hospital? This room is for people who are ill."

As he walked away, he stopped, turned to me, and said, "Oh, and don't baby yourself; you're very healthy, so do everything you would normally do. That includes scuba diving."

I was as determined as ever to get certified and to cope with my stress and stay out of hospitals. Anxiety attacks, or panic attacks, are real and can be dangerous. Heart palpitations followed by sweating and shortness of breath, were just some of the symptoms that I experienced. They are gone now, hopefully forever.

ᚤᚤ

I felt a certain sense of accomplishment after being handed my scuba certification patch. I wasn't feeling anxiety anymore; I was thinking about how to get the most out of life. It was important for me to keep busy, not necessarily to forget what had happened, but to put into some sort of perspective how dangerous stress can be. As I thanked God that I was healthy, I was reminded of a bumper sticker I saw days before entering the hospital: DEATH IS GOD'S WAY OF TELLING YOU TO SLOW DOWN.

With my certification behind me, I decided it was time to explore the deep, wherever I could, whenever I could.

In 1992, after being certified by the Professional Association of Diving Instructors, I traveled to Saint Petersburg, Florida, to visit my father-in-law, Eugene Grangenois, and decided to take advantage of good weather and clear waters. I called a local dive operation a few miles away and signed up for two dives the next morning.

When I arrived at the dock, there were eleven divers standing along the pier, setting up their tanks, buying bottled water, and loading their gear onto the twenty-foot boat.

Divers were talking to one another, but no one said a word to me. I smiled to everyone and started to unpack my brand-new Dacor equipment. Most of the divers on board were already paired up. There were a few, however, like myself, who did not have dive buddies, so the captain told us to select partners before we arrived at the dive site, a short twenty-minute trip from shore.

"Is there anyone who does not have a buddy?" the captain finally asked.

I raised my hand.

A dozen pairs of eyes looked down, looked out to sea, looked everywhere but at me.

I felt like the kid nobody wanted to pick for a sandlot basketball game. Because black divers are still somewhat rare, perhaps the divers assumed that I was not an experienced diver or that I would put their lives in jeopardy. Or maybe it was just that they didn't want to dive with a black person. I can recall one diver looking at me as if *I* were the problem, as if I shouldn't be on the dive in the first place, and that by not having a buddy, I slowed the process of getting into the water.

Unfortunately, it was a look that black divers have seen for years. This wasn't the way I wanted to start a seventy-foot dive.

After the captain asked for a second time if everyone had a buddy, a reluctant computer salesman from Houston asked if I wanted to buddy with him. I could have stayed on board, but I wanted to dive. We talked for a moment, agreed on a dive plan—seventy feet maximum depth for thirty-five minutes of bottom time—and hit the water shortly after he sealed our temporary partnership with a quick handshake.

But once we descended, it only took a few seconds for me to realize that we weren't dive buddies at all; we were just two people who happened to be diving under the same boat in the same ocean. Although we were only a few feet from each other during the dive, we were worlds apart.

Still, it was a pretty good dive. Folks on the return trip talked about the big fish and colorful coral. But still no one uttered a word to me. When we returned to the dock, the gentleman from Houston gave me his telephone number and suggested that I call him the next time I passed through Texas. It was a halfhearted gesture; I thanked him and walked away.

I could have become one of the many scuba dropouts that Doc Jones talks about: African-American divers who became weary of diving alone and tired of being snubbed in dive shops and on dive boats.

I'm not suggesting that all white divers are rude or racist; they are not. It's not to say that I cannot dive with white divers and enjoy the experience, because I have. Indeed, I have made several lasting friendships with divers of all backgrounds over the years from Pennsylvania, to Florida, to Texas, people I trust underwater. What was infuriating for me was that racism, a shadowy companion, seems to have also seeped into my recreational activities, my space, my time for peace.

∪∪

In 1988, when *Ebony Man* magazine published a profile about Dr. Jose Jones and the Underwater Adventure Seekers, applications for membership began to triple. By late 1989, the files in Jones's cabinets were overflowing with names and telephone numbers of future members of a national black divers' organization. Members of the Underwater Adventure Seekers were still gathering in the evenings at Jones's home, momentum was building, and talk of the formation of a national black dive organization dominated discussions.

On a sunny winter morning in Fort Lauderdale, in November of 1991, nearly 150 African-American divers began arriving at the first convention by cars, trains, and airplanes, unsure of what they were going to find but somehow having the knowledge that they were going to be part of something remarkably special and historically significant.

Black divers from across the country strolled into the hotel, shook hands, and introduced themselves. Within minutes, people were talking about dive destinations and dive sites they had in common. Divers from the same cities, who lived blocks apart, were meeting one another for the first time, tales of big fish were being swapped, and divers were holding discussions in the lobby about the ever-evolving scuba gear and the latest in technology.

But there was one refrain that seemed to echo throughout the hotel: *"I never knew there were so many black divers!"*

Instantly, Jones's theory that thousands of black divers were scattered around the country unaware that there were others was proving correct.

Though most of these divers had never met, it was a reunionlike atmosphere, with divers showing one another their equipment, exchanging business cards, and offering to help one another improve their scuba skills.

Many of the divers had gathered in the conference room of the hotel and were talking about exotic locations and the ever-exhilarating shark dives when Dr. Jones entered the room to deliver his first speech as co-founder of the National Association of Black Scuba Divers.

"He is soft-spoken with a youthful gleam in his eye when talking about black divers and scuba diving. He won't reveal his age, although he does possess a grandfatherly persona—he's quick to sit and advise students on any issue from diving to relationships, and when it comes to diving, he has more energy than most men half his years."

"It's no coincidence that we are here today to form a new organization of black divers. I think we've always known about each other from a distance," Jones told the group. "I think we've always known there are brothers and sisters who are divers out there, somewhere out there, but who may not be aware of one another. Today, we can make connections and put names to all these wonderful black faces."

Looking out over the roomful of black divers, one could see black men and women from across the nation dressed in shorts and T-shirts, sitting in silent amazement, thrilled to be part of something so extraordinary. There were doctors and lawyers, policemen and firefighters, educators and computer executives, chemists and engineers, postal workers and architects.

Jones spoke of winters past, of cultural connections, of links to our African forefathers. He spoke to black divers about challenging the same oceans where African people had perished. He talked of the slave ship *Henrietta Marie.*

He talked of spirits from another time, of soul mates with the sea, those who are still part of the raging Atlantic Ocean, which once flowed with the blood of African people.

"There's a ship not far from here, a slave ship called the *Henrietta Marie,* a ship that carried our ancestors from Africa to the West Indies three hundred years ago," Jones said. "It carried some of your family members and it carried some of mine.

"This slave ship has come to our attention at a time when we're forming a national organization of black scuba divers. There are no coincidences. This slave ship is a part of us, whether we like it or not."

There was a sense of unity that seemed to fill the room: a sense of family connection past and present, a feeling of friendship and camaraderie that no one could have anticipated.

"This ship represents a part of our past, a part of *your* past," Jones said as he began to pace the floor. "It's part of a place within each of us. This is an extraordinary opportunity—and the first opportunity—for black scuba divers to study a slave ship that represents a portion of our history, a history that has been written about extensively, analyzed, and interpreted by European writers.

"But today," he said, "we can help reconstruct this part of our history ourselves, because we can explore the ocean floor. What makes the *Henrietta Marie* so important is that this is not just about *our* history; it's a pivotal part of American history."

Every person in the room was beaming with pride. For them, the *Henrietta Marie* was not simply a story from a book, but something tangible that could be examined and observed underwater.

Jones paused for a moment and offered a suggestion, an idea that he had discussed weeks before with Oswald Sykes, a newly certified diver, and Ric Powell, a former navy diver. He didn't have all the answers for implementing the plan yet, but he felt that he should raise the issue anyway.

"What I would like to see is some kind of plaque—or memorial—placed at the site of the *Henrietta Marie*," Jones said "A commemoration from black people, black divers, to black people, African people, our people, that we can leave on the ocean floor."

What Jones was proposing was unparalleled. Never before had a group of black scuba divers honored their African ancestors in such a way, nor had any African-American dive group had an opportunity to study a slave ship firsthand.

For that matter, there are few monuments underwater that honor a significant part of American history.

"This is an opportunity of a lifetime and we can't let it slip away," he said. "We have to honor our people and we need a substantial memorial that will honor our ancestors and hopefully stand the test of time."

Jones suggested a monument be placed on the site of the *Henrietta Marie* the following year, when the organization would meet in Key West.

Oswald Sykes listened carefully.

A stout man with a soft, bulging middle, Oswald wears large glasses that seem to swallow his round, light-skinned face. A man who thoroughly loves to laugh, he would rather hug a friend than shake hands. He will be the first to admit that he can consume a plate of baby-back ribs in Olympic-record time.

He is a stickler for details, a perfectionist who sometimes grows impatient with those who cut corners. A bright and thoughtful person who has studied a range of subjects, Sykes isn't shy about sharing his knowledge.

Oswald, Dr. Jones, and dozens of African-American divers had listened to a lecture about the *Henrietta Marie* the night before, holding the artifacts and shackles in their hands and paying close attention to a presentation by David Moore and Corey Malcolm, two archaeologists from the Mel Fisher Maritime Heritage Society, who had arguably spent more underwater time on the wreck site than anyone.

It was the first time that Moore and Malcolm had met so many of the black divers. They had met photographer Howard Moss years earlier, however, and had supplied detailed information about the *Henrietta Marie* for a documentary that Moss was filming. This film was now being shown.

"When you see those shackles that were fashioned for children, it's kind of a mind-bending experience, isn't it?" said Moss as a pair of tiny shackles flashed across the screen.

Jones focused on the film. He was fascinated by the history unfolding before him, but he was also a bit distracted. He wanted to commemorate the African people aboard the *Henrietta Marie* and to pay homage to the African men, women, and children who had been thrust into the Middle Passage, stolen away into slavery, and whose cries for mercy had been muffled after they slipped beneath the sea.

He wanted to place a memorial on the site of the wreckage, something that would withstand time and the elements of the sea, something that would last in the oceans and in our minds.

All sorts of questions raced through his mind: How much should such a monument weigh to stay in place? How long would it take to get it to the wreck site? How much would it cost? How many divers would it take to lower it to the bottom? What about the strong currents?

"This is going to be one hell of a chore putting this thing together," Jones said to Powell. "We're going to need plenty of help and an awful lot of luck."

The following day, Sykes couldn't stop talking about the *Henrietta Marie*. He had already held the shackles in his hands and sifted through the glass trade beads that were bartered for African people. He had wiped away the tears that rolled uncontrollably from his eyes. He had imagined the torture of black people he would never know.

Sykes thought about the thousands of Africans who had been consumed by the currents. He was preoccupied with the water: It was the West African sea that had brought African people in shackles to America's shores; it was the Atlantic Ocean where Sykes and his wife, Marion, had learned to dive together. It was the cold Potomac River that had taken his father's life in 1959.

Sykes was twenty-three years old and had just finished graduate school when his father committed suicide.

One morning, while driving to work, his father had jumped over the side of a bridge in Washington, D.C., and drowned in the muddy currents of the Potomac. His father's closest friend watched him leap from his moving car at thirty-five miles an hour, run for the edge of the bridge, and leap over the steel railing. The last he saw of Oswald's father was his hand slowly disappearing into the river.

Oswald Sykes was a former water-safety instructor when his father died. He still believes he could have saved his father's life if he had been on that bridge over the Potomac River nearly forty years ago. He's never fully put his father's death to rest.

"There would have been nothing he could have done to keep me from saving him," Sykes said, tears in his eyes. "All that experience I had. I had some of the best training in the country and I couldn't do a damn thing about it. It's always been in my mind—here I am a water-safety instructor, and he dies by drowning. I wasn't there when he needed me most. This ship, this damn ocean, is forcing me to deal with feelings that I've kept in a box and never wanted to open. I guess it's finally time."

UU

The telephone rang several weeks after Sykes returned home from the summit in Fort Lauderdale. Jones was on the other end of the line.

"How would you like to chair the *Henrietta Marie* Shipwreck Committee?" Jones asked.

"Sounds interesting," Sykes said. "What would I have to do?"

"Everything!" Jones said. "Well, damn near everything."

"I can do that," said Sykes, laughing with a mixture of excitement and nervousness. "How could anyone turn down that kind of offer?"

Sykes proved to be the logical choice to head the committee. He spent hours each day on the telephone making long-distance calls and researching information about how to construct a monument and lower it into the sea, the best methods for adding a bronze inscription, boat costs, weather patterns on New Ground Reef, and licenses and approvals by Florida marine, environmental, and Coast Guard officials—work that wasn't sexy, but was necessary.

An announcement of plans to dive the site of the *Henrietta Marie* was published in the NABS newsletter in the spring of 1992, which I read for the first time after mailing in my application, having had a few conversations with Dr. Jones and joining NABS earlier in the year. Now word of the slave-ship dive was rallying black divers from across the country.

I began to have ongoing conversations with Oswald Sykes and Dr. Jones over the phone in 1992 because I had decided to write a feature story for *New York Newsday* about NABS and the dive on a slave ship that no one in New York—or the rest of the country—had heard anything about.

Jones was enthusiastic about the newspaper story, but he was more concerned with getting the memorial completed by the end of November. Each day, Jones would field dozens of calls from divers asking about the new date for the *Henrietta Marie* dive and, more important, whether there would be room on the boat for just one more diver.

"Everybody wants to go out there," Jones told Oswald one evening. "We're going to have to regroup and make some alternative plans real soon."

"What about the weather?" Oswald asked. "We need to take that into consideration, too. Right? It's hurricane season and anything is possible. Tropical storm winds could flip a boat in the time it takes to blink."

"If it's too windy, then we don't dive," Jones said. "But let's move ahead and check the weather as we get closer to the conference date."

"I guess we'll have to wait and let our ancestors give us a sign," Oswald said.

They both laughed nervously, realizing that they were beginning to feel driven by the power of the project, instead of taking the lead.

By the fall of 1992, I was starting to speak with Oswald regularly. He was spiritual in his own way and, like Howard Moss, he believed that it was no coincidence that black scuba divers were planning a dive on a slave ship.

"This is something that we're suppose to do," he told me one evening. "I'm sure it will become clear to you, if it hasn't already."

I could hear the subtle quiver in Oswald's voice each time we spoke over the telephone about the *Henrietta Marie*. He would sometimes stumble over his words when telling me stories about the ship's transatlantic route and the high mortality rate of its black cargo.

"They sacrificed so much," he told me. "They were so strong. They endured so much, for so long."

It was not unusual for Oswald to pause between breaths when talking about how the slaves were packed in the belly of the *Henrietta Marie*, while dogs were allowed to run free on deck; how African people were chained below with rats that picked at stale food that was placed on the floor beside them.

"I'm sorry," Sykes would tell me. "This damn ship has my stomach in knots. Let me take a deep breath...."

Each time we spoke, Oswald would offer more details about the *Henrietta Marie*. We were gradually piecing together a tale that I felt more connected to than any other story I had reported since my journalism career began in 1976 at the *Atlanta Daily World*, one of the oldest black newspapers in the country.

One night, Oswald called me with his trademark question: "Hey, Mike, gotta minute?"

"Sure, Oz. What's up?"

"I want to read you an inscription I wrote for the plaque," he said. "Tell me what you think."

I could hear the shuffling of paper in the background as Oswald cleared his throat and began to read slowly into the phone, his voice trembling slightly.

"Henrietta Marie: *In memory and recognition of the courage, pain, and suffering of enslaved African people. Speak her name and gently touch the souls of our ancestors.*"

"Well?" he asked. "Do you think they'll like it—the ancestors, I mean?"

"Oz, it's a wonderful tribute. Everyone will love it—including our ancestors."

From the moment I decided to learn as much as I could about the *Henrietta Marie,* I knew that I was about to embark on an extraordinary odyssey.

Here was a story that had to be told; a story that was waiting just for me.

1 2

It was November 1992, my first conference as a member of the National Association of Black Scuba Divers and the organization's second national meeting.

I walked through the sliding glass doors of the Holiday Inn about 3:00 P.M., loaded with dive gear.

There, in the hotel, standing everywhere, were black people with dive equipment—in the lobby, by the pool, in the restaurant, in the bar, talking, laughing, men and women, some with club logos on their T-shirts and caps, all black, all divers.

I had traveled to Key West dozens of times, having worked for the *Miami Herald* from 1980 to 1986, and in all my visits, I had *never* seen this many black people in Key West. And judging by the curious looks from most Key West residents, I assumed they hadn't, either.

In 1988, four years earlier, Anthony Nesty of Surinam had upset Matt Biondi of the United States in the one-hundred-meter butterfly at the Olympic Games in Seoul to become the first black swimmer to win an Olympic gold medal.

Breaking that barrier was considered a watershed achievement for blacks worldwide and particularly in the United States, where Al Campanis, the former Los Angeles Dodger executive, once appeared on television saying that blacks lacked the buoyancy to be competitive in the water.

Black swimmers and divers, I thought, have been proving Campanis wrong for years and the national meeting of black scuba divers I was witnessing was a true testament to black achievement in water sports.

As I signed in, paid my dues, and surveyed the schedule for a week of diving, I met Andrew Rhoden and Eugene Niles, two officers from the Aquatic Voyagers Scuba Club of New York, one of the first two NABS clubs to form, and the club that I would serve as president in the years to follow. We talked about the significance of the organization and the importance of training our own people to become stronger divers.

The weather that day was lousy—gray skies, heavy rain, and wild winds. We couldn't have picked worse weather if we had planned it. The forecast called for the weather to clear in five days—just in time to head home.

As divers, we were students of weather patterns, which basically meant that we were all consistent viewers of the Weather Channel.

On any other occasion, I would have been sulking because I had traveled for a dive trip and couldn't dive. But on this day, the weather didn't bother me. I was caught up in the excitement of meeting other African-American divers, people who would change my life in some measurable way this week, and rotten weather wasn't going interfere with something that was destined to be.

I introduced myself to other divers, and before long, I felt as though I had known some of them all my life. Hank Jennings, a data-processing technician with the Ryder Corporation in Miami, and Niles, a computer analyst from Chicago, were among the first people I met.

Broad-shouldered and funny, Hank had a quick, wide smile that covered his entire face. He was easygoing and seemed to know almost everyone in the lobby. Hank was someone you wanted to like. He was smart and offered more one-liners than Letterman.

Gene was beefy, wearing glasses, his club T-shirt, and a thick gold bracelet. He was pleasant, more reserved than Hank, serious-minded. His baritone voice filled the lobby area.

Dr. Jones was sitting alone in a corner of the restaurant, scribbling notes on a piece of paper and watching his dream of a national black scuba-diving organization unfold in the lobby of a Holiday Inn. I walked up to him and introduced myself. I had heard so much about him and had spoken with him on the telephone before leaving for Key West. He had encouraged me to attend the meeting.

"Hi, buddy. How was your trip?" he asked.

I wasn't sure exactly what I was expecting, but I didn't expect him to be quite so warm. This was the man they called "The black Jacques Cousteau," the former army diver who had logged more than five thousand dives all over the world, and here I was with less than twenty at the time.

Jones and I talked for about two hours. He shared his vision of NABS with me and asked me to look around the lobby and observe the results of those late-night meetings that had lasted for months at his home in Washington.

He was awash with pride. I couldn't help watching him watching us.

The next morning, we learned that fifteen-mile-an-hour winds were blowing five-foot swells around the reefs. We took a straw poll, and against our better judgment, we headed out to sea.

The weather was just damn rotten. We shouldn't have been out on the water. We learned that evening that we were the only divers—or fools—to leave the dock that day.

"Captain Billy will go out anytime, anywhere, with anybody and under any conditions," one dive-store operator had told us over drinks the night before. "He may not make the right decisions all the time, but he does have a sense for adventure."

We saw adventure up close. Sheets of rain were falling hard. We bounced to the dive site in about twenty minutes. A few folks in our group of fifteen were already leaning over the side.

As we strapped on our tanks and slipped into fins, the rain seemed to let up just a bit. We thought our luck was changing, so we took a quick poll and about half of us hard-core divers decided to make the dive.

The visibility had gotten worse. We lost sight of the anchor line within seconds of our descent and a monster current was sweeping us away from the boat and out to sea before we could get our bearings underwater.

Things were happening fast. My dive buddies, Rachel Scott, a bank executive from North Carolina, and Rosalyn Woolfolk, a businesswoman from Atlanta, were floating with me in about fifteen feet of silty sea, unable to place the anchor line and riding a strong current in the wrong direction.

I was the only one with a compass, but was not proficient in underwater navigation. At about fifty feet, the current vanished. We plotted a course with my compass and began to kick against the current back to where we believed the boat was anchored.

We swam and kicked constantly. We were sucking up air and we knew that we had a long way to go. Rachel and Rosalyn cupped their hands together, the hand signal that means, Where is the boat?

Five minutes later, Rachel yanked my fin and showed me her pressure gauge; the needle was inching toward empty. She was getting very low on air, and so was I.

We ascended slowly to about twenty feet and swam for three minutes as a safety measure. I instructed them to stay at that depth while I swam to the surface to see if we were anywhere close to the boat.

As my head broke the surface, rain was falling hard and the current was knocking me against the waves.

I did a 360-degree spin, searching for the boat, but the rain was blinding. I couldn't see anything but gray sheets in front of me. If I couldn't see the boat, then nobody aboard would be able to see us.

Rachel and Rosalyn were waiting below me. I had to indicate something to them soon. A few seconds later, in the distance—what appeared to be about two football fields away—was the bow of a boat rocking wildly in the sea.

At that moment, it could have been any boat; it really didn't matter.

I dropped back down to twenty feet, where Rachel and Rosalyn were waiting, and gave them the sign meaning "boat." I checked Rachel's air, gave her the okay sign, set a quick compass heading, and waved them to follow me. With two hands on my compass and kicking hard against the current, it seemed like hours before we reached the boat. Rachel and Rosalyn were kicking hard, hanging tough.

We stuck together.

Slowly, as each of us was sucking air fast, the boat came into view above us, along with the outline of the dive ladder, which was flapping in the current. We were the first dive team to approach the boat. Several others were waving in the distance, too tired to kick back to the boat.

People threw out towlines, and as the divers grabbed the lines, we closed in on the boat.

As we climbed aboard and stumbled to a few makeshift seats, the divers who had remained on board rushed over and helped us out of our gear.

We were coughing and breathing hard, shivering from the wind, which had turned cold, and trying to explain in rapid-fire order what had happened.

We were safe and alive. It was that single experience underwater in Key West that made me realize the value of diving with people sharing the same bond, diving with people you trust to keep you calm through adversity, people you know would never leave you when nature suddenly changes all of your plans.

Jones indoctrinates his students with one central rule: *Never* leave your buddy. He demands that all NABS divers stick to the buddy system, the fundamental cornerstone of safe diving practices.

Linda Freeman, a psychologist from New York, started the process for her scuba certification in 1970, but she scrapped her plans, saying she didn't feel comfortable or embraced by the other students. She was the only black student in her class.

In Chicago, in the mid-1980s, Freeman tried again; this time, she joined a group of black scuba divers, where she was the only woman.

"It gave me an opportunity to get back into diving," Freeman said. "I wasn't concerned that it was an all-male group; that was fun. What was important was that the group was black. It's a sport where you have to care for and communicate with other people. For me, learning to scuba dive, I needed to be with a group with whom I felt safe and comfortable. That's why this group is important to me."

The vision that Jones had for the National Association of Black Scuba Divers is being played out on dive boats across the country. There are now fifty-three clubs, representing thousands of divers.

But Jones still fields questions about the notion that establishing NABS was somehow fostering segregation. He has received a few racist crank calls on the organization's toll-free line over the years and he is always answering the same question over and over.

"Why do we need our own dive organization?" Jones asked aloud to his faceless critics. The answer is always stated with the same firm, unequivocal tone: "Why not?"

υυ

At the Mel Fisher Maritime Heritage Society, where the artifacts from the *Henrietta Marie* were being displayed, dozens of divers gathered around the relics, walking in silence, peering into the tanks where three-hundred-year-old shackles were soaking. People spoke in whispers, their spirits drawn to the shackles like their bodies to the sea. With black arms stretched around the shoulders of friends and some people wiping wet eyes, they stared hard at the rusted iron shackles, some of which were displayed on a long wooden table.

There was an unsettling sensation among the group. For the first time since word of a sunken slave ship had spread among the divers, they were standing within reach of the artifacts, which were no longer generic descriptions over the telephone or grainy photographs in newspapers; they were actual tools for the torture of our ancestors. They were real. They could be held in the palms of people's hands—black hands that shook nervously from holding a piece of a past that had somehow resurfaced as an inexplicable part of their present-day lives.

For several minutes, no one uttered a word. Hank, whose thirty-eight-year-old shoulders have carried plenty of dive gear, was studying the hard evidence of slavery. Standing over the artifacts, he shook his head, taking short glances and blowing long sighs. He wore a peculiar facial expression—a mix of sadness and frustration, anger and horror.

"I hope their prayers were answered," he mumbled to himself, "and that they are all at peace now."

Hank didn't know their private prayers, but there must have been many—most of them whispered in the night beside slow-burning fires inside dirt-floored shacks.

...From whence thou seest the miseries
To which we are subject;
The whites have murder'd us, O God!
And kept us ignorant of thee.

Not satisfied with this, my Lord!
They throw us in the seas:
Be pleas'd, we pray, for Jesus' sake,
To save us from their grasp.
—A Prophet's Plea to God

"We really don't have any idea of how horrible their lives must have been," Hank said to Doc Jones. "The power of these shackles sort of sneaks up on you. One minute you're walking along carefree; the next minute you're doubled over. They were our people. They could have been our blood relatives, our own family. We don't know."

"Just remember where you came from," Jones said. "Remember their sacrifices. Remember their pain. Remember their genius. Be very proud."

"Yeah, I'm proud," Hank said. "I'm extremely proud. But being proud doesn't always ease the pain."

13

From the edge of the pier, I could see a fury of five-foot waves rolling out of the Gulf of Mexico and crashing onto shore like a freight train rumbling off the tracks.

There is nothing coy about the ocean. It seems to relish demonstrating its ferocious power, forcing periodic visitors to the sea to think twice before plunging into an abyss where they are instantly dwarfed and irrefutably humbled.

But on this drizzly, wind-whipped afternoon, the sea appeared particularly angry, as nightfall arrived early, eclipsing my hopes of viewing even a sliver of sunset.

The five-day meeting of black scuba divers was drawing to a close and most of the divers were packing their gear and heading to the airport to escape the wet weather. But a band of thirty divers, including myself, was staying in Key West an additional three days, ignoring the impending storm and preparing to make a dive that was more for our spiritual uplifting than for entries in our logbooks.

This was a dive that would take us thirty feet down into the murky Gulf of Mexico, onto the sunken wreckage of the slave ship *Henrietta Marie*.

Much of the conversation at the meeting had been consumed with theories about the *Henrietta Marie*, mostly about how a slave ship that rested thirty-seven miles from the dock was somehow giving us a new perspective on the slave trade.

This was not about a deep dive; rather, it was about a merchant slaver that sailed the Atlantic Ocean long-ago that continues to creep into our consciousness today. In a sense, the dive to the *Henrietta Marie* had more to do with exploring the depths of our souls than the depths of the sea. Perhaps this day would offer the opportunity to dive on the remains of a ship that may have carried our family members to the shores of Jamaica.

We were black scuba divers preparing for a historical first: diving on the wreckage of a sunken slave ship, the only slave ship in the world that had been scientifically identified by name, examined, and excavated, the site of the largest collection of slave-ship shackles ever discovered. We were black scuba divers planning to dive a wreck that was part of our past.

I sat on the edge of the bed and stared out the window of the Holiday Inn. I was waiting for the storm to pass; the raindrops on the glass blurred the view of the beach, where hot sand had turned to mud. I could barely see the tall masts of the boats in the harbor, but I could hear the wind howling across the decks.

Shadows were blowing swiftly overhead. The flag that hung high from a pole outside the Holiday Inn was stretched out as if about to be framed. Boat captains clad in bright yellow slickers were double-checking the thick ropes that secured their vessels to the dock, and motorists who were heading for the highway pulled off the road to wait out the storm.

This was, after all, the middle of November 1992 and the tail end of hurricane season, which could bring winds of more than one hundred miles an hour, winds that could reduce a two-story town like Key West to crushed concrete within minutes.

These skies might have looked just as ominous over Key West three hundred years ago when hurricane-force winds ripped the decks of the *Henrietta Marie* to splinters, blowing her off course and bouncing the 120-ton ship across the sea like a bathtub toy.

As the rain fell outside my room, I watched tall trees bend like arches in the wind and wondered whether the spirits of my ancestors who had perished in similar choppy seas were trying to send me a signal, a warning to stay away from the reef this day.

Perhaps they were trying to tell me that they didn't want to be disturbed, that it's better to read about the history of the *Henrietta Marie* than to try to dive into it.

I quickly dismissed my theories as nothing more than amateur hocus-pocus and went looking for Oswald to get a more rational perspective.

Oz was looking pensive. I could see a big blue vein running along the side of his head. I knew that he was worried about something.

"The ancestors don't seem too happy today, do they?" Oswald said.

But in less than three hours, a group of black people were preparing to strap on air tanks and visit the site of a slave ship, where three hundred years ago, any black people associated with this ship would have been locked in chains.

We couldn't leave the past behind. It was the past that had helped shape our future and we wanted to learn—and feel—everything we could about our black ancestors, who brought African culture, art, stories, poems, and prayers to the Americas.

Black scuba divers, thirty strong, were assembled in Key West and anticipating a dive into our past. We were middle-class folks, yes. We drove nice cars, held good jobs, and had been to faraway places to explore underwater worlds that many will see only on the glossy colored pages of *National Geographic*.

We were baby boomers for the most part, having achieved some level of success in the workplace, although all of us were not making the major decisions or controlling the purse strings within our respective companies.

And no, we couldn't begin to know the atrocities that slaves experienced on these seas during the Middle Passage. We knew that.

"Good luck!" one of the divers yelled from the lobby of the Holiday Inn as a taxi driver loaded his bags into the trunk. "I hope you all get out on the site."

I had waited months for this opportunity. Many of us had already read almost everything we could get our hands on about the *Henrietta Marie*. It was a strange but fascinating feeling waiting to experience the unknown.

We had done wreck dives—shallow wrecks, deep wrecks, wrecks that were intact, wrecks that were so fractured, we couldn't even tell they had once been ships. But a *slave* ship? This was a concept that intrigued even the most cynical of divers. It was an opportunity for underwater time travel and unearthing a piece of our past.

Mid-November was not the best time to take a three-and-a-half-hour ride thirty-seven miles from shore in six-foot seas and blinding rain.

With each mighty wave that crashed onto the jetties, the chances of getting to New Ground Reef grew slimmer. I knew it. Everyone else did, too. Still, there was a feeling of optimism.

"What do you think about this weather, Doc?" I asked Dr. Jones, who was scrambling to get a weather forecast from the local boat captains.

"We're just going to have to play it by ear," he said in a solemn tone that wasn't very reassuring.

There was never a perfect time to dive New Ground Reef, even under normal conditions. Currents run fast without warning and an easy, stress-free dive could suddenly turn into a battle against nature.

Everyone in town seemed to know about the quick currents on New Ground Reef. And everyone in Key West also seemed to know a little something about the weather—or so they thought.

I didn't know much about the *Henrietta Marie* at the time, but I had studied enough to know that this was perhaps the most significant dive I'd ever make.

"We can still get a boat into the water and get you guys out there," insisted Charles Lee, a travel agent hired by NABS to help coordinate the dive.

As we waited for blue skies, the group was getting restless. We were pacing the pier as if we were at the airport waiting for an update about a delayed flight. Most of us had gathered at the dock and were awaiting word from Dr. Jones, who was huddled off to the side with Charles Lee, Ric Powell, and Oswald Sykes. They were talking alternatives.

"These waves are about nine feet out there today," Jones told me, pointing to the swells in the distance.

"It could get dangerous," he said. "It's a long ride to the reef under normal conditions, but this could be a disaster."

Jones, five feet eleven inches, broad-shouldered and muscular, looked out over the group of divers, some of whom had never dived in strong currents. People had begun to pull their cameras from their bags when

Moe Molinar in 1972.

The author's hands in shackles.

The memorial service where the monument was lowered into the sea.

Oswald Sykes and Michael Cottman cleaning the monument.

The plaque.

HENRIETTA MARIE

IN MEMORY AND
RECOGNITION OF THE COURAGE,
PAIN AND SUFFERING OF
ENSLAVED AFRICAN PEOPLE.

"SPEAK HER NAME AND GENTLY TOUCH
THE SOULS OF OUR ANCESTORS."

Dedicated November 15, 1992

Preparing for a dive off Goree Island in
West Africa.

Michael diving near the Door of No Return.

Diving off the coast of Dakar.

Returning from a dive in Belize.

Working on the book in the United
Kingdom.

A hole in Coral Wall, Goree.

Michael Cottman in the Bahamas.

A diver looking at the hull structure of
the *Henrietta Marie*.

Underwater at Goree.

The bell from the *Henrietta Marie*; the most significant artifact recovered.

Glass beads used by Europeans to trade for African people.

Michael gazes at shackles used on adults and children.

Part of the nearly one hundred pairs of shackles recovered from the wreck of the *Henrietta Marie*.

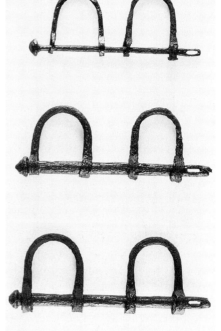

Shirley Lee, with Dr. Jones standing to her left.

Dr. Jose Jones and the original Underwater Adventure Seekers (Association of Black Scuba Divers, late 1950s).

Michael and Mr. Joseph Ndiaye in the Door of No Return.

The Slave House on Goree Island.

Looking out to sea.

The author in what was once a holding area for slaves.

The Door of No Return through one of the cells.

Front Door, Slave House, Goree Island.

Inside the Slave House.

Colin Fuller, a probable descendant of slaves aboard the *Henrietta Marie*.

Michael at the Door of No Return with Joseph Ndiaye.

The opening of the *Henrietta Marie* exhibit in Key West with Oswald Sykes.

Moe, Michael, and John on his boat, the *Virgalona*.

David and Michael, Bog Walk, Jamaica.

Michael Cottman in Belize.

Workers on the Tulloch Estate, Bog Walk, Jamaica.

Members of the Association of Black Scuba Divers heading for the site of the wreck of the *Henrietta Marie*.

Former president of the Association of Black Scuba Divers, Ric Powell, "calling the spirits" on the way to the plaque.

On the last trip to the *Henrietta Marie*, the day they located the box that had held the elephant tusks: Hank J., David M., and Corey Malcolm with the author.

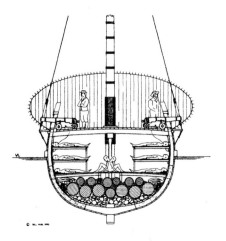

HENRIETTA MARIE (CA 1699)

The *Henrietta Marie* interior view of slave storage.

Consignment of slaves.

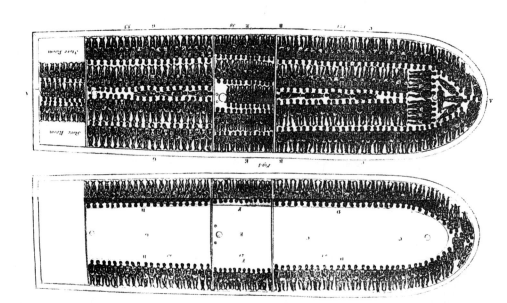

Slaves stowed on a typical slave ship.

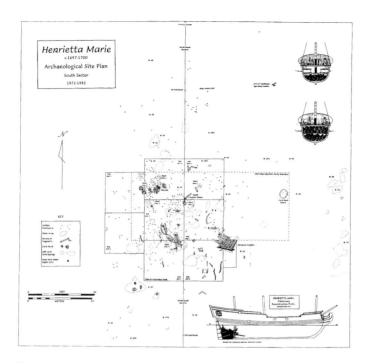

The *Henrietta Marie:* archaeological site plan—south sector.

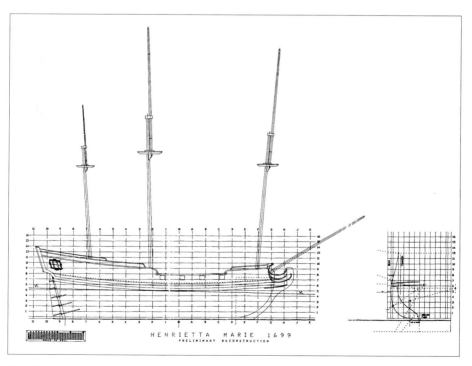

The *Henrietta Marie:* a reconstruction by David Moore.

Michael and his daughter, Ariane, age thirteen months, contemplating the sea.

Lee invited everyone onto an open-air ferry-style boat with a smorgasbord of sandwiches, cheeses, fruits, and cakes set up for the divers.

"This is really nice. We were starved," I said to Lee. "But where's our boat for the dive?"

Lee looked perplexed. He smiled and pointed to the ferryboat with arms outstretched, as if he were unveiling a priceless piece of art.

"This is it!" he said proudly.

"But there are no tank racks, no canopy to block the wind, no—What I'm trying to say is that this isn't a dive boat," I said.

Thirty people climbing onto this ferry with its plastic benches would have worked well as one of the rides at a water theme park, but trying to navigate it through bumpy seas for thirty-seven miles in the Gulf of Mexico was a death wish.

"We're not putting any of our people on this boat while it's moving," said Jones, making the distinction between eating lunch aboard *The Good Ship Sea Snack* and sailing on it. "Not a chance. This boat is not built for this kind of trip."

Ric Powell was stomping the pier. He was mad at the world. Ric had worked hard to make this event happen. He and Oz had stayed up late nights updating Doc about plans for the dive and trying to weave this forgotten piece of our past into our five-day convention.

Ric and Doc, two veteran military divers, were putting their best face on a discouraging situation. I almost got the impression that Doc would rather have returned to combat than cancel this dive.

"This really tears me up," Jones whispered to me, his eyes hidden behind dark sunglasses. "I wanted this dive for all of us."

I watched the reactions from the divers who were standing just within earshot of the always soft-spoken and kindly Doc Jones. It had been a long time since I'd seen such disappointment on the faces of so many people standing in one place. I saw tears in some eyes.

This wasn't a pleasure trip; it was an experience of a lifetime for most of us. People bargained for time any way they could—taking extended vacations, unpaid leave, or working overtime in advance—just to make the dive.

They were starved for a chance to learn more about our past through a sunken slave ship, yearning for some type of connection with ancestors they would never know, hoping for the knowledge about a generation of people who may have been family.

Oz was walking in small circles near the pier. Nature had roared into Key West and upset our plans.

His wife, Marion, was walking alongside of him, rubbing his back and speaking softly into his ear.

"We'll do this next time," she whispered. "We'll be back, you'll see."

I sat along the pier, waiting for the official word and staring off into the sea as I tend to do whenever I'm disturbed. The ocean always brings me a sense of contentment and helps me find peace during the toughest of emotional storms.

"The weather was looking good about a week ago," Ric said, pulling a baseball cap over his bushy grayish head of hair. "Storms blow in fast down here. This hurts. I've been telling my son, Victor, all about the ship and what it means to our people."

Less than one hundred yards away inside a maritime museum, some of the encrusted shackles from the *Henrietta Marie* were soaking in large metal tanks, while other artifacts such as pewterware, trade beads, musket balls, and the ship's bell were on display. Most of the divers had already walked through the museum to take a look at the artifacts before coming to the pier.

Ric had taken Victor, his twelve-year-old son, to see the artifacts and had explained some of the history of the *Henrietta Marie* and its significance for black people. Archaeologists Corey Malcom and David Moore and the museum's curator, Madeline Burnside, offered them a backstage tour of the second floor, affording them the opportunity of seeing things not on display.

Upstairs, Ric made a point of showing Victor a pair of shackles that would have fit snugly around his son's skinny wrists.

The shackles had been manufactured for black children about Victor's age, height, and weight.

Our planned dive on the *Henrietta Marie* was not only about brotherhood and sisterhood; it was about families like those of Howard Moss and his ten-year-old son, Kristopher, and Ric Powell and Victor.

Family has always been an important part of the black experience, both in villages throughout Africa and in communities across the United States.

Victor and Kristopher were talking and playing together along the pier while Howard, never without his cameras, began firing off dozens of frames. He was capturing the moment, not knowing exactly whether he would be shooting any film on the ocean that day.

I decided that if we weren't going out on the boat, I might as well grab a bite. I was starving, and the line for snacks was beginning to form. People slowly walked on board and nibbled at the cheese and sandwiches. It was quiet for a few minutes; no one really wanted to state the obvious—that we would not be visiting the site of the *Henrietta Marie* that day.

To describe the mood that day as disappointment would be a colossal understatement. Divers were numb. Some wore the pain on their faces, while others, like me, simply felt as if nature had robbed us of a chance to explore a more spiritual side of the sea.

"It's too bad. I was really looking forward to this dive, such a fascinating opportunity," said Sheila Walker, a woman with short curly hair and a warm smile. She was a diver and anthropologist from Houston. "Could you please hand me a napkin?"

We talked for a while between bites. Sheila was intelligent and thoughtful, the kind of person who can engage almost anyone in conversation without being overbearing. She was a student of the slave trade, cultural development, and African social customs.

"I came to the convention specifically for this dive," she said. "I feel like I'm leaving empty-handed, you know?"

"I feel the same way," I said, staring out over the whitecaps that were stacking up in the sea. "But we'll be back soon."

Sheila was disappointed, but she later talked of the slave ship in historical terms and put the discovery of the *Henrietta Marie* into perspective.

"To discover the remains of any historical phenomenon like this slave ship makes it real," Walker said. "We've read about slavery, but in the absence of the skeletons and bones of our ancestors, this makes it real. We can't deny it. I see the *Henrietta Marie,* something that has been hidden, finally coming to light.

"Africans believe that ancestors can do things, positive things, or if things go wrong, it may be because you've offended the ancestors," she added. "If you take this perspective, then what would an African say about a slave ship that had come back?

"Perhaps one would say that a slave ship has come back, or the ancestors have come back, to tell their story, because they didn't get a chance to tell it before. They came back at a time when they thought we needed it, at a time when they thought we could use it.

"The *Henrietta Marie* comes at a time when there is a wish to memorialize our ancestors in a way that says, Don't be ashamed to go back and fetch something precious that you left behind, something that can help you understand your future," she said.

"The *Henrietta Marie* is a concrete reminder of a past that a lot of African-Americans and non-African-Americans would prefer to forget. But archaeology is the art of digging up the past, and the past doesn't lie to archaeologists. The fact that the *Henrietta Marie* was a slave ship gives us a link, because, in a larger sense, we all came here on slave ships."

This was an important insight for me. For the first time, I could see a course being set for me. It was important for me historically and journalistically, but it was more important for me emotionally—to take on a challenge that had nothing to do with following an assignment but had everything to do with following my heart.

"Can I get everyone's attention, please," Dr. Jones shouted over the roar of the wind. I knew what he was going to say, but at least it would be official.

There was immediate silence. I stopped chewing and tossed a half-eaten sandwich into a trash can. I wasn't hungry anymore. Doc surveyed the crowd that had formed a semicircle around him and spoke loudly so everyone could hear.

"We've decided to postpone the dive today," Jones said stoically. No one wanted to make this dive happen more than Dr. Jones and Oswald Sykes and I knew that this decision was tearing Jones up inside. Oswald looked worn-out as he stood alone, off to the side.

"If it looks this bad near shore, I can tell you that it's ten times worse at sea," Doc said. "As slow as this boat is, it would take us six hours to cover thirty-five miles. We could get everyone on board, but then we wouldn't have any room for your dive gear, and even if we did, we couldn't guarantee everyone's safety, which of course is our first priority. We're going back to the drawing board. I'm sorry."

Damn.

Fifteen seconds and it was all over for the day. No boat. No diving. No *Henrietta Marie*. I felt as if we should be throwing dirt over a pine box.

There were a few hugs and handshakes after Doc finished talking; some wiped away a few tears. I guess at the time I never knew how much this dive meant to so many people. And then there were questions about the next attempt to get out on New Ground Reef from those who just didn't want to walk away.

"Can we stay and wait out the storm?"

"What about next month?"

"Can we all be included next time?"

Doc answered everyone with the same simple response: "I'll be in touch."

He walked away from the dock, wearing his trademark blue jacket with its dozens of colorful dive patches from around the world stitched on the front, down the sleeves, and across the back.

The rain had let up a bit, but the humidity was thick. Doc took off his jacket and folded it over his arm. This was an important day for him. It was only the second meeting for the National Association of Black Scuba Divers, and through the *Henrietta Marie,* Doc was searching for a deeper purpose for the organization.

I walked along the pier and collected my dive gear, which was soaked from the rain. I tossed my mesh bag over my shoulder while the other divers began to load up and head back to their hotels. Some were rushing off to change their flights, trying to get out of town as soon as possible.

I decided to stay overnight and talk to Doc about our options for the future.

I didn't know quite what to expect below the waters of the Gulf of Mexico, but the thought of floating underwater, touching planks of wood that were ripped from the hull of the ship, running my hands through the same sandy seas where African people may have leaped to their deaths to escape a life of bondage was the most powerful personal image I've known.

I had been searching for a journalistic venture to take the place of the routine stories that were increasingly common at daily newspapers. After nearly twenty years in journalism, I had finally found a spiritual road map, not one that would transform me from sinner to saint overnight, but one that would help guide me down a more solid path through life.

This was a day of setbacks, a day we would eventually put behind us, and we would return to dive again, but for the moment, I felt completely robbed by a force beyond my control, a force that I couldn't get my arms around and wrestle to the ground.

The site of my personal pilgrimage was scattered underwater, thirty feet below the ocean's surface, cloaked in sand and surrounded by millions of silent souls that have been drifting through time for three hundred years—faces I will never see, names I will never know, voices I will never hear. But their spirits, which are floating through the wreckage of the *Henrietta Marie*, will forever be a part of me.

One by one, the divers left the dock, some walking arm in arm, until the pier was nearly empty. Doc was alone and gathering his gear. Ric had stomped off, cursing under his breath. Oswald was pacing the pier and speaking of better days ahead.

"We'll be back, my brother," Oswald whispered, his arm wrapped around my shoulder. "We'll be back and our ancestors will be waiting for us."

I watched Oz disappear across the empty parking lot as thunder rumbled overhead and the storm that had threatened our dive to the *Henrietta Marie* moved closer to shore.

I took a seat on the edge of the wide-planked pier, wiping sea spray from my face and looking for comfort where I have always found my source of strength: from the power of the sea.

14

I stepped off the twenty-seat airplane and onto the short stretch of runway in Key West. It was almost noon—too late for coffee, too early for beer.

Two seasons had passed since we'd aborted our dive on the *Henrietta Marie*. It was now May, 1993, and Doc had decided that one of the major problems we had experienced with the first attempt to reach New Ground Reef was that too many people had been involved.

Only ten people had been invited to Key West this time.

I was waiting for Oswald and Marion, who were on a flight right behind mine. I was getting bored—I could walk around the Key West airport terminal twice in the time it takes to swallow.

I walked outside, took a few deep breaths, looked toward the sky, and posed a quick question to a bass player turned taxi driver who was standing near me smoking hand-rolled tobacco.

"So," I asked, my arms folded tightly across my chest, "how's the weather?"

"It's been decent," he said, taking his last drag from a stubby cigarette before grinding out the butt under his shoe. "Little rain, some sun, not too humid. All in all, it's been okay. You plan to do some fishin' while you're here?"

"No," I responded. "Some diving."

"Diving," he said, shrugging his broad shoulders and tugging on his ponytail. "I try to stay away from that stuff."

He was another dropout who had made his way south. Key West, the southernmost point in the United States, where Ernest Hemingway wrote novels, was filled with former flower children from the sixties, wearing peace signs around their necks and sporting tie-dyed T-shirts. Tunes by Steppenwolf, the Stones, and Jimi Hendrix blasted from beat-up Volkswagen buses.

By the time I collected my bags and read the *Miami Herald,* Oswald and Marion were walking off their flight and into the terminal.

Oz was hauling a couple of carry-on bags and walking as fast as usual, as if he was an hour late for a business meeting and the stock market would crash if he didn't get there on time.

"Slow down, Sykes," Marion shouted. "The boat doesn't leave until tomorrow."

"Okay," Oz said. "Okay."

I had always thought they made a nice couple. They were partners. They had that special something that seemed to work, even when it appeared as if they were arguing half the time. Oz would grumble, Marion would tell him to suck it up and get over whatever was bugging him, and, miraculously, all would be right with the world again.

"How ya doin'?" Oz asked, greeting me with a tight hug. "I feel good about this trip. Real good."

"If you feel good about it, Oz, then so do I," I said, kissing Marion on the cheek and taking one of her bags to the taxi stand.

"Look at the sky," Oz said, stabbing his finger into the air. "Our ancestors are telling us to come out to New Ground Reef. They're giving us some great weather. They're calling us!"

Oswald was always the optimist, and this time it was rubbing off.

We climbed into the taxi and turned onto the highway, with the Atlantic Ocean on our left. I could smell the salt water in the air. It was about ninety-five degrees, and we began rolling up the windows while the driver cranked up the air conditioning.

"Hey, aren't you the guys who got blown out trying to dive New Ground Reef last year?" the driver asked, his eyes trained on me through the rearview mirror.

"Yeah," I answered. "Do we still look beat to hell?"

He laughed. "Naw," he said. "I think you're in luck for this one. The weather has been great. We're rootin' for y'all."

We pulled up to the hotel and checked in. Doc and the others would be arriving a few hours later, so I decided to rent a car and drive over to the dock where we would be leaving the next morning.

"Oz, you wanna take a ride?"

"Sure," he said. "Where ya headed?"

"Over to Subtropics. I just want to check things out."

The owner of Subtropics Dive Center, Dr. Robin Lockwood, a physician from Key West, had heard about our aborted attempt to get to New Ground Reef and our need for money and two boats—one to transport the divers and the other to haul the one-ton concrete monument that we were going to lower into the sea.

Lockwood had been in touch with Ken Schultz, a boat captain, friend, and official NABS boat charter for the *Henrietta Marie,* who told Lockwood about NABS, the slave ship, and our plans to hold a ceremony at sea.

After a series of conversations, Lockwood agreed to donate his forty-two-foot boat, the *Island Diver,* to NABS for our dive. His generosity was overwhelming and I just wanted to meet him and thank him personally.

That a stranger, and a white man, saw a need to help a group of black people he had never met, for a commemoration to honor enslaved African people that meant more to us, was something special.

We had come through quite a partnership, a first of sorts, the black divers and the members of the Mel Fisher Maritime Heritage Society: black divers, white divers, meeting each other for the first time and sharing experiences that none of us would have guessed at just a month before; black divers and white divers exploring a slave ship and talking openly about slavery.

Oz and I pulled into the parking lot; the *Island Diver* was docked in the slip. It was clean and fueled. A gentleman wearing wrinkled shorts, a T-shirt, and weathered loafers was mopping the deck with a bucket of soapy water next to him. We got out of the car and walked along the dock.

"Hi," I shouted, as we walked aboard. "I'm looking for Dr. Lockwood."

"I'm Dr. Lockwood."

"I'm Michael Cottman and this is Oswald Sykes. We're with the National Association of Black Scuba Divers. I didn't expect to find you mopping the deck yourself," I said, laughing.

"Well, I knew this was an important trip for you guys and I wanted to make sure that everything was perfect," he replied.

Lockwood not only had loaned us his boat for eight hours but had showed up to clean it himself.

"We just wanted to come by and thank you personally for the use of your boat," I said. "It was extremely generous."

I paused for a moment, looking at the shiny deck.

"Dr. Lockwood," I asked, "why did you loan us the boat?"

"I was happy to do it," he said. "I heard about your project. It seemed like such a worthwhile one. It's history and it's important to everyone."

Such a simple answer and yet so important. If only everyone could see the big picture.

It was late afternoon and the other divers were beginning to arrive in Key West. Hank Jennings, Jim Beard, and David Harrison were driving from Fort Lauderdale. Howard Moss, Gene Tinnie, and Ric Powell were driving from Miami. Fred Duff was flying from New Jersey and Doc was flying in from D.C.

My phone rang about 5:00 P.M. as I watched the local, twenty-four-hour weather channel.

"Mike, it's Jose."

"Hey, Doc. What's up?"

"I'm here at the Santa Maria Hotel," he said. "Come on over."

On the way to the hotel, I drove along the shore and thought about how Doc's dream to bring us together as black divers to pay homage to African people had also become my dream.

I thought about how ten of us—nine men and one woman—would ride together on the same boat to New Ground Reef but would take our own personal journeys on the *Henrietta Marie*. I thought about African-American men and women and the two young boys who were with us; I thought about how blessed I was to be a part of this pilgrimage. I made a point of thanking Doc, but first I thanked God.

Doc answered the door at his hotel wearing his trademark patched jacket and told me to have a seat while he sifted through some of his gear.

"This is a rare opportunity for all of us, you know," he said. "We don't know if some of the slaves on the *Henrietta Marie* were members of our family. They could have been. But what we do know is that this is the first time black people have ever explored the wreckage of a sunken slave ship, the first time that *black* divers have ever researched their history underwater. For the first time, we're literally doing some diving into our past."

He paused for a moment while pulling his wet suit from his dive bag.

"The reason I asked you to come along is that I'd like you to record this dive for us," he said.

"Not just for the NABS newsletter but also for your newspaper and magazine articles. Maybe some of your notes could be used to chronicle history in the making here. I'm not a writer, but I do know that this is something special. I just don't want this dive and what it means to us and African-American people everywhere to end up underwater in sand for another three hundred years."

We decided to leave about 6:00 A.M. The *Island Diver* could hold about thirty people, but with the weight of the people, air tanks, scuba gear, and camera equipment, it was sure to be a long, slow ride.

We figured on three and a half hours out, four hours on New Ground Reef, and three and a half hours back. We planned to return to the dock by about 5:00 P.M., long before dark.

I checked my messages at my hotel. Hank had called and Howard Moss and Fred Duff were also in town. I returned the calls and invited everyone to share a meal together. I thought it would be good for us to get together for dinner before our journey the next morning.

That evening, Duval Street in Key West was packed with tourists: young people looking for drinks and rock-and-roll bands and lovers working their way to the beach for a moonlit walk.

We had dinner at Curly's, our favorite barbecue restaurant in Key West. Oz was eating ribs as if they were going to be banned the following day and telling us a story about shooting a pig in the head with a shotgun when he was a teenager.

I was draining my second twelve-ounce beer.

"All of those black families that were separated during slavery, do you think about that?" Hank asked. "It's amazing the black family experience is strong despite all the suffering through the years. Slavery is still horrible to think about; it still makes me uncomfortable. It's an uncomfortable subject for white and black America."

I didn't sleep well that night. I tossed and turned for hours. My chest tightened and my hands were sweaty. I was anxious, and for the first time, I couldn't predict what I would discover on my dive. I had dreams of pirates attacking ships in the night, restless dreams, the kind you attempt to analyze for a few minutes, then forget about as the day goes on.

We began to gather on the wooden dock outside Subtropics shortly after 5:30 A.M. as the crew was preparing the *Island Diver* for our passage to New Ground Reef. The sun was just beginning to make its debut.

Doc Jones and Dave Moore were sitting next to each other on the pier with a waterproof map spread out across their laps. They were plotting our course and had made a decision to enter the water before the rest of the divers to locate the site of the *Henrietta Marie*.

The last time that Moore had been on the site was in 1983. The yellow lines of rope that he marked the area with ten years prior to our dive may have been completely covered over with sand. Coral formations might have changed, he said, and the site could look totally different. Underwater, the world is ever shifting.

"Here's where we should get into the water and start our circle patterns," Moore said to Doc, pointing to a black dot on the map just off New Ground Reef.

"It's murky down there," Moore said. "The visibility will probably be about ten feet. We'll do our best to find the site so we can get the plaque into the water. A lot has probably changed since I was last out there, but there should be something down there I will recognize."

The crew was loading tanks and water onto the *Island Diver* and everyone was checking their gear for spare parts and making sure they brought along all their equipment. No one was going to miss this dive because of a ripped fin strap or a forgotten mask.

As Moore was folding up the map, members of the media began to show up. A television crew from an NBC affiliate out of Miami arrived along with a crew from CNN, an AP photographer, a freelance photographer, and newspaper reporters from the *Tampa Tribune* and the *Washington Post*.

They were all hustling to get on board.

It was five minutes to six.

"Let's do a quick roll call," Doc shouted to the group. "We should be pulling out of here in about ten minutes.

"Hank Jennings!

"Ric Powell!

"Victor Powell!

"David Harrison!

"Oswald Sykes!

"Marion Sykes!

"Michael Cottman!

"Howard Moss!

"Kristopher Moss!

"Fred Duff!

"Jim Beard!

"Gene Tinnie!

"David Moore!"

Everyone was accounted for. It was time to shove off.

I was excited about the trip, but I was also looking at these two small boys who were with their fathers, black fathers and sons, who were going to experience history together.

Often in the media, black men are not portrayed as caring fathers who spend time with their sons and daughters. It was heartwarming to see Howard and Ric with their boys, explaining the history of slavery and the history of the black scuba divers.

Watching Ric and Howard reminded me of spending time with my dad in Detroit. We shared a range of emotions together.

One afternoon, on April 4, 1968, I came in from the playground. My father had been sitting in front of our black-and-white television, his eyes red from tears. I knew something terrible had happened. He told me that Martin Luther King, Jr., had been shot and killed in Memphis, that he was murdered because he spoke out on behalf of black people across the country, and that the world had lost a great leader who stood for peace.

I cried, too, but not for Dr. King. I cried because I had never seen my father so devastated by a single event, and it troubled me. He was bothered by the violent direction the country seemed to be taking.

He had witnessed an old man being stomped to death during the riots in Detroit in 1967, a graphic image he never really forgot. He was struck about how callously young men can take a human life.

With wise words on the day that Dr. King was killed, my father taught me the meaning of social justice, and that evening we comforted each other. I took my dad along for the voyage to New Ground Reef. He was with me in my heart.

The concrete memorial weighed one ton and went out several hours ahead of us. It was attached to a tugboat by a steel cable and pulley system. Even though the concrete for the monument was donated to NABS, the bronze plate for the inscription was paid for after a painstaking two-year fund-raising drive where Doc collected checks and cash by mail. Doc and Oswald solicited funds from just about everybody, appealing—and pleading—to people through the NABS newsletter and by word of mouth.

Several months before the plaque was designed, money was oozing in like sluggish glue. But after Oz counted the cash, added some extra funds from his own pocket, and cut a deal to lower the original cost, the manufacturers made the plaque with the money that Oz had to work with.

We boarded the *Island Diver* one by one, carrying our dive gear, juice, sandwiches, chips, and fruit. By the time we were all on board, the lower deck was packed.

The captain advised us that it would be close to four hours to New Ground Reef and that we should relax, take a nap if we wanted, and drink plenty of water to keep from getting dehydrated. The next announcement would be on the site of the *Henrietta Marie*.

The engine sputtered to a start and the boat slowly pulled out of the slip and away from the dock. I stowed my dive gear under the bench where my tank was positioned, reached over to secure my gear, and watched the dive shop get smaller and smaller as we headed for open water.

After months of lousy weather, logistic miscalculations, ill-equipped boats, and a run of just bad luck, we were finally on our way to the site that offered more questions than answers.

We were taking our personal pilgrimage, a daylong journey to a sacred site. As the last strand of land disappeared in the distance, I replaced an old mask strap with a new one, slipped fresh batteries into my underwater flashlight, and reflected on my first visit to Goree Island off the coast of Senegal in 1985.

For more than three hundred years in that haunting West African slave port, tens of thousands of Africans were stockpiled inside narrow pitch-black catacombs and chained with leg shackles and iron collars, their backs crisscrossed with scars from repeated leather lashings.

They were forced to wait with little food or water until they could be shipped and sold. I recalled peering through tears into the smaller sweltering pits that were fashioned for children, who were forever separated from their parents.

I could almost hear the screams, feel the misery. I stood on the same sun-scorched shores where many African slaves took their last steps before perishing at sea aboard ships like the *Henrietta Marie*. Eight years later, as we prepared to hover over the wreckage of the *Henrietta Marie*, we believed the spirits of these African people were calling to us from beneath the sea.

I worked my way through the crush of people and headed toward the stern for some bottled water from the cooler. I had to step over two thick legs that seemed to stretch the length of the boat. They belonged to Eugene Tinnie, a six-foot-ten-inch educator from Miami whose curly gray-and-black beard covered most of his smiling face. He seemed to be standing even when sitting down.

Tinnie's close friend Howard Moss had told me earlier that Tinnie was trying to raise money to build a life-size replica of a nineteenth-century slave ship and was trying to negotiate a parcel of land for the construction.

"Hello, I'm Michael Cottman," I said. "I'm with NABS from New York."

"I'm Gene Tinnie," he said, offering his hand. "I'm an English professor in Miami."

Tinnie's hand was twice the size of mine. His fingers were as long as straws and three times as wide. His handshake ended halfway up my arm. He had a warm aura about him, though—easygoing, soft-spoken, and spiritual.

"Wanna sit down?" he asked in a deep baritone voice, clearing away the books and paperwork he had brought on board.

I sat beside Tinnie and watched people begin to stretch out, some lying across the bow and others lying faceup on the benches on both sides of the boat. Doc was resting on his back and using his scuba bag as a pillow. His cap was pulled over his face and he was still wearing his sunglasses.

"So I hear you're trying to build a slave ship," I said to Tinnie.

"Yes," he replied. "I'd like to construct a slave ship that's true to its actual size. It's a dream that I have. As you can imagine, funding can be difficult for a project like this."

Tinnie had dedicated the past two years to trying to raise $5 million to build a replica of the slave ship *Dos Amigos,* which sailed in the nineteenth century with 567 African people, each confined to an area that was three feet high and three feet wide.

Tinnie said the replica of the *Dos Amigos* would take the place of artifacts that went down with other slavers. He said the replica could serve as an educational tool, providing children with a more graphic perspective of the slave trade.

"History is the lifeblood of our culture," Tinnie said. "The human need for history—to know who we are, how we came to be—is as real as our need for food, clothing, shelter, and love."

Tinnie had known Howard Moss and Ric Powell for years. He is an intellectual by training, a student of Malcolm X and Marcus Garvey. He is also a history enthusiast, and he talked in great detail about the Middle Passage.

"For all the horrors of the slave trade, for all the disease, the filth, for all the atrocities, slavery brought the African genius to this country," Tinnie said while gentle waves splashed against the side of the dive boat.

"These early Africans made a painful contribution to this world and their gifts to America are still not yet totally realized," he said. "And in spite of all this pain, they made it and rose above the odds to achieve success. Without those African minds working with their hands, there would be no America as we know it. They built this country.

"The *Henrietta Marie* is giving us a purpose as African-Americans and African-American men. It's connecting us with our ancestors in the spirit world. We *should* be here today on this boat paying homage to our people. They *should* be treated with honor; they *should* be thanked for their gifts, because they were tortured until they died.

"As descendants of these African people, we need to ask ourselves, Where are the souls who died at sea?

"We don't always get the opportunity to talk about the slave trade from an uplifting perspective," he said. "We shouldn't bemoan our heritage, but, rather, celebrate our resiliency, strength, and tenacity.

"We believe the stories of wayward and restless spirits that have not come to rest," Tinnie said, shifting his long frame to a more comfortable position.

"Some call it silly superstition, but as African-American people, we have an obligation to visit this wreck site and remember that these Africans were honorable citizens who contributed greatly to our society," he said. "This slave ship should inspire us to regain our purpose as African-Americans, to help our sisters, to help one another, to study at our own schools, write our own books, chronicle our own history."

Listening to Tinnie speak reminded me of just how important it is for us to tell our stories to our young people and how we've drifted away from the art of storytelling and the oral accounts of history.

"Diving on this slave ship should force us to remember how people of low moral character had their way with African women belowdecks while African men were chained and powerless and watched helplessly, the consequences of which, I believe, we are still experiencing as black men today," he said.

"And like our ancestors before us, we are constantly being served notice that we're not in power, that we're still inferior, that we cannot anchor national newscasts, that we cannot head large financial institutions, that we cannot trade on Wall Street. But here we are today."

Tinnie took a swig of water from a tall plastic bottle. He poured some of the water into his two large hands, which, cupped together, resembled a huge brown bowl. He splashed the water over his face, the drops falling from his curly, damp beard.

"The *Henrietta Marie* provides a tangible connection for us," he said. "This is why we're here—to explore this incredible window into our past."

Nearly an hour had passed. We weren't halfway to New Ground Reef yet, but I told Tinnie that I needed to stand and stretch my legs.

The sun was sweltering on the deck, but we were being cooled by gentle trade winds as we made our way across the ocean. There was no land in sight in any direction.

Doc and Oz and Ric Powell were talking slavery—past and present.

"If it wasn't for the sacrifices of African slaves, we wouldn't be here," said Doc, who was standing on deck. "The *Henrietta Marie* tells us our history didn't start in America; it's a conduit to the past. We need to face the fact that slavery did exist and we should acknowledge the sacrifices they made.

"I consider New Ground Reef a grave site," he said. "We don't how exactly how many voyages the *Henrietta Marie* made before it got here, or how many people died on those voyages. The least we can do is commemorate these people, because we can't even begin to fathom the agony and misery they must have endured just to make it through the voyage."

"Slavery was complex then and its effect on us is still very complex today," Oz said. He had been trying to get a word in for a few minutes now.

"Whatever pain we feel—and the pain is deep—we can't allow it to hold us back or force us to become so bitter that we lose sight of the things that really matter in life," he said. "We still have to be educated. We still have to be politically and financially astute so we can compete in the workplace.

"We can be just as bright, just as savvy in business, and just as successful as white folks, but we can't do it walking around being bitter, cussing, and being angry. Each one of us has to find his own way to get past the anger and move forward. But we don't have to do it alone. We have one another. Right?"

"You're right, Oz. Well, we can't depend on others to help us economically, that's for damn sure," Doc said, speaking firmly. "We cannot depend on government; we cannot depend on corporations. We have to do for ourselves."

"That's what I'm saying," Ric said. "I'm not saying walk around angry all the time, I'm saying that we can't sit back and accept things the way they are. If we're going to be successful, then there will have to be some struggle. White folks ain't just gonna hand over partnerships in law firms and share the wealth. They need to be nudged."

Hank Jennings was off in a corner, making minor adjustments on his video camera.

"I'm not missing a minute, brother," Hank told me. "I want to be able to look back on this day forty years from now and watch a part of history that was unfolding. And if I'm not around to see it in forty years, someone in my family will be able to appreciate it."

Hank is a walking tank: five eleven, two hundred pounds, stocky, barrel chest, and a vise for a handshake.

He is the kind of guy who still believes in goodwill, that white people and black people can get along if we confront racism honestly. He still writes letters to his ten-year-old nephew Jamal.

Hank has a deep love for the sea and loyalty to family—his sisters, his aunts and uncles. He lost his mother to cancer in 1985, and his father was shot to death in 1964.

His father, Henry Jennings, Sr., was the first police officer to be killed in the line of duty in the Hartford Police Department's 103-year history. He was only twenty-eight years old when he was fatally shot while attempting to apprehend a suspect connected with the shooting of another Hartford police officer the day before.

Hank's father was an accomplished swimmer and an avid scuba diver—he was a member of the Winsted scuba-diving team—who spent his free time teaching Hartford teenagers to dive. One newspaper described him as someone who was trying to bring all members of the community together, "despite the racial tensions of the day." After his death, a national scuba-diving award was established in his honor to be given annually to the diver who contributed the most to community service.

A faded newspaper clipping from the *Hartford Courant* reported on the shooting and the response from his police officer friends who drove to Hank's mother's job to break the news.

" 'He loved life. He got a big kick out of every day,' said one friend, Lee Prettyman. 'He was the kind who would loan you his car and walk himself. You don't find them like him around anymore.' "

Hank was only seven years old when his father was killed, but before he died, he instilled within Hank his passion for the sea. Hank always felt that his father would have taught him to dive had he lived long enough.

Diving the *Henrietta Marie* gave Hank a spiritual opportunity to do something he was never able to do: scuba dive with his father, his role model even in death.

"I really miss him," Hank said, a rare time when his trademark smile was temporarily lost. "I mean, I *really* miss him, bro."

I have never lost a parent. Hank had lost both of his parents, and I couldn't pretend to know how it felt; I could only imagine.

"He was a diver," Hank said of his dad. "He's got to be with me, Mike. He was a diver who had a purpose in the community and I think I'm here because of him."

David Harrison had just walked over to us. He was more animated than I had seen him in quite some time. David always had something to say—sometimes it was profound; other times he was bragging. I got the impression that David practiced his swagger in the mirror the way some people practice tennis.

On this day, however, David was reflecting. And for once, I even agreed with him.

"You know, I wouldn't have missed this dive for anything. You ever stop to think that these African people from the *Henrietta Marie* could have been members of our families?" he asked. "You ever think that there is a link, something spiritual, something that we may never fully understand that brought us together at this moment?"

"All the time," Hank said. "But did *you* stop to think that *I* could be a member of your family, a distant cousin, something?"

"Our history is so complicated because our ancestors were carried off on different ships, dropped on different islands in the West Indies, traded at different ports, and sold on different auction blocks. Families were separated and never heard from again.

"You could be my cousin. Michael could be my cousin. Oz could be my cousin. We could all be related; hell, we just don't know. But what we do know is that the possibility definitely exists," Hank said.

"Well if we never get to sort out our bloodlines, at least we know for sure that we're related in spirit and it's in the spirit of this pilgrimage that we're here today," I said to Hank and David. "We know that this particular journey can never be duplicated and that we'll be forever linked by this experience."

"No question," David Harrison said. "There is something mystical—call it spiritual if you want—but something that's out of our control connects each of us to the others and to this ocean. It's no accident or coincidence that black divers are paying their respects to black people from the Middle Passage. We were brought here and I don't believe we really had a choice."

A tall brown-skinned young man rousted me from my daydream.

"Hi, I'm Jim Beard."

Jim was thirty then. Lean, even-tempered, soft-spoken, and straightforward, he is a financial analyst, married, and was one of the most serious thirty-year-olds I've known.

"I basically crashed this dive," Beard said, laughing. "I crashed the party, I'm happy I crashed the party and I'd do it again. I wasn't part of the original list. I read about the *Henrietta Marie* in the newspaper. I knew Hank and Howard and then I heard through NABS that Dr. Jones was going to give it another shot in May, after the problems with the bad weather.

"I knew I'd probably never get another opportunity to dive on a slave ship with other black men, so I told my wife that I just had to go for it," Beard said. "She agreed. I figured that no matter what happens to me in the future, I can always say I helped lay a monument underwater to commemorate my people. Not many other folks can make that claim. I'm proud to say I'm a part of this experience."

I scribbled some notes and gazed at the ocean while the *Island Diver* bounced over the white waves across the Gulf of Mexico. There was a calm in the air, there was activity on the deck of the boat, but for a moment all was quiet around me.

Strong black families have always been part of my life's experience. It is my family that has kept me focused. It is my family that encouraged me to tell the spiritually uplifting stories of African-American people. It was important for me at a young age to watch strong black men and women in my family, some who have since died but who left behind a legacy of spiritual strength and a lifetime of faith.

My family is special to me, but it is not unique in black communities. The tenacity of black families is the rule, rather than the exception. The nation is filled with loving, caring African-American families who send their children off to school with hot meals in their bellies and love in their hearts. Our families are often hidden from America's mainstream and viewed as drains on society by conservatives who blame "the breakdown

of the black family" for many of the country's social problems. And here
I was cruising to a site in the Gulf of Mexico to visit the remains of a slave
ship where black families were truly separated.

"Ten minutes to the site!" the captain shouted.

There were no high fives or shouts of joy or rushing for dive equipment. There was a silence I've never witnessed on a dive boat. It was as
if everyone was moving in slow motion, as if no one had really heard the
captain's announcement.

Jim Beard was leaning over the edge of our boat, taking a peek at the
clear blue water below.

"Would you look at this calm sea and all of this sunshine," he said,
waving me over. "Someone up there is certainly smiling on us today,
brother."

Oswald was writing down last-minute thoughts for our service at sea.
Doc was stretched out again. Hank was sitting at the stern, taking advantage of quiet time.

"There's no hurry," I said to Hank. "Our ancestors have planned a
perfect day for us. They've brought us this far after three hundred years
with faith and nothing more. They'll guide us the rest of the way from
here."

15

The call that beckoned us underwater to a ship of splintered wood and smothered souls didn't come from the telephone: It came from the sea.

It echoed from a thrashing surf seven thousand miles away on the African continent; a sea that raged from the banks of the Niger River, flowing into the mouth of the Old Calabar River, the Bight of Biafra, and the streams of Sierra Leone, racing along the Ivory Coast, slamming the jagged jetties of the Caribbean Sea and spilling into the Atlantic Ocean and the Gulf of Mexico, the place of our pilgrimage.

It was a punishing sea that left a nation of African bodies in its wake. It was a sea that snatched black children from the arms of their mothers, fathers from their sons, husbands from their wives. It was a sea that silenced a generation of black heartbeats.

It was—*and is*—a sea that never sleeps; a sea that spits swells; a sea that always stares back no matter from which direction you approach it; a sea with no back door.

The sea was dead calm by the time we anchored on New Ground Reef.

The wind was still; there was no land in sight, just miles of dark blue ocean in all directions.

As the engine of the *Island Diver* sputtered and shut down in warm

waters, there was only silence on the sea and one lone bird flapping its
wings across a cloudless sky, a streaking silhouette lost against the blinding sun.

There was something inherently peculiar about this place, New
Ground Reef, the site of slave-ship wreckage where the Atlantic Ocean
meets the Gulf of Mexico. It is a place of unpredictable currents, where
the sea churns without warning, where the success of a day's dive depends
not only on the state of mind of the diver but also on the attitude of the
ocean.

On this day, the sea was flat as glass. I could have skipped a stone
ninety miles and chased the trail of ripples to the shoreline of Cuba.

It was 10:00 A.M. I could hear the bulky steel-chained anchor rumble
over the side of the boat, securing us, temporarily, on the site of the *Henrietta Marie*, where we believed the tortured souls of those who died
aboard her were still submerged.

Seventy-five yards away was the tugboat that had hauled the concrete
monument to New Ground Reef. The memorial, with its bronze inscription, was floating inside a thick plastic lift bag connected to the underside of the tugboat by a steel line of cable.

I closed my eyes for just a few seconds, and while the boat rocked easily in the breeze, I paused to ask God to bless our pilgrimage to this
sacred site on the sea.

"Never underestimate the power of prayer," my father always tells
me. "Prayer can make all the difference in your life."

My father is right, although prayer hasn't always come easily for me.
I have to work at it.

Prayer was always part of my family's life. We never ate meals before
blessing the table. We attended church on Sunday mornings together. I
went to Sunday school. In the early 1970s, I would split my time between
two churches.

After the riot in 1967, which turned Twelfth Street into a smoldering
block of buildings, my mother and father couldn't agree on a church, so
we alternated between Hope, Mom's Presbyterian church, and Tabernacle, Dad's Baptist church.

Mom's Presbyterian church was sedate. The pastor's message was usually somewhat interesting, although subdued and difficult to apply to the

everyday life of a fourteen-year-old boy in Detroit. Oftentimes, I would fall asleep and awake to a subtle jab from my mother.

The people in the congregation were warm; they were friends of my family from our old church, St. Mark's Community Church. I missed the father-and-son banquets at St. Mark's and the Easter-egg hunts in the backyard of the church.

Dad's church was jumpin'. There were two levels and two packed services inside the sprawling Baptist church. The balcony was reserved for latecomers because the first floor was packed by 8:15 for the 9:00 A.M. service and crowded by 10:00 for the 11:00 A.M. service.

Baptist church services are not for the weak of heart. It's church up close and in your face. The rumbling bass sounds of the pipe organ echoed through the sanctuary at Tabernacle, the indication that the service was about to begin. The thirty-five-plus-person choir would enter through a doorway behind the pulpit and file into the choir area, clapping their hands and stepping in rhythm from side to side. Some members of the congregation were already shouting "Amen!"

I remember someone fainting every Sunday and being helped to a lower level of the church, a place I thought was sort of a makeshift infirmary for the newly spiritually healed.

Still, I was intrigued by the music and sometimes my eyes filled with tears as I listened to the organ and watched the older members of the congregation stand, walk to the front of the sanctuary, and testify to the power of their faith.

The pastor, draped in a glorious robe, would take the pulpit and begin a one-hour sermon that would start in low tones and build to a spiritual crescendo, with parishioners erupting with shouts of *"AMEN, brother!"* ... *"Preach, my brother!"* ... *"Yes, Lord!"*

There was no sleeping during a service at Tabernacle Baptist.

The minister's message usually pertained to me, to life in urban America, to growing up in need of a spiritual foundation, a guide through life. He often preached about the continuing survival of black people who embraced faith when they had nothing else.

I finished my brief prayer aboard the *Island Diver* on the Gulf of Mexico and looked toward my dive partners.

Each of us had our own personal reasons for visiting the *Henrietta*

Marie on May 15, 1993. Each of us was drawn to New Ground Reef by something more powerful than a simple invitation from Doc Jones. We were all searching for much more than artifacts.

This pilgrimage was an experience that meant more to me than simply documenting the day's event. I was involved with this three-continent odyssey that had led me on a quest for some form of creative freedom and spiritual discovery, a way to combine my passions for writing, history, and underwater exploration and to share my experiences and the uplifting stories about black people with people throughout the United States.

Officers from the Coast Guard and the Florida Marine Sanctuary were pulling alongside our boat to monitor the dive as Ric Powell went over the plan: Doc and David Moore would locate the wreck site and return to the boat.

But as David and Doc studied the map of the site carefully for about twenty minutes, David mentioned that it had been at least nine years since he'd last visited the site but that he planned to use his compass and natural navigation as a guide.

David was sure he would remember a large coral head that rested at the site of the *Henrietta Marie,* but after nine years, landmarks often change underwater.

"I still think we can find the yellow line that we marked the site with last time," he said. "The site is in twenty-eight to thirty feet of water and there's grass growing in a patch of sand near a large coral head."

"How large is the coral head?" Doc asked.

"About six feet tall and eight feet wide," David said.

David slipped into his wet suit; Doc sat across the deck, buckling his jacket. He spit into his mask—natural antifog solution—and pulled it over his face, giving David the thumbs-up sign. Slipping into their fins, they met at the edge of the dive boat as we helped double-check their air supply and wished them a successful search.

Within seconds, they rolled off the boat and splashed into the ocean. We watched their bubbles until they disappeared, speculating as to how long it would take them to locate the site.

"You think that yellow line will still be there after nine years?" Hank asked me.

"If it's not, we're going to be here overnight looking for this site, 'cause you know Oswald isn't leaving until we lay this plaque on the *Henrietta Marie*," I said.

It was 11:15 and the heat was already oppressive. We were all drinking plenty of water to keep from becoming dehydrated.

Forty-five minutes had passed and we were getting anxious.

"They've been down a long time," Oz said. "This may be a bit more difficult than we expected."

I reached into the cooler, grabbed an apple, then pulled out my notebook and scribbled some notes from conversations with Doc, Hank, and Oswald.

Fifteen more minutes passed when I heard someone from the stern shout, "They're back!"

I packed my notebook away and headed to the back of the boat.

Doc and David were soaked and breathing heavily as they climbed back on board the *Island Diver*. They didn't say a word until they both sat down and pulled off their masks and fins, water falling from their heads.

"We didn't find it," David said. "It's all changed down there so much. I didn't recognize a thing."

"What do you think, Doc?" David asked.

"We'll look at that map again, grab a sandwich, and give it another shot in an hour."

Unzipping their wet suits, David explained that they had done four square patterns of fifty yards each a few feet away from where he thought the site was located. But with visibility dropping to about ten feet and a current picking up, the conditions for searching for a faded yellow line and an old fire stove were looking bleak.

The captain of the tugboat across the way would wave from time to time and we'd yell that we were still waiting.

"We've waited all of our lives to get here," I told Hank. "A few more minutes isn't going to make much of a difference."

Doc and David Moore had finished eating and had reviewed their compass headings again. This time, however, they decided to swim east.

"Ready?" Doc asked.

"Yup," David answered, sliding a pair of faded blue knee pads over his thick, pale legs and popping his regulator into his mouth.

I heard two splashes, and they vanished under the sea.

We all figured it would be awhile before Doc and David returned. I claimed a piece of deck, stretched out on my back, and looked toward the sky, feeling the cool breeze on my face. And then a loud noise echoed across the sea.

Toward the bow, Ric Powell was wearing his African *kufi* and blowing into a large pink conch shell, his cheeks bloated as if he was doing a reasonably decent impersonation of Dizzy Gillespie.

Ric was creating a sound from the conch shell that he believed would summon our lost ancestors. He was trying everything he could think of to ensure a peaceful and successful experience at sea.

As Ric blew into the conch shell, the low-pitch sound reverberating around the boat, Howard Moss began to beat a leather-skinned drum and Gene Tinnie reached for a large tambourine.

Within seconds, they were re-creating the sounds of Africa, playing music with instruments much like the ones that African people use to lift their spirits and send messages from village to village.

The boat was transformed into a floating revival of rhythms, like an offering of fellowship to lost souls in the sea.

"We're calling our ancestors," Ric said. "We're letting them know we're here and that we understand their pain and suffering and thank them for the strength they have given us to survive."

There was a look in Ric's eyes that I hadn't seen there before. It was a look of intensity and pride as he blew his conch shell, pausing periodically to hug his son, Victor.

I was seeing another side of these black divers. This was a group of veteran divers, certainly not a group given to hugging and crying. These were people who had dived all over the world—deep wrecks in California, encounters with hammerhead sharks in Australia, strong currents in Cozumel and low visibility in North Carolina.

But on this day, there was an exhilaration that we had never known. This was no ordinary dive. As I looked out over a vast ocean, I thought about water as a part of our history, our heritage. I thought about our long three-hundred-year relationship with water, the oceans our ancestors were forced to cross and the rivers where they bathed.

We had been summoned to New Ground Reef as if we had heard the

beating of the drums, the drums that sounded in our neighborhoods of
Miami, Washington, and New York, like the messages sent throughout
the villages of Africa advising the community of meetings and prayer services. Like our ancestors, we heard the drums, and for this day, aboard
the *Island Diver,* we were a community, too.

Perhaps it was not a coincidence that I was guided to this site at this
time in my life, when a group of black scuba divers had formed a coali-
tion; perhaps we were always supposed to honor our ancestors together
underwater and find a more constructive way to revisit the issue of slavery: by celebrating our survival and strength as a people.

"They're back!" someone shouted over the music.

I helped Doc aboard the boat, his gear soaked and dripping. David
and Doc shared something in common this time: They were both smiling.

"We found it!" David Moore shouted as he climbed up the ladder into
the boat. He was breathing hard and his grayish blond hair was dripping
into a fresh towel.

"We found the yellow line from '82 and an old firebox that looks like
it could have been a stove of some kind. This was one of the artifacts
from the *Henrietta Marie* that we never recovered."

"It's down there all right," Doc added. "It's not easy to find. We need
to mark it clearly so we can find it again."

"What's the viz like down there?" Hank asked.

"Not so good," David said. "About ten feet, maybe."

They removed their gear and there was quiet celebration, many of us
looking toward the heavens. The wreck site had been located, we knew
we were on the site of the *Henrietta Marie,* and we were all anxious to
go underwater.

David let the captain know the site had been found and that we
planned to stay anchored on New Ground Reef for most of the day.

Oswald was standing alone reading over his notes. He looked a bit
nervous. We had made a decision weeks earlier to hold a brief ceremony
at sea before entering the water, something short but meaningful, a commemoration to our ancestors, a spiritual observance for the ancestors we
lost but never knew.

We were not ordained ministers or students of theology, but a group
of black scuba divers who were drawn to the site of the *Henrietta Marie*

as if it were a life force calling for each of us to visit our collective past.

It seemed a natural progression of events: black divers exploring the remains of a ship that had transported our ancestors across the Atlantic. We owed these people our prayers, our appreciation, and our love.

We were aware that enslaved African people did not actually go down with the *Henrietta Marie* on New Ground Reef, but we knew that African men, women, and children had died aboard the ship earlier and that countless numbers of African people from the *Henrietta Marie* had perished in the Atlantic.

And there was a larger, symbolic issue: It was a time to remember a global injustice of immense proportions, and also to take note that all of us were descendants of a great people who had a determination to survive.

For the first time as black divers, we were actually drawing a connection to the sea, instead of simply exploring it.

Oswald had spent late-night hours crafting the writing for our ceremony. He wanted our ancestors to know they hadn't died in vain, that we appreciated their sacrifices, and that after three hundred years we had come to honor them in our own way.

He walked over to the center of the bow and asked each of us to stand in a tight circle and join hands.

"We are here today, members of the National Association of Black Scuba Divers, to pay tribute to millions of people—men, women, and children, black people, our people—who lost their lives during the Middle Passage," Oswald said, his voice cracking. "Many of these innocent people lost their lives in this ocean, and many more lost their lives on this slave ship whose spirits lie below us."

Oswald hadn't finished his first sentence when the waves came.

From a dead calm, the sea shook and small swells appeared from nowhere, rocking the *Island Diver* from side to side and forcing us to balance ourselves on one another's shoulders.

Waves slapped the bow, the boat swaying in its own wake as if we were being acknowledged—or welcomed—by a phenomenal force. There was an abrupt change in the ocean's current—and an abrupt change in our perspective of the day.

I've never been one to discredit or reject phenomena I don't truly understand. I believe there are connections that cannot always be immediately explained—links to our souls that raise more questions than answers on New Ground Reef; rare moments where a warm feeling in the pit of my stomach is the only barometer for knowing I've experienced something extraordinary.

"If African-Americans have survived the centuries since slavery began, it is in large measure due to the courage and strength and thoughtfulness of those people who were forced to travel the sea routes of death and suffering in vessels like the *Henrietta Marie,*" Oswald read.

"They were determined to live," he said, wiping his face, which was drenched from a mix of sweat and tears. "We believe the spirits of a multitude of African people who died in transit are still with this sunken vessel."

We paused for several minutes, each of us spending a moment to offer a private prayer.

Oswald closed his folder.

The winds subsided and calm returned to the sea.

"Mike, *you* did feel that, didn't you?" Hank asked. "I'm just making sure it wasn't my imagination."

"No," I said. "It was very real. The ancestors have blessed us."

"We were being welcomed!" Oswald said, looking perplexed but exhilarated. "They were expecting us. They know we're family."

Oswald reached for his dive gear. Doc and Ric Powell were suiting up and getting ready to jump off the stern, and the captain of the tugboat was waiting for their signal before he began to slowly lower the monument into the ocean.

"Those were fine words," Doc whispered to Oz before he went over the side. "See you down there."

Doc and Ric swam to the tugboat, gave the captain the thumbs-up sign, and within minutes the lift bag filled with air and the monument slowly disappeared beneath the surface.

I had already zipped myself into my wet suit and was slipping on my fins when I looked across the deck at Oswald, who seemed a little slow to get ready.

"You all right?" I asked him.

"I'm fine," he said. "I'm fine."

He didn't sound convincing.

"I'll wait for you if you want," I said. "We'll buddy up, dive together."

Oz was always a bit slower than the rest of us getting dressed; we'd tease him, saying all those pork ribs he liked to eat weighed him down.

But this was different. He appeared reluctant to get into the water, but he assured me that he was ready for the dive.

I met Oz at the stern.

"That was a wonderful observance to lead us into an extraordinary day," I said.

He didn't say much; he just nodded and asked if I was ready to dive. We checked our air, popped in our regulators, and took a giant step off the *Island Diver* into the Gulf of Mexico.

The water was gentle, there was a light current, and there were no waves at the surface. We swam over to Doc and Ric, who were just beginning their descent. The monument floated inches above their heads.

Within a few seconds, we had slipped beneath the surface and were dodging half a dozen jellyfish at five feet.

As we descended past a depth of fifteen feet, I followed Doc's bubbles, which had encircled me. I lost Oswald momentarily in the blur of the ocean. Through the silt and haze, we appeared as shadows with long webbed feet, making a graceful free fall past a squadron of shiny barracuda.

We couldn't see more than ten feet in any direction. We kept our eyes on Doc and Ric and the huge memorial as we floated over them in midair.

I drifted with the rhythm of the currents, moving in slow motion as the salt water gently washed over me while I sank deeper into the ocean. The ocean was silent, except for the cadence of my own breathing and the thumping of my heart.

I'd looked up every so often to glance at the ringlet of bubbles floating toward the sunlight and watched them burst like tiny balloons before breaking the surface. Just for a moment, I spread both my arms like wide wings and steered myself toward Oswald.

I didn't have to be in the air to soar.

The water on New Ground Reef was warm, but as we glided toward the seafloor, the site was strangely familiar. I felt as though I were returning to this place after many years, like family that had been away for a while.

I felt embraced by gentle currents as we propelled ourselves with short snaps of our fins. I felt a kinship, a welcoming of sorts, although I had never visited the site of this wreckage before.

For the ten of us, the visit to this slave ship was a dive of the spirit, one that we could feel but not see. It was a pious pilgrimage: baptizing ourselves in the same seas that had engulfed an immeasurable number of our ancestors.

I cleared my mask to release the excess water and I could barely see Hank in the distance. We were all floating just above Doc and Ric, who were holding on to each side of the monument, slowly guiding the one-ton memorial to a sandy patch on the ocean floor.

I was struck by the sight of the black divers dropping effortlessly onto a site of soggy planks of wood that had once made up a ship that hauled my ancestors into slavery. I was struck by the power of the sea that kept this ship hidden from us for three centuries. And for a moment, it felt as if we were surrounded by an energy that gave me a quick chill, even though the water temperature was 80 degrees.

I lost sight of Oswald at twenty-five feet, but then he reappeared, wearing an expression I had never seen. It was a cross between anxiety and reluctance.

At thirty feet, as we dropped to the ocean floor, I could see sand and thin strands of grass. Doc glanced at his compass as he and Ric positioned the monument to the east, facing Africa.

When Africans were buried in the Americas, their families placed them inside coffins and laid them to rest with their heads facing east toward Africa, their homeland. We believed the monument to our ancestors should also face Africa.

We hovered in the still of the ocean a few feet above the weighty memorial, our bodies and our souls soothed by the sea. We shifted with the current and watched the concrete pledge of our appreciation pound the ocean floor, the silt swirling from the bottom as the monument made its solid impression in the sand.

In teams of two, we toured the memorial, each of us reaching out to touch the hand of the brother next to him; all of us stopping momentarily to read the inscription that was etched into a bronze plaque and bolted into the concrete:

Henrietta Marie: *In memory and recognition of the courage, pain, and suffering of enslaved African people. Speak her name and gently touch the souls of our ancestors.*

Inside the memorial was a steel case with a sheet of paper listing each of our names, brothers who came to honor family, brothers whose eyes filled with tears through tempered masks. Beneath us, scattered along the ocean floor, were planks of wood and perhaps more shackles, trade beads, and cannons—artifacts more precious than any amount of shiny treasure.

It was a moment that seemed to last for hours. I watched each of the brothers swim past the memorial, stopping for a moment to offer private thoughts, as I ran my hands through the layers of sand.

Oswald and I were the last two divers to visit the monument. Everyone had viewed it, touched it, and prayed before it and now was heading back to the surface. But Oswald seemed slightly disoriented and unresponsive.

He rounded the memorial twice, then dropped to his knees, resting in front of the shrine and running his hands gently over the inscription as if he were stroking the face of an old friend. Thirty feet below the ocean's surface, Oswald was lost in a swirl of silt, lost among millions of silent souls.

As if the currents had pulled him deep into the past, he seemed mesmerized by the inscription, which was glistening from soft flashes of sunlight. Wrapped in his own watery cocoon, Oswald ignored each of my signals to ascend.

I waved my hands in front of him, but he didn't seem to notice I was there. I allowed him a few more minutes, but then it was time for us to begin our ascent. I circled the memorial one last time and rubbed my hand along the stone, taking a final look at the inscription.

I positioned myself next to Oswald, and after thanking God for blessing our day, I tugged on his shoulder. He took his time looking up from the monument, then snapped into focus and looked at me as if seeing me for the first time.

I pointed toward the surface and rose slowly from the ocean floor. Oswald grabbed my hand and squeezed it tightly. I held on to him as we ascended, watching the monument until it gradually disappeared into the silt.

As Oswald and I broke the surface, all of the divers were floating in the Gulf of Mexico, too consumed by emotion to climb aboard the boat immediately. It was like a reunion on the ocean's surface. We had been apart for just about forty minutes, but it seemed like hours, having traveled back in time.

We didn't realize it then, but as black divers and in the spirit of our pilgrimage, we had created a mini Million Man March at sea—expressing our thoughts for self-reliance, personal responsibility, and the importance of giving back to the community and commemorating our African ancestors, who, through their pain, showed us the way to peace.

"There's an eerie connection associated with this site," said Howard Moss. "There's a powerful presence down there. A *powerful* presence.

"If I never dive this site again; this experience will last a lifetime," he said. "There is no question in my mind that for me something phenomenal happened down there."

"What was going on down there?" I asked Oswald.

"I thought you had left. I didn't know you were still there," he said, his voice quivering. "But I'm glad you were there."

"Come again?" I asked.

"They were down there—our ancestors; they were watching us; somebody wanted us here today," he said, speaking in broken sentences.

"My legs turned to jelly," Oswald tried to explain. "I couldn't kick. I couldn't do anything. It was as if I was paralyzed, like something was holding me down there."

We climbed aboard the *Island Diver* one at a time and began to unzip our wet suits and dry off. We all moved to the center of the deck, shaking hands, hugging; some were just sharing a quiet moment.

But in a rather unorthodox way, for us, this pilgrimage had become a spiritual experience: a collective reflection, an emotional cleansing, a chance to be one with the ocean, a rare opportunity to confront and touch our history.

"It gives us a new dimension into what our history is all about," Oswald said. "This dive on this slave ship allows black people to get beyond our anger and put ourselves in the shoes of our ancestors, to some extent; to wonder about the nature of greed, to cry and touch their souls."

"When we anchored on New Ground Reef, there was a dead silence and the entire energy on the boat changed," Hank said. "And underwater, I could almost see images of people through the haze. I remember the dead silence before we entered the water, that eerie feeling that other people were down there. There was a spirituality that manifested itself in the water and something touched our world. It was like two dimensions touched at the same time—a spiritual world and our world touched at that precise moment in time.

"My mom, bless her soul, she passed away in 1985. She raised me to be proud of my race and my culture," Hank said. "She always made a point of making me aware of our history. And she always said that my dad would be with me the rest of my life.

"I think I left the *Henrietta Marie* saying, Mom, you were right. It was like a confirmation that my mom was right about being able to connect with the past. She's passed on, but I believe she and my dad were both with me on the *Henrietta Marie*.

"If I dive that site one hundred times, I don't expect to experience that feeling ever again. But that one time was enough to let me know not only that there is a God but that there is also a world beyond ours where our ancestors spirits exist—and I've visited that world."

We were all in the water for the same amount of time, give or take a few minutes; we all traveled on the same boat, yet we all took personal journeys to the site of the *Henrietta Marie*.

"I experienced a tremendous feeling of peace," Oswald said, pulling his fins from his feet. "It was a feeling that something was around me, a presence that I couldn't put my finger on. It was as if a warm feeling washed over me. It was like a key that was capable of opening all kinds of emotions.

"I was thinking about my father and how he committed suicide," Oz added. "I was just out of grad school; I was twenty-three. There's still a lot of pain there. We knew that something was wrong with my father before the suicide, but it was difficult to deal with.

"A few days before he killed himself, my mother found a gun in his room, and one evening, she thought she had heard him cock it. So she went into his room and took it out of his drawer without him knowing it; then she came into my room and gave it to me. I still own it—a Spanish-made thirty-two automatic. I still pull it out and look at it from time to time.

"I cried for hours after his death," he recalled. "Years later, I learned that all he needed was a little medication for depression. I don't know whether I'm trying to defeat water or not, but this experience has forced me to think about it. I'm amazed that I'm finally talking about it. The *Henrietta Marie* has forced me to confront some old issues associated with water."

Jim Beard was also thinking about a lost relative while standing on the bow of the boat. He was remembering stories about his great-great-grandmother, whom he never met. He knew only that she was a slave.

The closest that Jim ever came to meeting her, he said, was diving the site of the *Henrietta Marie*—swimming the same seas that perhaps his great-great-grandmother had been forced to sail three centuries ago.

"I wondered about her prayers," he said.

"I wonder whether my great-great-grandmother was in this same part of the ocean, whether she ever had an opportunity to look into this same sky, or whether she was in shackles in the hull of the *Henrietta Marie,* or a slave ship like it.

"I wonder what was traded for her life. I remember reading that a black man was worth seventeen dollars back then, and black women even less, and I wonder if there was anyone on the *Henrietta Marie* related to me," Beard said.

The kids, Kristopher and Victor, were tugging on their dads, Howard and Ric. They had snorkeled above the site while the divers were below. They could see the divers descending into the water but had lost them in the haze. Now, while helping them out of their gear, their fathers were telling them what they had seen.

"I felt overpowering feelings," Howard Moss told his son. "We paid homage to the African ancestors, but I felt connected to their souls. It had a cleansing effect on me. While I was underwater, I thought about how this powerful piece of history had been washed away with the currents and covered up by sand for so long."

Hank walked over and offered me a drink of water.

"I wish I could bottle this feeling and savor it," he said. "I wish I could take it back home and pull it out whenever I want to. I wish I could keep this feeling in perpetual slow motion."

We stood on the deck in a semicircle, the wind cooling our hot skin, and I talked of forever being linked with the *Henrietta Marie* because a black diver named Moe Molinar was guided to a mound of rusted shackles in the Gulf of Mexico; because a black man recovered spiritual treasure that we can always call our own, treasure that can never be sold or stripped from us.

"Moe Molinar helped bring each of us here today," I said, pouring cold water over my head. "The man who always wanted black men to share in his treasure hunting was somewhat responsible for us taking this underwater pilgrimage today. We should think about Moe, as well as our ancestors, as we head home."

Thirty minutes after our underwater pilgrimage to the *Henrietta Marie,* as we bounced across the waves, heading back to Key West, Oswald sat in the only quiet corner of the boat, his dive suit dripping wet, his head buried in his sea-wrinkled hands. He spoke softly of how we reclaimed a rare and unforeseen power in the still of the ocean.

"I know they're down there," he muttered to himself, a stream of salt water and tears rolling from his cheeks. "Our ancestors waited for us; they waited a long time, and we finally came to join them.

"Michael," he whispered, "I could feel their souls."

16

slav-ery (slay'vuh ree, slayv'ree) n. 1. the condition of a slave; bondage 2. the keeping of slaves as a practice or institution 3. a state of subjection like that of a slave 4. severe toil; drudgery.

Dawn in Dakar brings burnt-orange skies to the distant edge of the sea; it brings the cool spray of salt water and a rhythm of winds that whistle through the shoots of the baobab trees—winds that flapped sun-scorched sails and steered a horde of hellish ships to the shores of West Africa; winds that warned of impending sins; winds that still carry the cries of my ancestors.

With the dawn come layers of white-capped waves that roll like blankets over the slick black jetties—a natural, choreographed wonder that never gives the same performance twice. These waves have splashed the feet of generations of black children and bathed a multitude of mothers and fathers, daughters and sons.

It was shortly before six o'clock in the morning, July 19, 1996, and I had only been in Dakar about twenty-four hours. I was looking at a roaring ocean along the West African coast and listening to the sadness being broadcasted on CNN.

Ninety minutes before I was preparing to board the flight to Dakar from New York's JFK International Airport, I learned that TWA Flight

800, bound for Paris, had crashed in the Atlantic Ocean after taking off from a runway less than a mile away from me.

From the window of the Air France lounge, I had seen emergency vehicles with flashing red lights racing through the airport as people in the lounge closed their books, folded their newspapers, reached for liquor, and sat in silence.

At the time, I had no idea that everyone aboard Flight 800 had died in the midair explosion. I knew only that a tragic incident had occurred on an aircraft and that I was preparing to board a plane for a seven-hour flight to Africa.

Later, when I learned what had happened, I couldn't help thinking about the arduous and eerie task of scuba divers who would undoubtedly be called to help recover wreckage from the aircraft and to search the ocean's depths for the bodies of passengers. I cringed at the thought of diving for the dead.

Then I remembered the one question that is asked most often about diving on the wreckage of the *Henrietta Marie*.

"Did you find any bodies?" a child will ask.

"Were there any skeletal remains?" a scholar will inquire.

The answer, so far, is "No."

Perhaps in years to come, the wreckage of Flight 800, which rests 140 feet below the surface of the Atlantic Ocean, will become a memorial for those lost lives, as sacred as the sunken remains of the *Henrietta Marie* have become to me and my diving brothers.

Minutes before a pleasant voice announced the departure of my flight, I had recalled that although I was flying Air Afrique, Senegal's national airline, I had told several friends and family that I would be flying through Paris en route to Dakar. I rushed to a pay phone to call my mother and father in Detroit.

It was close to 10:00 P.M., late for my parents. My mother answered the phone.

"Hi Mom," I said. "It's me."

There is only one *me* when I call home. I'm the only child of Howard and Roberta Cottman, so I can't be confused with anyone else.

"I just wanted you to know that I'm okay and I'm flying Air Afrique tonight at eleven. I just wanted to check in with you…well, in light of the accident, of course."

"What accident?" my mother asked.

It was the first she had heard of the crash. I was regretting my decision to call home.

My parents are not television people, they don't own a VCR, and I'm constantly dragging them into the twenty-first century with talk of compact discs and voice-activated telephones.

"A plane went down near the airport here," I said. "And they're saying it looks grim."

I heard my mother shout to my father to pick up the phone.

"Hey, Mike," my dad said, sounding stronger than he had in months. "What's going on?" I shared the news for a second time. My father paused before posing his question: "Well," he said, "do you still want to make the trip?"

There was no need to contemplate his question. I had made my decision long before I walked to the pay phone.

"Yes, I do," I said quickly. "I've postponed this trip three times already for a variety of reasons, and I really need to complete my research and finish the book. You know that Africa is the most important segment of my journey. I think I have to go."

There was a short silence on the other end of the phone. I sensed that they wanted to ask me not to get on the plane, but they wouldn't. And they didn't. My father has always believed in the power of faith and the human spirit.

When I was a child, he would come into my bedroom every evening and kneel beside me. We would say our prayers together, aloud, thanking God for health and strength in our family, and families everywhere, before he tucked me in for the night.

His words on the telephone at JFK were as comforting as my childhood blanket on those cold winter nights in Detroit.

"God has watched over you for two years during your travels for your book," my father said. "God will be with you during your pilgrimage to Africa and bring you back home safely."

My wife, Mireille, was traveling to Miami on business and hadn't yet checked into her hotel. There was no way for me to reach her.

"Call Mireille for me, please," I said, "and tell her that I'll call her from Dakar."

"We certainly will," my mother promised. "And Michael, please call us, too."

We shared a prayer and I could hear the concern in my mother's voice.

"We love you," she said.

"I love you, too."

I walked down the Jetway and onto the plane, thinking about how important it is in these fast-paced times of transcontinental travel to remind our parents how much we love them, because tomorrow is not guaranteed.

After a smooth takeoff, I unbuckled my seat belt high above the clouds and paced the narrow aisle for a few minutes, stretching my legs in preparation for a long flight. I ordered red wine, put on my headset, and reached for the first CD I could find. It was John Coltrane. I turned off the overhead lamp, sipped my wine, and eventually fell asleep while listening to Coltrane's soothing rendition of "My Favorite Things."

The Air Afrique wide-body airplane touched down on the runway in Dakar at 7:30 A.M. on July 18, 1996, twenty minutes early. Although I enjoy flying, I was relieved to be on the ground.

As we taxied to the gate, I could see families with children inside the terminal building, waiting for their loved ones. Men were dressed in flowing robes and *kufis,* some carrying briefcases and the local newspaper. Women were wearing colorful boubous and rows of bracelets on their brown arms. Little girls wore silver in their pierced ears. It was a heartening feeling to see black people everywhere—almost like growing up in Detroit.

I was tired, but I also felt welcomed by a place I had visited eleven years earlier, a place that many African-Americans call home.

The terminal wasn't very crowded; in fact, many of the passengers on my flight stayed on the plane and were heading on to Abidjan, Ivory Coast, a two-hour flight from Dakar.

I walked through the first checkpoint and looked anxiously toward the baggage area to see if my luggage had arrived on the conveyor belt. I was more concerned about my scuba gear arriving in Dakar; I could always buy slacks and shirts.

I cleared immigration in two minutes. The young black man behind the desk only needed to clarify my role as journalist, which I had entered on the immigration form under "Occupation."

"Who do you work for?" he asked, staring me directly in the eye.

I paused for a moment.

For the past twenty years, I have routinely answered that question with the title of a major newspaper, but for the first time, I found myself offering a different, yet satisfying, response.

"I'm an author," I said. "I am writing a book about *our* history and my research has lead me to Dakar."

"I understand," he said, stamping my passport with a slight smile. "Good luck with your research and welcome to Africa."

"Next in line!" he shouted sternly.

I walked into the terminal building and was greeted immediately by a friendly face.

"Mr. Cottman?" a voice called from a small crowd of people waiting for family.

"Yes," I said. "I'm Michael Cottman."

"I'm Chicka." He was in his late thirties, stocky, brown-skinned, and wore a serious expression.

He extended his hand.

"Welcome to Dakar, Mr. Cottman. I hope you had a pleasant flight," he said. "I'll be arranging your transportation, your schedule, your interviews, and your—well, do you speak French?"

"Very little," I said.

"Then I will also arrange for a translator," he said, handing me his business card. "If there is anything additional that you will require, Mr. Cottman, please contact me."

"Thank you. I will. And call me Michael."

We loaded my luggage onto a cart and proceed to the exit signs. "Follow me," he said, "and please do not stop for anyone asking to carry your bags."

I wanted to remind him that I had just flown in from New York, the capital of all scams.

It was a warm day, slightly overcast, but no rain was falling. We stored the luggage in the trunk of a small four-door Toyota and drove out of the airport. I was introduced to my driver, Mr. Som, an extremely patient and pleasant gentleman who spoke more English than he let on and was more familiar with American customs and politics than he cared to admit.

As we drove along Senegal's shoreline, I watched the regal women carrying large straw baskets on their heads, the children in blue-and-brown uniforms walking to school, and the men lining the sidewalks with tables loaded with jewelry, art, clothes, and books for sale.

As we turned a corner that overlooked the sea, I asked to stop briefly. I wanted to step out of the car and smell the salt air, to stand firmly on African soil, to thank God for my safe passage, to look at the Atlantic Ocean from the *other* side, and to appreciate, for a moment, the home of my ancestors—my home, land of my pilgrimage.

I stood quietly, looking out at the sea from a shoreline that nature has not altered since the *Henrietta Marie* sailed by in the late 1600s. For me, this was a familiar place. Perhaps someone related to me had stood on this same coastline.

This was, after all, the *same* ocean that had swallowed my ancestors; the *same* sand that had been trampled by slave traders; the *same* air that had filled the lungs of my forefathers; the *same* sky that African mothers and fathers had looked toward in the night, praying for a morning free of misery and a life free of chains.

In the late morning, I arrived at the hotel twenty minutes from downtown Dakar. I was tired.

"*Bonjour,*" I said, feeling very comfortable communicating in French—as long as the woman behind the counter didn't ask me any questions.

"*Bonjour,*" the woman responded, quickly switching to English. "Please fill out the registration card while I get the key for your room."

Chicka waited for me to get settled at the hotel and advised me that a guide would be coming for me promptly at eight the following morning.

"A very bright young man will pick you up tomorrow," Chicka said. "His name is Ibrahima Top. He will be in the hotel lobby at eight A.M. He is always on time. Do you know your schedule for tomorrow?"

"Yes," I said. "I'd like to visit Goree Island."

"That is no problem; I will pass that along," he said. "Rest well and I will speak with you in a few days."

I thanked him for his help and went to my room. I called my parents to let them know I had arrived in Dakar safely, then left a message on my voice mail at home for Mireille. I climbed into bed for a long nap.

The telephone rang the next morning at 7:30. I was already awake, having watched the sun rise over the Atlantic Ocean. The sea can be so therapeutic, and in the morning, when all is peaceful, the ocean has a way of calming me, giving me the strength to face any calamity the rest of the day may bring.

I answered the phone.

"Good morning. Mr. Cottman?" a voice asked.

"Yes, it is."

"This is Ibrahima Top. I hope your flight to Dakar was pleasant," he said. His voice was deep and deliberate. He spoke with a sense of authority and sincerity. I was looking forward to meeting him. "I am downstairs in the lobby, but please take your time. The ferry to Goree Island doesn't leave until ten A.M."

I got dressed, grabbed my camera, extra film, notebook, pens, and tape recorder, and took the elevator five floors down to the lobby.

Ibrahima was standing near the front door of the hotel. He was dressed in gray slacks and a striped pullover shirt.

"Mr. Cottman, it's a pleasure to meet you," he said.

"It's a pleasure to meet you also," I replied.

Ibrahima was tall and slender. He was six seven. His face was dark, his skin flawless, and his features very sharp. He carried himself with the poise of an ambassador.

He leaned over to shake my hand. "Everyone calls me Top, but if you prefer Ibrahima, that is perfectly fine," he said.

"I'll remember that," I said quickly, "if you remember to call me Michael."

"I'll try, Mr. Cottman," he said, laughing.

I knew from that moment in the lobby of the hotel, Ibrahima Top and Michael Cottman were going to get along just fine—regardless of what we decided to call each other.

But I'd settle for a simple seven-letter word: *friends*.

I climbed into the backseat of the Toyota. We pulled out of the hotel parking lot and cruised along the shoreline, winding our way downtown, through diesel-choked streets crowded with pushy merchants, businessmen, and women sitting along the sidewalk selling magnificent handcrafted jewelry.

"I want to make sure that your stay here is pleasant and productive," Ibrahima said. "Please tell me about your book. The more I know about your research, the better prepared I am to assist you."

I told him about the *Henrietta Marie,* about its travels along the west coast of Africa. Then I told him about the black scuba divers, about my dive travels and my experience with retracing the history of the ship. I recounted a personal odyssey that had started two years earlier and explained how Africa was the most spiritually significant portion of my journey, which we called "my pilgrimage."

"It is quite fascinating," he said. "I am glad you are here to tell this story."

This was my second visit to Dakar in eleven years. The first was in 1985, the first time that an all-black group of American journalists toured the country and reported on the Sahara Desert's adverse impact on Senegal's environment and its people.

Much about life in Dakar I still remembered: the beautiful people, the spicy fish and rice, the culture, and the unique rhythms of Senegalese music. Each visit, however, is special, and memorable in its own way.

My trip eleven years earlier had been a wonderful whirlwind of meetings with dignitaries, press briefings, interviews with residents, and tours from downtown Dakar to villages along the dusty road to the neighboring coastal resort of Saint-Louis.

"Come quickly," Ibrahima said now, opening the door for a fast exit. "The ferry to Goree Island gets very crowded."

I remembered those crowds from my last trip as I watched the mass of humanity swell near the ticket window. Ibrahima stood near the window, making a fast transaction with the ticket agent and sidestepping the commotion that was beginning to build around us.

With a wave of his large hand, he signaled for me to cut through the crowd. I didn't mind waiting my turn, but he assured me that if I stood patiently, we would never make the 10:00 A.M. ferry. As it was, we were the last to board.

The double-decker ferry was packed by the time we left Dakar for our twenty-five-minute crossing to Goree Island. I climbed the metal stairs to the upper deck to get some fresh air. I also wanted to get a closer look at the infamous island that stretches eight hundred meters long and three hundred meters wide.

For three centuries, an estimated 15 to 20 million African men, women, and children were crammed inside stone chambers, shackled by the necks and ankles, and routinely flogged, raped, and murdered on this island.

The sense of mass suffering is so overpowering on this weathered rock of ruthless history, so disturbing and so personal, that even grown men who visit this place have surrendered to tears.

"I have watched many African-American people come here to cry," Ibrahima said as we stood on the top deck, looking straight at Goree Island.

"They are crying because this is not a visit for trinkets, but because this is a personal pilgrimage, as it is for you, Mr. Cottman. They are crying because they feel the pain of three hundred years of black suffering; they are crying because they know that we are all the same, African people and African-American people; they are crying because they know—as do we—that the African holocaust was the most heinous crime against humanity in the history of the world, and it can never happen again."

He spoke in polite detail about the history of Goree Island, starting with a detailed account of how Goree was named by the French who claimed the island in a war with the Dutch in 1677.

At twenty-nine, Ibrahima is a diplomat by instinct and a historian by training, having earned master's degrees in history and English. He is fluent in five languages and speaks several African dialects, including Wolof, Dakar's native tongue. He is a devout Muslim, a student of black culture, a man who is focused on family.

"I wish every African-American person could have the opportunity to stand on African soil," I told Ibrahima. "We share the same history, we share the same culture, and we share the same blood. We are all brothers and sisters in spirit, and we must continue to share our sense of connection with one another as part of the stories that we tell ourselves.

"Our history has been ignored, misinterpreted, and fabricated. We must rewrite centuries of wrongs while also writing the truths of today for the children of tomorrow," I said.

Ibrahima smiled, placed his hand on my shoulder, and looked me square in the eye.

"Why are you smiling?" I asked.

"Because you are obviously here for a larger purpose and I am pleased that you have come to the motherland," he said. "Africa needs her African-American sons and daughters, brothers and sisters, mothers and fathers to share in our joy, to share in our sorrow, to write our stories, to assist us politically and economically, because we are all the same people, with many of the same social concerns. I am no different from you, and you are no different from me. We have been separated only by time."

The boat pulled up to the dock on Goree Island. It was the first ferry of the day. I could hear the waves slapping the rocks below and I could see young boys swimming in the sea, a rhythm of black arms in synchronized strokes.

A few vendors were beginning to set up their tables and display their wares. Children ran from the beach to meet the ferry and to ask strangers for coins.

I had been here before; I had already heard the brutal stories about the slave quarters and felt the gut punch of sorrow in my soul. But this pilgrimage was different. This time, I was retracing the route of a slave ship. This time, I was traveling along an uncertain path to learn more about the past—and myself.

I followed my research to Dakar because historians believe the *Henrietta Marie*—like hundreds of other slave ships—once sailed along the west coast of Africa to replenish supplies, including water, and to give the ship's carpenters time to make necessary repairs. Historians cannot say with certainly whether the *Henrietta Marie* actually took on enslaved African people from Goree Island.

Scholars do know the *Henrietta Marie* made her way along the coast of West Africa and may have anchored off Dakar en route to New Calabar—present-day Nigeria.

In *Trade Without Rulers*, David Northrup notes that New Calabar was closer to the interior markets and could provide better food supplies for the slave traders.

> *... Very few ships go as high as new Calabar town, preferring instead to anchor inside the mouth of the estuary at a place where they are less molested by mosquitoes and could draw upon slaves and supplies from New Calabar, Bonny and lesser towns.*
>
> *There was also considerable rivalry among the European nations trading in Rio Real at that time; Barbot estimated that the Dutch have the greatest share in the trade; the English next; and after then the Portugese....*

In one of his most chilling revelations, Northrup writes that 15 percent of the enslaved African people were children.

According to historian Nigel Tattersfield, "In Old Calabar River, John Barbot reported, 'The air . . . is very malignant and . . . New Calabar was much molested with the mosquitoes.'"

Tattersfield wrote:

> *John Barbot's nephew, James, supercargo aboard the* Albion Frigate, *reached Calabar in mid-June 1699, a mere five months before the* Henrietta Marie *would have anchored in the Bandy River, saluting the town with "three, five, or seven guns . . . the blacks being fond of such civilities, and it contributes much to facilitate the trade."*

"Barbot," Tattersfield wrote, "drew upon recent personal experience when he wrote of the coastal people being a 'very good civiliz'd sort of blacks any man may safely venture to trade, either for slaves, elephant teeth, or provisions.'"

Tattersfield wrote:

> *John Barbot records as being the favored currency of account in Calabar, "The blacks there reckon by copper bars, reducing all sorts of goods to such bars; for example, one bar of iron, four copper bars; a man slave for thirty-eight; and a woman slave for thirty-seven or thirty-six copper bars."*

Children as well as adults drowned in the Atlantic Ocean and in the rivers of West Africa, where innocent black people were tied and floated to waiting slave ships, according to historians.

Rivers were the primary mode of transportation for slave runners. The main rivers, like the Niger, provided a network of waterways into the interior, where slave raiders and oil traders commanded the area and navigated in their fleet of large canoes.

I once sailed along the Niger to Timbuktu, the ancient, onetime wealthy, and mysterious city that sits on the edge of the Sahara Desert, the site of Africa's first university and still home to three of the oldest mosques in West Africa. The city, whose name has become synonymous with an inaccessible place, is still hard to reach.

From the boat, sailing along the Niger, the sun high and sweltering, I could see women with babies on their backs bathing and washing clothes in the river, while older men and women carrying metal pans waded through waist-high water to sift through plants for rice.

Along the banks of the river, men sliced two-inch slabs of salt for sale at the markets and pushed off from shore in slender, worn canoes for a day of fishing, carefully keeping an eye out for the hippos that fill the waterways.

On the river, I was reminded of a story shared by an African-American minister, the Reverend Curtis Jones of Baltimore, who was approached by a little African girl who asked, "Where is your village? Who are your people?"

When Reverend Jones hesitated, the little girl asked again, "You know, where are your people from?"

The minister was dumbstruck. Rarely caught speechless, he had few answers, he told me. There was an immediate realization that because of slavery, it is nearly impossible for African-Americans to pinpoint the origin of our forefathers.

We cannot identify a country in West Africa where our individual ancestors were born, let alone a city or a tiny village. We can name only the west coast of the enormous continent.

Where do my ancestors come from? Are my people Ibo, from Nigeria; or Fulani, from Mali; or Wolof, from Senegal; or Ashanti, from Ghana? I may never know. What is important is my appreciation for my culture and my need to draw strength from ancestors who survived mind-numbing atrocities.

I wish I could identify a country in Africa where my ancestors were born. But I can only speculate that they came from countries along the west coast of Africa, where the largest slave ports existed and where trading was heavy, and so I have a connection of sorts to republics like Senegal and Ghana.

There are many African-American people who have forsaken their African heritage, preferring to concentrate on their American home, rather than try to relate to a home they never knew.

I am not African, but my spirit is. I am not planning to change my name, nor am I going to trade my suits for African robes or move my family to Africa to live permanently. But it is important for me to make my personal connection with Africa, to acknowledge my ancestors and their tremendous sacrifices.

I do embrace the richness, beauty, and brilliance of the African culture—my culture. It makes me whole; it is a part of who I am as a black man. I could no more dismiss my African heritage than I could the color of my skin. It is who I am and it is important for me to find out as much as I can about my ancestors so I can pass our rich history along to my daughter, Ariane.

Each time I visit Africa—each time I stand on the soil where my ancestors walked; each time I swim in the ocean where my forefathers jumped from slave ships; each time I stare at the stars from under the African sky—I am reminded that I am a product of kings and queens, or poets and preachers, or artists and astrologers, like the Dogon people of Mali, people of an elaborate and complex culture who, some scholars believe, were once great astronomers, having located and identified stars with the naked eye centuries ago.

I have climbed into the cliffs where the Dogon people live. I have seen the houses of mud and flat roofs supported by beams. I have seen the fine handcrafted doors and stools and statues.

I have walked through the villages, shaking hands with children, some who smiled and others who cried and trembled from sickness.

It reminded me that *my* purpose, in part, is to tell stories of my people—the stories that are ignored, the positive stories of strength, tenacity, and genius; to tell the stories that my African ancestors could not tell themselves.

I made this latest pilgrimage to Africa, and in particular to Goree Island, in part because the route of the *Henrietta Marie* led me there, but also because I needed to be reminded that there were more African people enslaved on Goree Island and at neighboring Cape Coast and Elmina than perhaps anywhere else in the world and because an estimated 6 million African people may have died on Goree Island from beatings, starvation, and suicide.

What attracts me to Africa is a calling, not a religious calling; perhaps it's a spiritual calling, which has led me to a land whose people have been overlooked by historians and who have not been properly acknowledged for their tremendous contributions to the world.

17

Nigeria presented far too many problems in 1996.

Even though historians believe the *Henrietta Marie* sailed to New Calabar in Nigeria, where her captains traded for African people, I steered clear of Nigeria and looked for other ports in West Africa where the *Henrietta Marie* may have docked or sailed near.

The decision was made for me. Nigeria was suffering from political, social, and economic instability. The infrastructure was crumbling, the currency was unstable, the University of Calabar, which was to be my base, was closed indefinitely because educators were on strike, and the airports were being closed routinely due to safety concerns.

But more important, in 1995, some of the most prominent African-American leaders, Trans-Africa president Randall Robinson, Congressman Charles Rangel, the Reverend Jesse Jackson, and Maya Angelou among them, announced a boycott of Nigeria to protest years of government-sanctioned tyranny, violence, and the murders of innocent citizens of Nigeria, corrupt law-enforcement officials, extortionists, and drug running into the United States. It was the first time in history that African-American leaders had boycotted an African country, so I decided instead to conduct my research in Senegal, where the *Henrietta Marie* sailed past and perhaps anchored during its two transatlantic voyages.

Most evidence from the cargo of the *Henrietta Marie* points to its

African port of call as being New Calabar in the delta of the Niger River. New Calabar was one of the most important ports in the region. It was especially frequented by the "Ten Percenters," whose ships were not always welcomed at the posts where the Royal African Company controlled the Gambia River and constructed forts and castles protected by soldiers where enslaved African people were warehoused while waiting to be taken to the New World.

The *Henrietta Marie* would have sailed more than ten thousand miles to complete the triangular route from England to New Calabar, then from New Calabar to the West Indies, and finally from the West Indies back to England.

A family friend, a Nigerian doctor who lives in Detroit, returned to his home in New Calabar one month before I was scheduled to travel to Nigeria and called to warn me of severe infrastructure problems, government extortion at the airport, chaotic fluctuation in currency, and hotels that were no longer acceptable.

"I would advise you to travel elsewhere in West Africa if possible," he said. "Even I encounter great difficulty, and I'm Nigerian."

I listened to my friend and decided to travel to Senegal.

Walking along the pier on Goree Island, I watched dozens of young African boys swimming fast against the rolling waves, some of them as young as seven or eight years old; others were teenagers, all of them swimming with polished style, strength, and endurance, many of them swimming more than a mile into the Atlantic before heading back to shore.

I wasn't surprised. I was impressed. They swam like champions.

"I wish I could take these young brothers back with me and sign them up for the swimming competition in the next summer Olympics," I told Ibrahima. "The myth among some in the United States is that black people can't swim."

"That is absurd," he said. "I wish you could take them also. They could use guidance, and you would have a fine team. You should spend a moment watching them if you wish. They are extremely gifted swimmers because they swim every day."

We watched the boys swim for a while and then we took a tour around Goree Island, taking the long way to the Slave House, where I was scheduled to meet with Mr. Joseph Ndiaye, the curator there since 1961, one year after Senegal obtained its independence from the French.

We strolled past precious brown boys and girls, some running down the road in diapers and screaming after being startled by the flash from my camera.

"Bonjour," I said to one little boy who smiled and ran off.

"Speaking French will get you whatever you need, but speaking Wolof will earn you the respect of Senegalese people," Ibrahima said. "French is not our language, although we speak it fluently. Wolof is *our* language; Wolof should be *your* language also while you are in Senegal. This is the language of *your* people. If we are all family, then you should speak your family's language also."

"I'd like to learn a little Wolof before I leave Senegal," I said. "When do we get started?"

"Immediately," he said without hesitation.

"When we say, 'Hello. How are you?' we say *'Nang-ga-def.'* Nang—ga—def. Okay?"

"I think so," I said. *"Nang-ga-def."*

"Good," Ibrahima said. "Now, when we respond saying, 'I'm fine, thanks,' we say, *'Mangi-fi-rek.' Mangi-fi-rek."*

"Mangi-fi-rek," I repeated several times.

"Very good," he said. "Now, when we say, 'Thank you,' we say, *'Jerry-jef.' Jerry-jef."*

"Jerry-jef," I said.

"Okay," he explained as we walked along a dusty road, "if you feel uncomfortable by an aggressive vendor, you say very firmly, *'May-ma-jam!' May-ma-jam!*—which means 'Leave me alone.'"

"This I will remember," I said. *"May-ma-jam! May-ma-jam!"* A few vendors from down the road looked at me with surprise.

"I think you're catching on." He laughed. "You are speaking Wolof."

We walked for about thirty-five minutes before stopping in front of an old brick building. There was a large sign on the front of the two-story building that was written in French: MAISON DES ESCLAVES.

The House of Slaves.

Ibrahima opened the door.

Our conversation ended very abruptly, both of us walking through the door in silence. There was a large courtyard in the House of Slaves that was surrounded by a dozen or more dark stone stockades of various sizes, shapes, and dimensions. These cells were once used for African men and African women. They were all dark, all disturbing.

I walked along the dusty ground and followed Ibrahima to the center of the courtyard. I didn't want to take a closer look into the cells. Not yet, anyway.

"We don't have the monopoly of commerce or the monopoly of communication to explain our holocaust. So African-Americans who come back to Africa, to see how their ancestors suffered, take the stories back with them," he said.

"The best way for African-Americans to know who they are is to come back to Africa. We must not forget our past."

I pulled a notepad from my back pocket to scribble down a few thoughts and glanced at a three-word notation I'd made for myself in New York.

It read simply: "Rock for Hank."

Hank Jennings, my friend and dive buddy, had asked me for a favor before I left for Dakar. He called me one evening a few days before I was scheduled to leave for Africa.

"Mike, what's up?" he said in his trademark upbeat manner.

"Just reading and getting ready to pack my dive gear for the trip," I said.

"I wish I could make this trip with you, brother," Hank said. "I've never been to Africa, so I want you to bring me something back."

"Name it," I said. "What would you like?"

"When you get to Goree Island, Mike, just look on the ground and pick up the first rock you see. Pick it up, take it back to the hotel, and pack it somewhere safe. I just want a rock. I want a piece of the earth from the motherland, I want a piece of the ground where my ancestors walked. I want something that will always be a part of Africa and something that will always be a part of me. That's all I want. Just a rock."

"I wish you were going with me, too, brother. I'll get a rock for you. We all need something from *our* continent that we can hold, that we can touch and call our own; something that will link us with our ancestors and stay with us forever. Some of us will never get that chance. You'll travel to Africa one day, but until that day comes, I'll bring you back a rock."

As I looked on the ground for an appropriate rock to take back to Hank, I was distracted by the sound of clanging chains. A German television crew was filming a documentary about the slave trade inside one of the concrete cells. There were several black actors, men and women, stretched across the floor, covered in chains, with red makeup smeared over their bodies. I stared at them for a few minutes, disturbed by the graphic scenes that were being filmed as German directors were instructing the actors to cower and cry.

I couldn't help noticing the absence of black people *behind* the camera—no black assistant directors, no black cameramen, no black technicians, just black people playing the role of slaves.

I turned away as Ibrahima signaled for me to step into a small downstairs office. Inside, stacks of papers filled the top of a wooden desk and letters from prominent African-Americans who have visited Goree Island were thumbtacked to the wall: handwritten notes from Danny Glover, Harry Belafonte, Angela Davis, and the late Ron Brown, and a photo of Stevie Wonder.

A dark-skinned man about five eight with a weathered but thoughtful face stood up from behind the desk and walked toward me. He wore a blue cap and large dark sunglasses that shielded his face from the already-oppressive morning sun.

"Mr. Cottman, this is Mr. Joseph Ndiaye," Ibrahima said.

He took his time giving me the once-over, then shook my hand with a firm grip, the kind of handshake my father said could tell you a lot about a man's character.

"I never trusted men who don't look you in the eye when they're talking to you and who don't shake your hand firmly," he once told me. "You shouldn't, either."

His handshake was followed by a polite and warm welcome to Africa, to Goree Island, and to his modest office of many years.

"It is a pleasure to meet you," Mr. Ndiaye said with a comforting smile. "You are at home here."

"It is a pleasure to meet you also," I said, with Ibrahima quickly translating my response. "And thank you. I feel very much at home."

I looked outside his office and saw a group forming in the court-yard. They were French tourists waiting for the daily guided tour by Mr. Ndiaye. He asked me to join the thirty-minute tour and said that after-ward, or the following morning, we could have quiet time to talk. He said he would arrange for tours in the afternoon to allow us to spend part of the day touring the Slave House alone.

"Good morning and welcome to Goree Island," he said in flawless French to the twenty-five tourists. "If you would please follow me, we will begin the tour."

He started the tour with history: Goree Island, during the 1500s to 1700s, was the most important commercial destination in West Africa. The Slave House was built in 1526, the only original slave house left on the island. The largest room was for men, he explained to the group. They would be weighed when they first arrived and forced to eat if it was felt they were underweight.

The rooms, with barely enough fresh air for one man, would hold up to twenty-five men for as long as three months.

The Africans were naked when they arrived on Goree Island, he told the group, and stripped of their identity, given new names by their Euro-pean oppressors—names they could not pronounce and didn't under-stand.

They were packed next to one another, with chains around their necks and legs. They were allowed to leave the cells only once a day to relieve themselves. They were fed once a day, and because there was little fresh-water on the island, many African people died from lack of water.

"They were treated like animals," he said.

I decided to take my own personal tour the following day, leaving the French tourists to learn more about our history.

I walked upstairs to the second floor, a place that once served as office space for merchants who casually conducted their routine business trans-actions, oblivious to the horror that was happening on the ground floor.

Mr. Ndiaye was standing in the back doorway of the Slave House, a doorway that faced the ocean. He was telling the French tourists the sig-nificance of "the Door of No Return."

When ships docked just off the rear of the Slave House, African men, women, and children walked through the door and climbed aboard ships bound for the West Indies, never to see their homeland, never to visit Africa, never to see their families again. Some threw themselves into the sea and were savaged by sharks, rather than face a lifetime in bondage.

"We call this door 'the Door of No Return,'" Mr. Ndiaye said, pointing out into the sea, "because African people never returned."

He paused for a moment, shook his head, and pointed to me. He spoke for a minute or two in French. The tourists clapped, turned to look at me, and smiled warmly. I didn't understand what he had told them. Ibrahima translated his words.

"I must apologize," Mr. Ndiaye told the French group. "For years, I have referred to this doorway as 'the Door of No Return,' because African people did not return to their homes after walking through this door.

"But today, there is a young man, a writer, an African-American, standing behind you who has returned home to Africa. He has returned home to write the story of his ancestors; he has returned home because his roots are in Africa. He and I are cousins; we share the same culture, the same civilization and blood.

"He has returned to Africa to reclaim his heritage and connect with his African family. And because this African-American writer has returned home to us, I can no longer call this doorway 'the Door of No Return.'"

He smiled at me and continued on with his tour, the French tourists stopping to offer friendly nods as they walked passed me, almost in tribute to our rich heritage and distinguished traditions.

Inside the Slave House, I felt a rare power that comes with a tremendous sense of pride. I ran my hand over my face, wiping water from my eyes. I put on my sunglasses, then stepped away from the crowd and into an empty corner of shade.

I stood for a moment watching this seventy-four-year-old curator with the quick mind, his words provoking thought each time he opened his mouth; the man who seemed to relish telling me that fifty-five is the mandatory retirement age for government employees in Dakar.

Ibrahima and I walked out of the Slave House and down the dusty road to the ferry. It was a quiet walk. Ibrahima sensed that I wanted some peaceful time, so he didn't talk at all for a little while.

I was walking and thinking about the African men and women who watched through agony and tears as their children and family members were hauled onto different ships, through the Door of No Return, never knowing what would become of their families, wondering silently whether they would live long lives, wondering whether they would ever be freed.

We returned to Dakar on the last ferry. I watched dozens of young boys dive from the top deck of the ferry and swim two miles back to Goree Island.

"We will return to Goree Island tomorrow, Michael?" Ibrahima asked.

"Yes," I said. "As early as possible."

"I will see you in the lobby at eight A.M.," he said. "Mr. Ndiaye will be expecting you. He has arranged for you to have all the time you need at the Slave House without interruption."

I returned to my hotel, then took my notebook, pen, and CD player to the pool. There were thoughts that I wanted to get down on paper. It was about 5:00 P.M., the end of the day, and the pool area was nearly empty.

I ordered a Flag, the national beer of Senegal, and was preparing to slip a Miles Davis CD into my portable player when a man wearing shorts and a polo shirt approached me.

"How are ya?" the man asked in a thick drawl that sounded textbook Texan.

"I *was* doing fine," I said, pulling out my headset and trying to send a signal that I was not expecting, or planning to receive, company.

"I noticed you were writing the other day," he said.

"Yes, I was," I said dryly.

"I'm from Houston. I'm a consultant for Shell and I'm looking for oil," he said. "They've spent a shitload of money and we ain't found oil yet. I'll probably be packing up in a day or so. What kind of work are you in?"

I'd known it was only a matter of time before he'd get around to the occupation question. I had seen it coming all the way from the corral.

"I'm an author," I told the gentleman from Houston.

"Hey, honey, he's an author," he said, shouting to his wife. "Have I read anything you wrote?"

"I doubt it," I said. "Heard of the Million Man March?" I asked.

"Oh yeah," he said with a hint of disdain. "I've heard of it."

"Well, I wrote a book about it," I explained.

"That's real good," he said, quickly changing the subject. "Working on a book now?"

"Yes, I am," I said. "It's about a sunken slave ship that was discovered in Florida." Another topic I figured would have him running to the nearest oil well.

"Oh...slavery," he said, sounding like an authority on the subject. "Well, I'll tell ya, I hope you're going to tell the truth in your book. I hope you're gonna say that your people sold your own people into slavery and that it wasn't just white people who did it. You all did it to yourselves, too, you know."

He was right, but I wasn't in the mood for lecture about the slave trade from a white man from Texas. Not today.

I had just returned from a somewhat haunting yet spiritually uplifting afternoon on Goree Island with Ibrahima and Mr. Ndiaye, a day that was nearly spoiled by a white man who was not only telling me how to write my book but also telling me how to write a book about *black* people.

Perhaps I was also angry because privately I conceded the point that some African chiefs took part in the slave trade and bargained their own people into bondage, but I wasn't in the mood for historical insight from a stranger whom I suspected was about as interested in preserving our history as Jesse Helms.

Every story needs perspective. Slavery was a widely used form of labor in Africa before the arrival of the Europeans. But African slavery differed dramatically from New World slavery because the enslaved people, who were usually prisoners of war, lived out their days within a culture similar to their own. Moreover, a person who was enslaved could eventually buy or work themselves out of slavery.

Some scholars believe that African chiefs were often duped into selling their people into slavery, believing the practice of slavery in the New World was similar to their own customs, unaware of the brutality and atrocities their people would endure.

Most of the slaves sold to Europeans were acquired through wars and raids among African tribes, according to historians. European slave traders encouraged wars through the sale of guns and gunpowder.

A slave-ship captain once wrote: "I verily believe that the far greater part of the wars in Africa would cease, if Europeans would cease to tempt them with goods for slaves."

It is through encounters with people like the gentleman from Houston that I realize how important it is for us, as African-Americans, to tell our own stories.

"I'll make a deal with you," I told the gentleman as I took a long swig from a tall bottle.

"Yeah?" he responded, trying to anticipate my next sentence.

"I won't tell you how to drill for oil if you don't tell me how to write a book about my own people. How does that sound to you?"

"Well, uh, sure," he said, looking a bit on the red side and walking away.

I sipped my beer, jotted down some notes, and listened to Miles Davis while watching the sun drop slowly out of the sky.

18

Morning came quickly.

The brilliant sun broke through a twelve-inch space in the curtains and woke me up shortly after 7:30 A.M. I was running late. I showered, grabbed a pen and notepad, and rushed downstairs to the lobby.

It was 8:10—not bad—and Ibrahima was waiting patiently in the lobby.

"Nang-ga-def," I said with a smile.

"Mangi-fi-rek," he said, sporting a smile wider than mine. *"Nang-ga-def."*

"Mangi-fi-rek," I responded.

"Very good!" he said. "You are becoming more Senegalese every day!"

We drove back downtown and parked near the ferry. We told Mr. Som that we planned to spend the day at Goree Island.

"I will see you this evening," Mr. Som told me.

"Jerry-jef," I said.

He chuckled, nodded his approval, and waved as he drove off.

We boarded the ferry for Goree Island. The crowd was as large as the day before and the heat seemed more intense. As we relaxed on the top deck of the ferry once again, I pulled a book from a yellow folder and handed it to Ibrahima.

It was a copy of my first book, *The Million Man March*.

He stared at the book for a moment, flipped through it briefly, and then closed it to read the name of the author on the cover.

"*You* wrote this book, the book about the Million Man March?" he shouted, his long arm wrapped around my shoulder.

"Yes, the first book to be written about it," I said.

"This march will be remembered as one of the most historically significant events in the history of the world for black people—and America," he said.

I was aware that Mr. Ndiaye had attended the Million Man March, although I did miss his early-morning speech, which was translated for the massive crowd.

The ferry was pulling up to the dock again and we walked down the stairs and onto Goree Island. This time, there were no detours; we walked directly to the Slave House.

It was quiet inside as we walked through the large doors. Mr. Ndiaye was waiting for me inside his office. It was empty and peaceful, just as he'd promised.

"Come in and sit down," Mr. Ndiaye said in French. "I've been expecting you."

He had just hung up when Ibrahima spoke to him in French. Hearing Ibrahima's news, Mr. Ndiaye stood up from behind his desk, smiling. He clapped his hands, politely excused himself, and hurried off for a few minutes.

"What was that all about?" I asked.

"I told Mr. Ndiaye about your book," Ibrahima said. "And he is very excited about your book and your pilgrimage to Africa. He said that he will return in a moment."

A few minutes later, Mr. Ndiaye returned wearing a Million Man March T-shirt with an aerial photograph of a sea of black men on the front and a white baseball cap that read MILLION MAN MARCH in bold black letters.

He was beaming.

"You have a mission in life to write about *your* ancestors, to tell the truth and correct stories about Africa that have been falsified over the years," Mr. Ndiaye told me that day in his office.

"Africa is a continent in transition," he said. "It was strip-mined of many of its resources during colonization, which left it economically bare. The United States has always placed a greater economic priority on the well-being of European and Middle Eastern nations, and by comparison, it has done little to help improve the economic and social conditions in Africa, barely acknowledging that Africa exists, despite constant pressure from African-American leaders.

"You must tell the world the truth about how whites consider Africa to be underdeveloped—and it is—but let's talk honestly about why it is so underdeveloped.

"It is because white Europeans came to Africa and enslaved African people; Europeans took the best of what Africa had to offer, stripped us of our strongest people, depleted our resources, disrupted our civilization, and separated us from our families," he said, his voice stronger and more deliberate.

"Our holocaust was the biggest crime against humanity. They can continue to call us an underdeveloped continent. The reasons that Africa is underdeveloped are very clear to us and should be clear to anyone who reviews history honestly."

He was taking deep breaths. His words were powerful yet measured, and they seemed to cloak any anger. There was a tone of authority in Mr. Ndiaye's voice, a hint of outrage, and a sense of hope. He is a man who understands history and his place in it. His words are passionate and spiritual, even as harsh realities stare him in the face each morning when he arrives for work.

We talked for nearly two hours. I could tell he had calls to return and I was planning to tour the Slave House alone.

"I'd like to share something with you before you go outside," Mr. Ndiaye said.

"I grew up in this house. This was a slave house like many others" he said, pointing to the courtyard area. "I lived here from the age of nine until I was fourteen. My mother and father lived upstairs and I lived downstairs. Downstairs was very dark. I used to run because I was afraid of the dark. Today, this house is still a symbol of the atrocities that black people endured."

I stepped out of his office and into the courtyard. All around me were the dark, tight concrete cells, some larger than others, but each of them with just slits of sunlight being cast along the dirt floor from the slender window that faced the sea.

I turned into one of the larger rooms, the room reserved for men, and stood on the dirt floor, staring through a small window where there was hardly enough air for one person, let alone twenty to thirty people all gasping for what little air was available.

I noticed numbers that were scrawled on a board that hung from the wall. It was a chart where slave runners had listed the height and weight of African men like horses at an auction.

Why shouldn't I be outraged? Why shouldn't I still be angry?

I could hear the wind ripping through the window and images of black people being packed inside these dust-choked rooms filled my head. It was almost inconceivable that human beings could have been treated with such cruelty and heartless disregard for human life simply because they were black.

I stared down into a five-foot-high, five-foot-wide pit where black men who resisted their brutal incarceration were flogged and held for days at a time without food, water, or sunlight.

In the very back of the dark, tight hole with no windows and dusty air was a rock half the size of a compact disc. I crouched down, my knees cracking, and inched my way slowly to the back wall of the small holding cell, trying to avoid hitting my head on the low ceiling.

I reached down and picked up the rock. I held it in my hand, blew off some of the dirt, and, before stuffing it into my pocket, wrapped it in the piece of paper from my notebook that read "Hank's Rock."

It was quiet in the Slave House. There were no tourists, no one taking photos, and no tour groups asking questions about the past. There was only me—and the spirits of millions of African people who in this hell-hole suffered agonies that I couldn't even begin to imagine.

I was drenched with sweat and I was having trouble breathing. I told myself it was my allergies, but clearly it was something different, this rush of emotion, this overpowering feeling of isolation. My chest tightened and my eyes were tearing. I couldn't blame it on the dust.

This was a place of mass sufferings and tormented souls.

Goree Island is a place where some claim to have heard the cries of a multitude of African souls. I sat alone in a cell where the atrocities against African people were incomprehensible, where murder had been routine, where human life had been traded for a pouch of silver shillings.

In the bowels of this shadowed pit with only time and silence around me, I bowed my head and prayed for the souls of millions of black people who were robbed of everything they knew, even something as personal, and as basic, as their names. I rubbed my hands over the gray walls that confined African people who yearned for freedom. I could hear the cries of at least one African soul: the African soul inside of me.

The walls were closing in on me. I backed out of the dark pit; there was not much room to turn around. I wiped the sweat from my face and took a deep breath of fresh air. I had been inside the cramped, windowless cell for only twenty minutes and I was ready to get out. My forefathers had endured this hell for a week at a time, maybe more.

After three centuries of this kind of oppression, it's a testament to our inner strength, resolve, and will to live that black people have survived at all, that we are successful, that our families are spiritually whole, and that although we still have to use emotional energy to beat back racism, we still excel in the workplace.

I looked out at the Atlantic ocean and there, again, were young black boys swimming hard against the waves. I thought of my mother, who taught me to swim at the YWCA in Detroit when I was a child not much older than the African boys swimming nearby.

I would watch her cover her curly black hair with a pink rubber bathing cap and swim laps in the pool like an Olympian. One day when I was eight years old, playing on the side, she told me to let go and swim across. I couldn't believe my mother was ordering me to sink.

That I was reluctant is an understatement. I was scared as hell.

But as I looked into her eyes, I saw a calm instructor who believed in me. I trusted her. And after a few minutes, I pushed off from the edge of the pool and kicked and kicked with little legs, moving my small frame through the water as if she were holding me up from below.

I reached the other side, giggling uncontrollably because I had achieved my first real sense of accomplishment—and adventure—all because I had trusted my mother, and myself. Her warm hug from that proud moment has lasted a lifetime.

I am reminded of that first accomplishment in water with my mother each time I dive.

I took those thoughts with me to Africa, where I prepared for my first underwater experience on the continent of my ancestors.

I had done my homework before leaving home. Dr. Jones had put me in touch with a dive operation in Dakar called Oceanarium de Dakar. The owner was Haidar El Ali. Dr. Jones had traveled to Dakar twice before and had used Haidar's operation both times. He assured me that Oceanarium was a reputable operation and that I would be in for pleasant, safe diving.

"Just remember," Dr. Jones said, "Haidar's boat is not a luxury liner; it's an old fishing boat that happens to take divers out to sea. It's the old roll off the back, no tank rack type. You know what I'm talking about; you've done it before."

Indeed I had. It didn't mean I had to like it.

A month before I was to leave for Africa, I received a fax from Dakar. It was from Haidar, who outlined the types of dives he offers, along with a price list. It seemed like a nice note and I appreciated his professionalism, but there was one problem: The fax was in French.

I called Doc immediately.

"Doc, it's Cottman."

"Hey, buddy," he said. "What's going on?"

"I got a fax from Haidar, but I can't read it," I told him. "It's in French. Does Haidar speak English? Does anyone in his operation speak English?"

"Oh," Doc said, sounding as if he was preparing to deliver a eulogy. "Didn't I tell you?"

"Tell me what?" I asked.

"Haidar is a very nice guy and one hell of a diver, hell of a diver, wonderful personality and works hard, works like a Trojan. But his English is a little rusty."

"How rusty?" I asked, already knowing the answer.

"Well, you might want to bone up on a little French," Doc suggested.

I had dealt with the language barrier on a dive before. In 1993, Mireille and I traveled to France and I decided to dive in St. Tropez. There were forty people on board for two dives that morning and no one spoke English. And, of course, my French was rusty.

There was lots of pointing and plenty of bad English and bad French to go around, but divers have a way of communicating with a universal nonverbal language. Now I called my hotel in Dakar and asked the manager to phone Haidar and to tell him of my plans. I planned to charter his boat for a day or two. I didn't just want to dive; I wanted to dive Goree Island—beneath it, around it, next to it, and I didn't want to dive with a crowd.

I also knew that Goree Island was not listed as the typical underwater dive site for out-of-town divers. But I wasn't going to leave Africa without diving Goree Island. It was as much symbolic for me as it was archaeological.

I was to meet Haidar at 9:00 A.M. the next morning.

I arrived at the dive shop an hour early. It was a forty-five-minute drive from my hotel to Oceanarium and we didn't want to be late. I was somewhat anxious about my first dive in Africa, as I was planning to celebrate this, my two hundredth career dive, in the motherland.

Haidar's shop was just as Doc had described it: small, rustic, with a long table near the edge of a series of steps that led to the dock. The dive shop was a peeling one-story building that resembled a warehouse. Everyone was friendly.

Ibrahima glanced at his watch and told me that he would return at 4:00 P.M., which gave me about seven hours with Haidar. Still, he said, he would stay until Haidar arrived.

"Is that the boat you will be diving on?" Ibrahima asked, pointing out to sea.

"Looks like it," I said.

Anchored just offshore, about one hundred yards from the dive shop, was a wooden boat about twenty feet long. The blue and yellow paint was peeling and the four-step ladder was rusted. It looked as if it had weathered many storms.

"Is this boat suitable for diving? Do you normally dive on boats this small?" Ibrahima asked reluctantly.

"Yes, it is, and I try not to make a habit of it," I said.

There were several Senegalese men standing near the compressor, filling tanks with air, hauling gear from the storage room, and loading the cooler with Cokes.

We waited awhile, looking out at an island that, I realized after a few minutes, was actually Goree Island. I didn't know that Oceanarium was so close to it. Dr. Jones had told me that Haidar could get to Goree Island in about fifteen minutes, and he was absolutely right.

"Bonjour!" a voice shouted from the top of the steps. *"Bonjour!"*

A stocky man, a bit on the short side, with a mop of blondish gray hair, came bounding down the steps. He wore a beat-up baseball cap, a faded T-shirt, baggy shorts, and a wide smile.

His tanned, muscular arms looked as though he worked out, but the cases of beer stacked against the wall of the dive shop gave him away. His hands were stubby and rugged, the kind of hands that have pulled up many anchor lines bare-handed.

"Hello, I'm Haidar. You must be Michael," he said, extending his right hand.

"I'm a little early," I told him.

"No problem. It's good to meet you. Where would you like to dive?" he said in broken English.

"I'd like to dive Goree Island," I said. "I'd like to charter your boat for a day."

He nodded. A friend and co-owner of the dive shop spoke clearer English than Haidar and tried to translate our conversation.

But Haidar had a better plan. He took a stick and drew a circle in the dirt, then an X as he pointed to Goree Island in the distance. He stood up, pointed to the building, and returned moments later with a pen and a large sheet of white paper. He placed the paper across the table and drew a makeshift map of the island, then pointed to the real island about half a mile east.

"You see?" he asked.

"I see."

He scribbled a few dots around "good diving" near Goree Island, most of them somewhat farther away than I wanted to be. I wanted to get as close to Goree as possible.

"Can we anchor near the Door of No Return at the Slave House?" I asked.

"The Slave House?" he asked. He was clearly stunned.

"Door of No Return? You dive there? Not good diving," he advised.

We shared an understanding of what good diving is all about: clear water, plenty of fish, and exotic marine life. But he didn't quite understand my desire to dive a site where the *Henrietta Marie* might have sailed, a place where thousands of ships docked, a place where untold numbers of black people lost their lives in the sea.

I borrowed his pen and drew a dot near where I thought the Slave House was located. He was able to communicate to me that authorities frowned on docking too close to the Slave House, but he said that he was willing to accommodate me in any way he could.

"You are the customer," he said with a smile.

We spent the next half hour negotiating the price for a private all-day three-dive trip that would also include a videotape of the diving and still photographs from the sites. I agreed to pay three hundred dollars in cash.

Haidar motioned for me to collect my gear and select a tank for the dive. I wasn't sure whether my regulators would fit on the European-style tanks that Oceanarium stocked. I pulled out my gear, and one of the employees, a tall, dark man with sharp facial features, said, "Ah, you need American tanks!"

I was ready to dive.

It was a brilliant day, sunny, no clouds, a light breeze. I grabbed a tank, hooked up my regulator, and checked the air pressure. Plenty of air. A tall, dark Senegalese man helped me with my equipment, walked down the twenty steps to the shore, and loaded the gear into the boat.

The small wooden boat was anchored in about three feet of water. I used the wobbly ladder to try to climb aboard, but I ended up throwing myself over the side and into the boat.

Haidar pulled up the anchor and gave the signal for one of his mates to fire up the single outboard engine and head to Goree Island. It was 9:45 A.M.

"We'll be there in fifteen minutes," Haidar said. "I will say when to get ready."

Haidar's wooden boat skipped over the whitecapped waves as I was reminded of the horrific journey that my ancestors were subjected to on these same seas.

We anchored just offshore, about twenty-five yards from Goree Island. Haidar tossed the rusted anchor over the side of the boat and yanked hard on the line, making sure that we were secured over the site.

"Close enough?" Haidar asked.

"This is fine," I said. I turned around to a view of the Door of No Return from the position in the sea from which African people must have seen the Slave House. It was a perspective that I had not seen before.

"You can get ready now," he said, taking some time to load his cameras and check the visibility and the direction of the current.

I reached for my mask and fins. I felt strange. My mouth was dry, and I was anxious. This is only a thirty-foot dive, I thought to myself. I've been to 120 feet, surrounded by sharks, and didn't feel this edgy.

I slipped six pounds of lead around my waist and put on my fins; then I rinsed my mask as one of Haidar's assistants helped me into my BC jacket and double-checked my supply of air.

It was 10:17 A.M. There was a slight current and there were no other divers around. This site was not on the list of Haidar's underwater tours and he seemed to be perplexed by my interest in this particular area. Still, like any good businessman, Haidar believes the request of the customer comes first, and service always comes with a smile.

"Whenever you are ready," Haidar said, rolling off the back of the boat. The water was cloudy, the visibility about twenty-five feet; I had seen worse.

I switched my computer to dive mode and rolled off the back of the boat into the warm Atlantic waters. Floating just above the surface, I could see the Slave House, and the edge of the Door of No Return.

It was an eerie moment floating in front of the Slave House, swimming in the same seas where sharks once waited for the hard splashes of black bodies. It was disturbing to look into the archway of the Door of No Return, through which so many black people, so many of my ancestors, had been herded like cattle. It was a peculiar moment, where everything was quiet as I looked around me, wondering how many African people had been victims of this same sea.

I sank below the surface and drifted close to the ocean floor. Haidar was waiting for me, but I could barely see him through the silt. I moved alongside him and pointed west, heading toward the Slave House.

Underwater was a blur of marine life. Spotted stingrays buried in the sand were everywhere; I lost count after the first dozen. Rugged rockfish inched their way along the ocean bottom, leaving squiggly trails in the sand, while a few feet away, a baby octopus was twisting its tentacles inside a half-cracked glass bottle.

I hovered in twenty-five feet of water, flying in midair and looking down on a rusted rifle butt wedged in the sand and wondering if it was a weapon from a slave ship.

I released what air I had left in my BC jacket and sank gently to the ocean floor, my depth gauge flashing 30 FEET on the bottom. I could see Haidar adjusting his camera equipment. I shifted steadily with the currents, moving slowly through the water, my heart pounding harder than usual for a shallow dive with a light current.

There was no one around me. Haidar was nearby photographing nature, but there was an unexplained presence that was pulling me.

My chest pressed against the ocean floor, I moved along with the current, my eyes shut tightly, running my hands through the tiny grains of sand that had covered so many of my ancestors, feeling the same ripples of water that had engulfed African people.

There was something special about these waters off Goree Island, something warm that was guiding me like an internal compass through the ocean, directing me to underwater crevices and peaceful places.

I allowed myself to drift with the currents, my eyes still closed, my hands filled with tiny shells while sand flowed fast through my fingers. And then I stopped. I rested in the still of the sea.

Kneeling on a sandy patch, I bowed my head and prayed where the spotted stingrays lived.

I thanked God for our survival and success as a race of proud and distinguished people; I gave thanks for our global contributions of the past and for our achievements in the future; I prayed for the souls of African people who are trying to find their way, just as I was being guided through the Goree Island waters—and through life.

I didn't have to come all the way to Africa to pray, but on this day I felt compelled to reach out to a force larger than myself, because I felt a force was reaching out for me.

I checked my depth gauge. I had been underwater drifting, thinking, and in some way communicating for sixty-four minutes; my two hundredth dive logged in waters that were new to me, yet strangely familiar.

For a moment, I thought I heard someone calling, but I was alone, surrounded by silt and a tiny trail of bubbles. Perhaps I was listening to the muffled sighs of souls that were much farther away than Haidar— sighs that I had heard before in Atlantic waters six thousand miles away, tired sighs that seemed to echo from the tortured wreckage of the slave ship *Henrietta Marie*.

They were inner sounds that brought peace to my wandering soul where, in thirty feet of ocean, I kept my eyes closed for a few last minutes, floating silently, with no heading in mind, and yet somehow I returned directly under Haidar's boat.

I smiled, thinking this was a great coincidence. Who could say for sure? The only true barometer was the feeling within me. It was a sense of inner peace—a calm: no anxiety, no stress, a sense of comfort with my technical and spiritual direction.

I was feeling some release of the anger that had been building within me since I sat inside the slave quarters just a few yards away. With baby steps, I was slowly beginning to appreciate more the resilience and brilliance of African people, how their pain had been turned into my strength, how their suffering had turned into my passion for our culture and history. From the sea, I looked at the Door of No Return, and in my mind I saw a community of distinguished black faces instead of bruised arms and legs bound by chains.

Perhaps this was the emotional purification I needed to move along in life: an underwater catharsis in seas where my ancestry began, a long history with oceans that has become part of me.

One thing was clear: This was no ordinary underwater experience; it was no ordinary dive. I suppose it was never intended to be.

19

Little Senegalese girls dressed in bright pink skirts and little boys wearing thin ties over white-collared shirts stood on tiptoes at the ocean's edge to watch history unfold.

They were watching a white man with silver hair, America's charismatic and controversial leader, offer his hand in friendship to the people of Africa. They were watching Bill Clinton, the first United States president to step onto sub-Saharan African soil; the first United States president to tour a onetime West African slave port; the first United States president to stand on Goree Island and speak of the pain of slavery.

I was watching, too.

"We cannot push time backward through the Door of No Return; we have lived our history," President Clinton told a gathering of American and Senegalese dignitaries and dozens of Goree Island residents who waved tiny American flags.

"America's struggle to overcome slavery and its legacy forms one of the most difficult chapters of that history. Yet it is also one of the most heroic, a triumph of courage and persistence and dignity.

"Goree Island is as much a part of our history as a part of Africa's history. From Goree and other places, Africa's sons and daughters were taken through 'the Door of No Return,' never to see their friends and families again.

"Those who survived the murderous Middle Passage emerged from a dark hold to find themselves, yes, Americans. But it would be a long, long time before their descendants enjoyed the full meaning of that word. The long journey of African-Americans proves that the spirit can never be enslaved," the president said under a cloudless sky as the waves slapped the shore where the journey began.

Clinton's visit to Senegal in early April of 1998 was the last stop on a historic six-nation, twelve-day tour of sub-Saharan Africa, a journey designed to highlight the political progress the continent has made and the economic promise it holds for investors.

And although the president did not formally apologize for the atrocities of the slave trade, as some critics have argued he should do, he did apologize for America's history of limited financial support for Africa and its reluctance to assist—or even acknowledge—the continent. In Uganda, Clinton admitted that the United States "has not always done the right thing by Africa."

The president sought to highlight Africa's positive sides—the rich culture, its art and music, its brilliant scholars and writers of literature, from novels to poetry. But he also noted often that he hopes that political and economic reform in Africa will increase American trade and investment opportunities.

After peering from a narrow passageway overlooking the Atlantic Ocean, where African men, women, and children were taken in leg irons from Goree Island and loaded onto slave ships anchored off the coast, Clinton, with his wife, Hillary, at his side, expressed remorse for centuries of black suffering and acknowledged Africa's rich contributions to the United States.

Less than two miles from the busy modern city of Dakar, Goree Island is a place apart, a disturbing remnant of the slave trade.

Goree Island is an empowering place for African-Americans; it always has been, perhaps it always will be.

There is an extraordinary energy on Goree Island that compels black people to take a journey through time, to cry, to release themselves to the calling from within, to give in to a hidden yet overwhelming power, to do the unconventional.

It was the power of Goree Island that compelled a group of African-

American journalists to stand side by side outside the Door of No Return, to bow their heads and bless a bottle of water before pouring it over stacks of rocks at the edge of the ocean to commemorate their ancestors.

For the four African-American White House correspondents covering Clinton's visit to Africa, their self-initiated ten-minute service signaled a retreat from traditional journalism's coverage of an international political event.

We often take ourselves out of the equation, covering stories without emotion, void of any passion or sensitivity or sense of collective involvement. We are usually detached and far removed from any public sentiment. We're just recorders of facts, scribes in the back of the room, in it but not of it.

But perhaps sometimes we should stop and think.

Perhaps as black journalists, we should let down our stoic shields every now and again and explore the essence of our surroundings; pause to embrace our history and our place in it; break for a moment to understand the significance of our work as we write about our own culture and heritage.

Perhaps as we write and report and gather facts, we should stop, every so often, to think about how a particular story affects our lives, how the stories we cover will affect the lives of those who will read our words and study our historical analysis.

Perhaps we all should take ten minutes out of our schedules, as these White House writers did in Africa, and remember that we are people with a rich past, descendants of people who made valuable contributions to the United States, even as we continue today to contribute to this republic ourselves.

"Goree Island is such a significant place," said Bill Douglas, a White House correspondent for *Newsday,* who was part of the Goree Island prayer service.

"I'm not sure where my family came from, but I know this place holds our incredible history. Our ceremony just seemed like the appropriate thing to do, and the Door of No Return was the appropriate place to do it. We were very moved, and one reporter in particular was moved to tears."

As an African-American writer who understood the purpose—and the need—to connect with our past in a rather personal way, I stood on the shores of Goree Island listening to the president's words and wondering if this symbolic trip with its heartfelt language would ever transcend into the much-needed financial resources that Africa desperately requires for education, health care, and infrastructure.

As gratified as I was to stand steps away from where President Clinton was speaking to the people of Africa, I was skeptical about whether United States legislators would actually embrace the needs of the beautiful black children who were seated around me.

"The many faces that Hillary and I have seen...I have seen in them beauty and intelligence, energy and spirit and the determination to prevail. I have seen the faces of Africa's future," Clinton said. "I will always remember the faces of the little children, the light in their eyes, the smiles on their faces. We owe it to them, you and I, to give them the best possible future they can have.

"The people and the leaders of Africa are showing the world the resiliency of the human spirit and the future of this great country," he continued. "They have convinced me of the difference America can make if we are a genuine partner and friend to Africa, and the difference Africa can make to America's future.

"I am very proud of America's ties to Africa," President Clinton said. "There is no area of America achievement that has not been touched by the intelligence and energy of Africa, from science, to medicine, to literature, to art and music....We will reach over this ocean to build a new partnership based on friendship and respect."

That President Clinton visited Africa and talked of slavery, the pain that it has caused even today, was the subject of numerous newspaper articles and editorials, television and radio stories, and magazine features.

It was the first time I could remember that so many stories about Africa not associated with famine, violence, or political unrest appeared in so many news reports.

The mere fact Clinton visited Africa heightened the discussion about America's relationship to Africa and shined a bright light on America's benign neglect.

But it was the issue of slavery that Clinton evoked that made some people cringe. Some black people urged Clinton to apologize for slavery, while some white conservatives and columnists criticized the president for even entertaining the notion and suggested the entire discussion is meaningless.

The United States doesn't need empty apologies for slavery, and it does not disturb me that President Clinton does not want to issue a formal apology. What the country does need is to acknowledge this underresearched, underreported, and underdiscussed part of world history. America needs an education.

"There are United States congressmen who still ask me what the capitol of Africa is," Mamadou Monsour Seck, Senegal's ambassador to the United States, told me in Dakar.

Slavery is a disturbing subject. Some whites still harbor some vague sense of guilt for the slave trade; others do not want to be strong-armed into discussing the issue. Some black people feel ashamed and would prefer not discussing the fact that we were once enslaved, while still others argue that we should not be sidetracked by past horrors when we have many more pressing issues in the United States.

The mere idea of Clinton considering making an apology for slavery brought out the worst in America, from radio call-in programs to newspaper columnists whose visceral reactions amounted to an arrogant dismissal of the very notion that Africa could have contributed anything to Western development.

The debate over whether Clinton should or should not apologize for slavery raises the basic question of whether the United States is interested in becoming racially tolerant and concerned with learning about the history of others while acknowledging that the world is changing demographically.

It is an uncomfortable subject, but perhaps people need to be made uncomfortable.

"So, what is your book about?" people asked at a recent dinner party where I was one of only two African-American people in the room.

"I'm retracing the history of a slave ship. It's about the slave trade," I answered.

A few seemed genuinely interested. But in general, my answer triggered a polite response and a quick disappearing act. Some looked at their watches and excused themselves, while others made it clear through body language they didn't care to talk about it.

Clinton cannot force white America to acknowledge one of the world's most graphic illustrations of man's inhumanity to man, but he can argue from his White House perch that this country should confront the legacy of slavery and racial injustice today.

ΰΰ

Slavery is not an ancient, abstract topic for history classes. It permeates our lives and conversations to this day. I asked several Americans, black and white, to talk about race. Listen to their voices:

Michael Eric Dyson, author and professor of African-American history at Columbia University, said there are lessons to be learned from the relationships forged between the black divers and the white divers who originally worked the underwater site of the *Henrietta Marie*.

"The brilliance of white and black divers exploring, going down literally into the depths and retrieving those things that have been lost to us, is that it shows that American history was made in black and white.

"The beauty of the black and white divers going down excavating this slave ship and using these resources together acknowledges that we made this country together. That, in other words, it's not simply made by white folk; it's made by the contributions of black folk, too," Dyson said.

"It unites America, too, because America can never be what it needs to be without acknowledging its debt and its responsibility to African-American people."

Dr. Madeleine Burnside is trying to come to grips with the past—and the present. As the executive director of the Mel Fisher Maritime Heritage Society and the person who facilitated the first exhibit—and the national exhibition—of the *Henrietta Marie* artifacts, Burnside has probably spent more time fielding questions—and criticism—than anyone else associated with the slave ship.

Burnside is British, born in London, a white woman spending more time learning about the slave trade and talking about race with black people than she ever imagined.

"It is a part of our history that has not been open for discussion because, honestly, nobody wants to go there.

"Some of the conversations are very productive, but it's an extremely complex issue, slavery and race, and some people come to the exhibition with some hostility, which I've tried to understand. It's made me look at the entire issue differently.

"We've had conversations with strangers and acquaintances who said, 'Why are you stirring things up?' or, 'Don't get black folks all riled up.' I was surprised by some of these comments. There are people who do not want to learn or come together.

"But I also believe that race relations have improved. Some of my friends, black and white, say that race relations are getting better, and then other people say we're much more polarized. I actually tell people that if we don't explore the issues of slavery and race, we will never progress."

Throughout the exhibition, Burnside said she was criticized by some African-Americans for paying closer attention to the British perspective in analyzing the slave trade.

She explained that her intent—a courageous one—was to try to expose the mentality of those involved in the slave trade, from the dock-workers who loaded supplies aboard the *Henrietta Marie* to the men who manufactured the shackles—and the people who benefited from the slave trade.

"There were people who made choices, the men who arranged for the pewter, the wives who packed the pewter in crates. Did she know that these crates were going on a slave ship? Where did she think the money to buy new dresses came from? The *Henrietta Marie* has reminded us of how much we don't know about this part of history, how much we need to learn, and how much research there is to do."

Burnside learned about the slave trade at a young age. When she was thirteen years old, she walked past an antique store in Ipswich, on the eastern coast of England, about two hours from London. In the window of the store was a saucer filled with silver coins. She collected coins. She bought the saucer of coins for five shillings.

When she got home and began sifting through the saucer, she noticed that one of the coins—the one the size of a U.S. fifty-cent piece and pierced with a small hole to be worn around the neck—was very unusual. On one side, there was a man in chains with a message: "Am I Not a Man and a Brother?" On the flip side, there were two hands shaking, a black hand and a white hand. The message: "May Slavery and Oppression Cease Throughout the World."

The coin was made in England in the 1780s, and people passed it around as currency to get mixed with change in cash registers throughout England. It was designed by abolitionists to call attention to the anti-slavery movement.

"The coin and many others like it were passed along as change each day. The thinking was that if you saw this coin, you might think of a slave ship and slavery and might want join the fight against the slave trade. It was a cosmic thing, I suppose. That coin was my first introduction to the slave trade and I've always wanted to learn more. I still have the coin. I pull it out to look at it every now and then.

"The *Henrietta Marie* has been a vehicle for people both black and white to explore a very complex issue, but what's important is that people are beginning to talk to one another, even if we're only starting to scratch the surface."

I have worked with Madeleine Burnside and David Moore for several years. When we first met, there were perhaps some reservations, and today, there may still be those within the Mel Fisher Maritime Heritage Society and the National Association of Black Scuba Divers who are reluctant to discuss their true feelings about race and who are also unwilling to trust one another.

But the truth is that the *Henrietta Marie,* for most of us, has become an extraordinary experiment in race relations.

We are collectively dealing with one of the most emotional issues imaginable, a subject that sparks the most visceral reactions, and yet through an unconventional partnership, we have worked above and below the ocean to piece together a wrenching puzzle from the past.

We still do not agree on every issue, nor do we have to, but what we are doing is taking a first step—black and white divers learning about a sunken slave ship together.

"For me, placing the plaque underwater with the African-American divers was kind of strange. On one hand, I felt a part of it because I was the principle investigator of the *Henrietta Marie* and the one who brought the knowledge of the ship to the NABS group during their '91 symposium in Fort Lauderdale," Moore said.

"On the other hand, I felt apart from the overall ceremony because I am white. I am not of African-American descent. No matter how much studying or how much research I do, I have not lived that experience," he said.

"These African-American divers are descendants of the people who were brought over here on the *Henrietta Marie*. They are physical remnants, if you will, of the slave trade—of the African diaspora. Even though I was feeling things emotionally about what the site signifies, it could never mean to me what it means to anyone of African descent.

"But through this project, I have met people in the African-American community whom I would ordinarily not have met, and have become close friends with them. I'm really appreciative of that," Moore said.

"Hopefully, the *Henrietta Marie* will serve a much greater purpose than any of us ever realized was possible. And perhaps it will foster a more constructive dialogue between the races."

Cheryl LaRoche, a New York–based archaeologist who has done extensive research on the trade beads found on the site of the *Henrietta Marie* as well as studied the African Burial Ground in Manhattan, says the legacy of the *Henrietta Marie* is one of survival.

"For years, we have been told that African-Americans don't have a past," LaRoche said. "And even though we have been taught that the Middle Passage severed our links, the *Henrietta Marie* provides us with a rare opportunity to connect the dots. And in fact, the line was never severed. I now see African-Americans reconnecting these dots and filling in the holes that slavery and the Middle Passage have left in our history."

LaRoche, who is black, has worked closely with Burnside and Moore and says both were open and receptive to different ideas.

But she acknowledged that "it's very hard for European-Americans who have been grounded in the Western sort of scholarly perspective to break out of their Western views. I think Madeleine understands this and the exhibit reflects that—that it's difficult for people to move away from their own Eurocentric bias to analyze something like the *Henrietta Marie*."

The issue of slavery, says Cornel West, author and professor of African-American studies at Harvard University, is inseparable from the conditions of African-American people in America today.

"There is no doubt in my mind that anytime you raise the issue of African slavery in America you open Pandora's box, because it forces each and every one of us to explore the wilderness inside of us, the conscious and unconscious that has been so deeply shaped by white supremacy.

"It also forces us to come to grips with our history. It's very painful to do that. It's discomforting to do that. But there's no other way to come to terms with that history than to go through the pain and discomfort and to talk about the enslavement of Africans, which is why many people don't want to talk about it.

"To talk about slavery in addition to genocidal attacks on indigenous peoples is to talk about the two problems of evil that sit at the very heart and core of American civilization.

"History is about blood, sweat, and tears. It's about scars, and bruises and wounds. And to talk about genocidal attacks on indigenous peoples on the one hand and to talk about slavery on the other is to talk about these two foundations that are, in part, a series of scars, and bruises, and wounds.

"When we look back on slavery, we should not see people of African descent solely as victims. Because in many ways, the story of people of African descent, in the New World, given the tremendous hatred that has been directed our way, has been a triumph of the human spirit.

"In that sense, black folk are really not supposed to be here, given what has been coming at black folk.

"But we have, somehow, been able to look the situation in the face, given all of the sadness, and sorrow, and suffering, and still not allow that sadness and sorrow and suffering to have the last word, even if all we could do at the moment was sing a song, or crack a smile, or say a prayer, or preach a sermon. Or just be silent.

"That's what America, for the most part, has not yet come to terms with. That's why we don't have a national monument to the transatlantic slave trade and the institution of slavery, because America still is in a certain state of denial, even as, thank God, we are a bit more willing to talk about it now than we were ten, twenty, thirty years ago.

"The dialogue about the legacy of slavery and its relations to democracy has to proceed on every level. It has to be among everyday folk in their collective settings, right across the board.

"In the end, we go up together or down together. There is a certain sense in which the American experiment is on the *Henrietta Marie*. All Americans in a certain sense, their destiny, were there. And that's what people don't want to come to terms with. Our white brothers and sisters in vanilla suburbs talk about how these issues exclude them, but they aren't excluded. We're stuck together and the challenge everyone's.

"We have to take seriously those folks on that ship who tried to keep their eyes on the prize during very dark and difficult moments," West says.

"The legacy of slavery ought to serve as a springboard or launching pad for accenting the triumph of the human spirit and the ways in which decency and dignity and grace can be preserved even under the most adverse circumstances."

Several hundred miles away, in a living room where the walls are covered with the works of prominent black artists and the shelves are stuffed with books by distinguished writers, John Hope Franklin crossed his lanky legs and weighed in with insight and passion.

"The important point about the institution of slavery is that so many people today are saying, 'Don't blame me for slavery; I didn't do it.' Well, they might not have done it, but they benefited from it, and their families benefited from it, and I'm not going to let them off the hook because they were born in 1900 or 1950, because their families held slaves and they set up the institution to make it possible for whites to enjoy a lifestyle that black people did not enjoy.

"Constructively, we have learned that black people were surely among the most significant forces in the economic development of the country. The forests would not have been cleared; the fields would not have been plowed; the crops would not have been harvested. Africans taught whites about agriculture and they brought with them their literary and cultural experiences and their artistic expertise."

In the quiet of the North Carolina evening, Franklin shared vivid memories of the racism he encountered forty years ago as if it were yesterday.

It was in 1957, and Franklin had made front-page news by becoming chairman of the fifty-two-man all-white history department at Brooklyn College. He was also trying to buy a house near the college.

"I simply wanted to walk to work," he said.

The next few months were agonizing, as he and his wife, Aurelia, were refused by dozens of real estate agents who told them houses they liked were spoken for.

They finally got to see one, he said. "Do you know, the entire block was waiting outside the house to see us, a black couple, walk out. There were people everywhere."

Franklin decided to look only at homes for sale by the owner. They found something they liked on New York Avenue.

"I rang the doorbell and the owner came to the door and said, 'Did you just call a few minutes ago?' I said yes. He closed the door, went to the kitchen, and drank a drink down and then came back and let me in."

The owner agreed to sell them the house, but it took a lawyer's intervention to get a mortgage. That done, the Franklins' new white neighbors went to war.

"When we moved in, my next-door neighbor would not move his car so the van with the furniture could move into the driveway. We had to unload the furniture from the middle of the street. Two weeks later, my son was riding his bicycle. They taunted him, trying to make him fall off the bicycle. That's when my wife decided it wasn't worth it. We paid a high cost."

Today, eighty-three years old, the professor emeritus at Duke University, whose *From Slavery to Freedom* has sold 3 million copies in five languages and remains the definitive text on the African-American experience fifty years after it was published, insists that African-Americans are still paying a high cost.

More than a year has passed since Franklin was appointed by President Clinton to head a seven-member White House advisory board to the President's Initiative on Race, convened to explore race relations for one year and lead an "honest dialogue" on the issue.

Franklin knows it's a difficult assignment, but he accepted the appointment because he believes Clinton truly wants to put the issue at the top of his domestic agenda and believes that cultural and ethnic differences can be resolved through honest discussion.

"This is not an organization that is out there in the bushes trying to create a new Eden," said Franklin, a man who speaks firmly about race, yet without raising his voice.

"We are trying to tell the president some things we think he can do to improve the conditions of people in this country as they relate to one another. We hope to acquaint ourselves with some assessments of race relations: How much discrimination is there in colleges? How much discrimination is there in the workplace? What is the relationship between hate crimes and racial problems?...But this is a historical piece; you can't get around it."

Born on January 2, 1915, in the all-black town of Rentiesville, Oklahoma, Franklin was the grandson of an escaped slave; his father was a lawyer and his mother a teacher.

His father's law office and the family's future home were torched during the 1921 riots in Tulsa, which claimed more than one hundred black lives. Once, Franklin helped a blind woman across the street. When she asked his race and he answered honestly, the woman pulled away and told him to take his black hands off her arm. He was twelve years old.

Today, this man who knew W. E. B. Du Bois and who enjoys a close relationship with President Clinton sits near the paintings of Henry O. Tanner, Romare Bearden, and Jacob Lawrence and says he still encounterers discrimination often.

"There are people who are living discrimination every day, living humiliation every day. White women ask me to hang up their coats; they think I'm a servant. Or a man sees me in a hotel lobby and says, 'Here, boy, go and get my car.' In New York, a woman said, 'Here, take this trash and throw it away.' I told her to throw it away herself....Everything is not all right.

"One woman sent me a letter saying that blacks should express gratitude for being taken out of savage Africa. She said her people came here in 1906 from Europe. I wrote her back telling her that by the time her people got here, we had already been dragged over here, had cleared the fields, harvested the crops, and helped to build the cities so her people could step off the boat without getting their feet wet."

Only time will determine whether Franklin's panel will be successful in creating the kind of national discussion that can ease racial tension. But Franklin is clear that it's worth the struggle.

"One day, my doorbell rang," Franklin said. "A white man was at the door; he asked to come in. I invited him in and he sat down. He said, 'I wish you well in what you're doing. This is the most important thing you could be doing, because you don't know how many white bigots there are.... We're not going to have peace in this country until we do something about these bigots,' he told me. That man was telling the truth."

Franklin believes Americans cannot begin to address issues of race adequately unless we approach them from a historical perspective. "People don't understand that the first step toward improving ourselves is knowing our past," he said.

Randall Robinson, a longtime activist for social justice and outspoken advocate on issues pertaining to Africa and United States policy, is also the author of *Defending the Spirit*. Trans-Africa was founded by Robinson in 1977.

For years Robinson has traveled extensively throughout Africa, has met with world leaders, and has helped influence United States policies toward Africa at the White House level. He has been credited with bringing apartheid in South Africa to the forefront of America's political consciousness and directed the movement that ultimately resulted in Nelson Mandela's release from prison.

"I have never distinguished myself from Africa or the Caribbean; when I see them, I see myself," Robinson said. "And so, I never divide the black world in pieces. We're all the same people as far as I'm concerned, and that's not an academic application, it's how I feel.

"From my earliest childhood in Richmond, black people were never indifferent to Africa; some of us may run away from it, some of us feel tortured, but not indifferent. We either aggressively want to associate with it, or disassociate from it, but it's there, it's part of us, and it's not to be ignored.

"One of the great disabilities that our communities suffer unlike any in the world, is having our lines to our ancient history and accomplishments obliterated, blocked, and totally obscured," Robinson said.

"People read history and build monuments and memorials for very good reasons—because people have a need to be extended from antiquity, extended from accomplishment and collective prestigious endeavors, hence all of the courses in college you are saddled with about Western civilization, the Roman Empire, and so on; white America teaches this to themselves because that makes them feel tall and important and powerful and ancient and old and significant. We don't have a sense of any history before the slave trade," he said.

Robinson feels very strongly about the link between the past and the present. "We think our history starts with slavery in this country; we can't see the distant past, and it has stunted us as a people in the way we see ourselves. And I know the value to Africa, because we had a glorious past.

"When you think there's no memorial on the Mall to slaves; we are this country's holocaust victims; we are so traumatized by our own victimization that we don't think enough of ourselves to call attention to it," Robinson said.

"We've got a Holocaust memorial but the Holocaust did not occur in the United States but slavery did, and there's no memorial to that. That says a lot about what afflicts us and the way we see ourselves, and most of us think they don't know our history because they think we don't have one. We think we don't have one.

"…Something very bad happened and it was slavery, and we're still paying for it, but to survive it we have to know we are not the problem, that we have accomplished and wonderfully."

Michael Eric Dyson sees more evidence of constructive discussions about race—until the topic of slavery is broached.

"We are addicted to amnesia," Dyson says. "It's true. As Barbra Streisand said in her song, 'What's too painful to remember, we simply choose to forget.'

"And the reason we need to talk about slavery right now is, first of all, we've never healed from that open wound. We've had a lot of salve, a lot of balm, we've had a lot of attempts to put Band-Aids on, but we've never had a kind of cleansing of the wound in our own history.

"And slavery is important for a number of reasons. Slavery is central to documenting and defining what we even mean by freedom. We have no conception of freedom in Western society without understanding what slave culture was all about.

"American identity is so intertwined with the notion of who black folk are that we have never owned up to the contributions that black folks have made to American society. And as a result of that, we are ashamed of this. Many African-American people themselves are ashamed of slavery.

"What should we do with it? Unless we come to grips with slavery, we're not going to come to grips with American identity. And finally, I think, it's important to talk about slavery right now because many of the particular problems, many of the possibilities of black life, indeed American life, are tied up with understanding how we were shaped in the tragic crucible called slavery—that is, black folks' identities, patterns, habits, dispositions, behavior. And not only the so-called pathological but the good stuff. The very important accent on family. That despite the fact that we were outlawed from reading, we read. And yet when we look at our literacy rates now, we know that part of the tragedy comes from having a culture that discouraged us from reading.

"If America is to ever come to grips with the brutality and the hideous nature of that black holocaust, of the suffering they imposed on black people, the only thing a conscientious American could say who's white is, 'Why haven't these people tried to destroy this country, undermine it?' Unlike the Tim McVeighs of the world, who have had all the privileges, relatively speaking," Dyson said.

"African-American people who have been so despised in this country have worked to build it up," he said. "If whites would come to understand that, they would not only appreciate the ingenuity of black survival; they would appreciate the love that black people really have for a country that treated them like stepchildren."

ʊʊ

We have come a long way, blacks and whites. Perhaps what we need is a vehicle, some type of thought-provoking mechanism to bring us to the table to discuss race.

For the black and white divers who explored the *Henrietta Marie* together, for the members of the Mel Fisher Maritime Heritage Society and the National Association of Black Scuba Divers, for the countless number of African-American and white people who have participated in lectures during the *Henrietta Marie* exhibit across this country, that vehicle for cultural understanding has been a sunken slave ship.

Perhaps we will find more mediums like the *Henrietta Marie* to inspire us to better examine the issues that confront us as a people.

Donna Britt, my dear friend, the woman who introduced me to my wife, Mireille, and a columnist with the *Washington Post,* has written extensively, passionately, and wisely about race for several years.

Donna is perhaps the most optimistic person I know when it comes to issues of race relations. She has an honest, refreshing view of multicultural America and believes there are more issues that unite us than divide us. She believes, for example, that most people are basically well intentioned and that if we had an opportunity to communicate, we would have a more peaceful coexistence.

She has friends who are white and black, and, as she explains, this should be the rule, not the exception: people of all ethnic backgrounds communicating, exchanging ideas, sharing thoughts, socializing.

Still, she is well aware of racism and bigotry.

"I vacillate between optimism and being overwhelmed by my desire to move to another planet altogether. It depends on what you encounter at any given moment or on any given day," Britt said.

"I live and work in a wonderful environment, around many clear-thinking and progressive white people, who not only have thought through issues about race but who on a personal level work to confront and help change things.

"So when you have good friends who are sincerely seeking betterment for relationships between black folks and white folks, to be a total pessimist would be a lie; to be a total pessimist would be to ignore how far we have come; to be a total pessimist would be to ignore the sacrifices and the creativity of black people and white people who helped get us to where we are today.

"One of the most incredible examples is in my own house," Britt said. "People who are African-American, white, Jewish, and Dominican, people from all over the globe, are friends of my children and friends of mine.

"My husband and I are just as likely to be invited to dinner by white friends as we are by black friends," she said. "And I hesitate to say that, because it could sound to some as though I'm not down with the brothers and sisters, but the truth is that our pessimism is turning into a cynicism that could negate the very bridge building that we seek and that ultimately we need for this society to survive.

"Pessimism runs counter to my sense of spirituality and everything that I believe in," Britt added. "So I have to be optimistic about people's potential for good."

∪∪

I used to do a television show in New York called *Flashpoint*. Along with interviews with guests, it featured verbal sparring between me and my cohost, Eric Briendel, an ultraconservative yet brilliant debater and gifted writer who died of cancer in April 1998.

Our guest for one segment in 1995 was former mayor Ed Koch. When the session was over, we chatted about our various projects. When the conversation turned to this book, Koch—a flamboyant man never at a loss for words—was stunned.

Koch couldn't imagine that a story about black scuba divers, underwater explorers examining the remains of a slave ship, could be real. He couldn't imagine that black people were actually instrumental in bringing an archaeological and historical phenomenon to light. He couldn't imagine that black divers were involved in a scientific endeavor beneath the sea.

This man who had run a city of more than 7 million—more than half of them people of color with roots in every part of the world imaginable, with vibrant histories and monumental accomplishments—turned to me and exclaimed, "Wow, what great fiction! How did you ever come up with an idea to create a story about black scuba divers?"

My response was simple. "I lived it, Mr. Koch."

20

Three years after we placed our monument in the sea, after following forks in the road across three continents, after interviewing
dozens of people and poring over hundreds of documents, I
returned to the site of the *Henrietta Marie.*

There were five of us this time—my dive buddy, Hank Jennings; my
archaeologist friends and research partners David Moore and Corey Malcolm; boat captain Cristian Swanson; and myself.

I remember taking staggered steps across the wooden deck of the
forty-two-foot *Rattle and Hum,* the narrow walkway testing my equilib-
rium each time the vessel shifted with the sea. I made my way to the outer
deck and pulled up a chair.

It is so peaceful on the ocean at night. I heard the waves slapping gently against the side of the boat and I watched the assortment of busy
marine creatures dart about beneath me as I shined my flashlight into the
ocean.

Under a black sky sprinkled with tiny specks of light, I could see the
flickering lamps from shrimp boats in the distance; the closest was ten
miles away. I had been on the road on one project or another for those
three years. I'd been searching for artifacts and documentation of a slave
ship.

I'd been traveling with Dr. Jones to Central America to dive remote parts of Belize. I'd dived deep walls in Grand Cayman, raced the currents in Cozumel, held a baby octopus in the palm of my hand in Curaçao. I'd videotaped our shark dives in the Bahamas and led divers to a 327-foot wreck 120 feet off Key Largo.

I had dived the Sunken City in Port Royal, Jamaica, where rubble and cobblestone streets still remain from an earthquake in the late 1600s; dived off the coast of Africa—Senegal and Goree Island, where enslaved people drowned; plunged into Carlisle Bay in Barbados, where the *Henrietta Marie* anchored; descended into the chilly waters in St. Tropez, France; and completed book tours for *The Million Man March* and *The Family of Black America*.

Out on the sea, the hazy glow of Cuba hung over the Gulf of Mexico like an early-morning fog. Cuba was sixty miles away; Key West thirty-four miles; New Jersey two thousand miles. I was a long way from home. Yet home was closer to me than ever.

Just days earlier, my wife, Mireille, had walked into our living room with her hand over her mouth, her eyes wide, waving a plastic strip with two solid blue lines in the middle of a tiny square window.

"I'm pregnant," she said, laughing uncontrollably.

"I'm pregnant!"

I had given up on parenthood—we had both been so busy and so consumed with professional growth.

We had been concerned about our age, had sat around in the evenings and had hard discussions about whether to have children at all—whether a child of ours could be healthy, whether we would have the stamina to raise a child, give it the constant attention a child would require, or whether it would be selfish not to share our good fortunes with a child.

All the while, time had passed quickly. We had shared the joy of friends and family who'd had babies; they shared the assumption that Mireille and I would probably adopt another cat.

I jumped up from the couch and hugged her tightly. All at once, I was overjoyed, even giddy—and completely terrified.

"I'm going to be a father?" I asked myself repeatedly. "Me? An only child? Me? A man who once thought Huggies was a sitcom?"

I knew the satisfaction of freedom; my dive gear was always packed and the phone ringing with offers of investigating shipwrecks and deep waters waiting to be explored.

And then, there I was, at sea—drifting in the middle of nowhere and yet more rooted than ever. I sat on the deck of the *Rattle and Hum* and took in a deep breath of salty sea air, a lungful of fatherhood. Forty years old and all grown up.

David, Corey, and I had talked for months of returning to the site of the *Henrietta Marie*. After recovering more than seven thousand artifacts from the only slave ship so far scientifically documented and identified by name, there is still so much to learn; there are still so many questions that remain unanswered, still so my more artifacts to be uncovered.

We wanted to identify and explore the precise area where her splintered hull remains buried under six inches of sand on the ocean floor.

I was to learn it was fitting that we made the trip aboard the *Rattle and Hum*. We asked Cristian about his boat one night, late, when the telling of good stories at sea replaces television and radio.

It turns out she has quite a history herself. The *Rattle and Hum* was custom-built for Jimmy Hoffa in 1959. The boat was originally christened the *Jersey Devil* during his labor years. A fishing-club patch worn by the vanished leader of the Teamsters hangs on a wall on her port side.

"No telling who else boarded it," Cristian told us.

Best of all, the dive platform on the *Rattle and Hum* once belonged to one of the boats used in *Sea Hunt*—from the very same underwater adventure series that had so captured my childhood imagination.

We had filled up the boat—four hundred dollars' worth of premium fuel—and pulled away from the dock at 12:35 P.M. on a wind-whipped October 2, 1996, after four days in town waiting out bad weather—twenty-mile-per-hour winds on the far fringes of Hurricane Isadore.

Weathered seamen, knowing waiters, and the guy who filled our tanks and sold me ice looked at us cross-eyed when they learned we were heading out.

"We'll give it a shot," Cristian said, pulling his cap over his blond locks and looking toward the increasingly gray skies. "We may have to turn right back around and go back home."

I climbed up to the pilothouse, where Cristian was reprogramming the global positioning satellite, our only means of locating the *Henrietta Marie*.

"I've got to get this thing working," he said. "I need about twenty minutes. You ever steered a boat?"

"Not lately," I said.

"Keep your eyes on the compass heading. Stay the course."

The compass read 270 degrees northwest. Looking around at miles of empty ocean and knowing there wasn't a chance in hell of running into anything, I confidently took the wheel—and watched the compass spin wildly.

"Try not to run the boat aground!" Hank shouted from below.

After a quick 360-degree turn, I set my sights on a cloud directly ahead. I followed that cloud for nearly twenty-five minutes; the compass stayed on 270. Cristian reappeared with the GPS in hand, working perfectly.

Three and a half hours later, we anchored on New Ground Reef within one hundred feet of the monument we had set in 1993. After thirty minutes in the water, Cristian yelled out, "I found it."

We all plunged into the ocean and followed Cristian to the ocean floor, where the concrete monument with its bronze inscription was resting right where we'd left it.

What an amazing sight, this symbol of camaraderie, strength, and history that sat on the seabed.

I swam around the memorial, touching it gently. And in the comfort of the sea, I was reminded of why I had started scuba diving in the first place, recalling the words of fellow diver Terry Sneed.

"Diving—and the ocean—is therapeutic; it's good for the body, the mind, and the soul," she said.

Lowaunz V. Koger, a good friend and a member of the National Association of Black Scuba Divers since 1994, was philosophical and spiritual when talking about her experiences beneath the sea.

"Diving is visceral," she said. "When I'm underwater, I'm viewing Planet Earth from the inside out. Water, being the strongest element on earth, empowers me. I feel the strength of the elements within me each time I'm underwater.

"It makes me feel complete and whole," she explained. "It gives me confidence and courage even after I leave the ocean, and it gives me balance and strength through life."

EPILOGUE

"Why do I scuba dive?"

After logging nearly three hundred dives from Florida to France, I still take a moment to ponder the question each time someone inquires about my most profound passion—exploring the obscure and ever-shifting world beneath the sea.

But it is perhaps best answered mathematically: Three-fourths of the earth is covered by water. Why should we limit our physical and intellectual exploration of this planet to land?

I dive for many of the same reasons that astronauts travel through space in search of new worlds, or why archaeologists dig deep into the earth hoping to uncover ancient treasures.

I dive to experience the phenomenal and peculiar pleasures of the underwater wilderness; to expand my knowledge of the sea and all of God's wondrous creatures; to embrace life with an unrestricted passion.

I dive to quench my perpetual thirst for adventure; to float into a free fall of absolute freedom; to be challenged by nature; to be dwarfed by its magnificence.

I dive to step away from the security of my home and plunge into the sanctity of an unpredictable underwater world that has been waiting for me all of my life. And when I ascend, I am humbled by the sea's vast fluid power, which can caress or crush me in the time it takes to draw a manufactured breath of precious air.

This is a world that I can experience for only about forty minutes at a time, but a wonderful world that belongs only to me. I am wrapped in the mesmerizing silence. I am wrapped in nature's glorious cocoon. I am wrapped in a crescendo of life.

Why do I scuba dive?

Because the oceans, and all they have to offer, are the last great undiscovered places on this planet.

ᴝᴝ

Nightfall was coming fast and it looked like a storm might not be far behind. Cristian piloted us to a sheltered area in the tiny uninhabited Marquesas, where Hank killed the time playing CDs, introducing Corey to reggae and Latin music, dancing Latin-style, mocking the macarena, and scratching the three-day stubble on his usually bald head.

At 9:00 A.M., October 3, 1996, sore from a night of being tossed around on a slender bunk by the rocking boat, I had a quick breakfast of bananas and muffins and we slipped back into the sea.

We were searching for a box—the iron box we believed was used to carry a load of ivory elephant tusks aboard the *Henrietta Marie*. If we found it, we would know that the structure of the doomed slave ship lay all around us. The box had been located by divers before but had been lost for years.

The water was calm and clear and Hurricane Isadore was no longer a threat.

A rickety raft was floating just a few feet away from where we were drifting on the surface. It was a floating artifact from another horrible crossing, a precarious passage made by choice.

For months, people had been fleeing Cuba by the hundreds. They were leaving the island at night and sailing the Florida Straits with nothing but rusty handheld military compasses and the stars to navigate the ninety miles to Key West, the closest point of the United States.

Families, some with tiny babies, packed themselves onto flimsy rafts of chipped plywood and old tires, bedsheets fashioned into sails. Some of the rafts that floated empty in the ocean were cluttered with soda cans and diapers.

We radioed the Coast Guard, but we never learned whether the people who had sailed in this particular raft had already been rescued or were lost at sea. I could only hope they were safe as I swam toward the raft to get a closer look.

I was reminded of the millions of African families that were separated by slavery, separated by the sea, as I thought of the Cuban families who perished during their crossing, their dreams of freedom ending in the dark Gulf of Mexico, and their lives, too, separated by the sea.

Minutes later, Corey was pointing furiously to a rectangular object covered with algae and tall strands of grass. I couldn't see it at first.

"This is it! This is the box!"

It was a wonderful discovery—a significant artifact located from the *Henrietta Marie.*

There it was—some thirty-six feet long, thirty-eight inches wide, and thirty-six inches deep.

As I descended over the box, I could tell that the *Henrietta Marie* was buried all around me. I remembered prior dives on the site, how I had unearthed soggy planks of the *Henrietta Marie*'s wood from three inches under the sand, and how splinters from her savaged hull had filled my hands.

For three years, this slave ship—this horrible, precious piece of my history—had nagged at me, haunted me, even pricked me under the sea.

She did so, I believe, to remind me to be uplifted, not discouraged, energized, not angry, that I am part of a long line of proud and distinguished African people who survived and overcame a history of brutal oppression.

She pricked at my consciousness so I would remember to tell America, and the world, that it needs an education about the African holocaust to understand fully the racial hostility of today; to say that if there is no attempt to understand this most underreported piece of world history, then we are doomed, never to live in peace.

Everyone needs a special place, a place of peace—a room in a home, a cabin in the hills, a bench in the park, a sanctuary from pressures and problems, somewhere to reflect, to bury the past or plan for the future, a place to confront troubles or conduct a private celebration, to pray, to cry.

For the past three years, this place for me, my place of peace, has been thirty feet underwater on the site of a sunken slave ship. I know with certainty that New Ground Reef is a spiritual site for me; an underwater refuge of hidden wisdom that shapes my consciousness and soothes my soul; a place where I am never really alone.

On the site of the *Henrietta Marie,* I reaffirmed that the anchor in my life is family. Under the mighty waters of a vast ocean, I comforted the souls of my ancestors, said good-bye to the past, and prepared to greet the future, my yet-to-be-born daughter, who will join the next generation of African-American people, a new wave of young black men and women who will follow their own paths.

I hovered over the sands in which a force greater than any of us had safeguarded the shackles of slaves until they could be placed into Moe Molinar's hands, until black divers could come and pay tribute and a black writer could tell the story, knowing that answers to all of life's questions would not be revealed on that day.

And yet I somehow knew, the knowledge as faint and as clear as the rainbow arched over the *Rattle and Hum* and across the sky above me, that this was not the end of my journey, but, perhaps, just the beginning.

BIBLIOGRAPHY

Adams, Russell P. *The World of the Henrietta Marie: Trading Routes and the Middle Passage* (unpublished manuscript). Washington, D.C.: Research from Howard University, 1994.

Bureau of Historic Sites and Properties, Division of Archives, History and Records Management, Department of State, Record of (Log) Daily Activities, 1972–73.

Burnside, Madeleine. *Society Sense and Sensibility: The Ethical Context of Chattel Slavery in 1700* (unpublished manuscript). Key West: Research conducted for the Mel Fisher Maritime Heritage Society, 1994.

Burnside, Madeleine and Rosemary Robotham. *Spirits of the Passage: The Transatlantic Slave Trade in the Seventeenth Century.* New York: Simon & Schuster, Inc., 1995.

Campbell, P.F., "The Merchants and Traders of Barbados," *The Journal of the Barbados Museum and Historical Society/Records of the Vestry of St. Michael,* 1699–1700.

Connell, Neville, "Father Labat's Visit to Barbados in 1700," *The Journal of the Barbados Museum and Historical Society* 24, no. 4 (1957).

Crossley, David and Richard Saville, "The Fuller Letters: Guns, Slaves and Finance 1728–1755," Sussex Record Society, 76 (1991).

Dow, George Francis. *Slave Ships and Slaving.* Cambridge: Cornell Maritime Press, 1968.

Dunn, Richard S., "The Barbados Census of 1680: Profile of the Richest Colony in English America," *William and Mary College Quarterly Historical Magazine,* 26, no. 3 (1969).

Edwards, Paul, ed. *Life of Olaudah Equiano, or Gustavus Vassa the African.* New York: Addison-Wesley, 1990.

Forde, Daryll, ed. *Efik Traders of Old Calabar*. London: Oxford University Press, 1958.

Franklin, John Hope. *From Slavery to Freedom: A History of African-Americans*. New York: McGraw-Hill, 1994.

Hair, P.E.H., Adam Jones, and Robin Law. *Barbot on Guinea*. London: The Hakluyt Society, 1992.

Handler, Jerome S., "The Amerindian Slave Populations of Barbados in the Seventeeth and Early Eighteenth Centuries," *The Journal of the Barbados Museum and Historical Society* (1970).

Hennessy, James Pope. *Sins of the Fathers—How Curiosity Became Geometry: A Study of the Atlantic Slave Traders, 1441–1807*. London: Weidenfeld & Nicholson, 1967.

Konstram, Angus. *The Armament of the Henrietta Marie* (unpublished manuscript). London: Curator of Weapons, Royal Armouries, Tower of London.

Mel Fisher Maritime Heritage Society. *A Slave Ship Speaks: The Wreck of the Henrietta Marie*. Key West: The Mel Fisher Maritime Heritage Society, 1995.

Moore, David D. *The Henrietta Marie: Vehicle of the African Slave Trade* (unpublished manuscript). North Carolina Maritime Museum, 1994.

Ndiaye, Joseph. *The Slave House of Goree Island* (unpublished manuscript).

Northrup, David. *Trade Without Rulers: Pre-Colonial Economic Development in South-eastern Nigeria*. Oxford: Clarendon Press, 1978.

Radick, Jerry and Rose-Mary. *See the Sea: Adventure Log*, 1987.

Rawley, James A. *The Transatlantic Slave Trade: A History*. New York: W. W. Norton & Company, 1981.

Reynolds, Edward. *Stand the Storm: A History of the Atlantic Slave Trade*. Allison & Busby, 1989.

Tattersfield, Nigel. *Account of the Slave Ship Henrietta Marie of London: 1697–1700* (unpublished manuscript). Key West: Research conducted for the Mel Fisher Maritime Heritage Society, 1994.

Thornton, John. *Africa and the Africans in the Making of the Atlantic World, 1400–1680*. New York: Cambridge University Press, 1992.

Thornton, John. *African Background of the Slave Cargo of the Henrietta Marie* (unpublished manuscript). Millersville: Research from the Millersville University of Pennsylvania, 1994.

Wilder, Rachel, ed. *Insight Guides Barbados*. New York: Houghton Mifflin, 1994.

Zach, Paul, ed. *Insight Guides Jamaica*. New York: Houghton Mifflin. 1995.

INDEX

Photo Credits

Courtesy of the Mel Fisher Maritime Heritage Society: "Moe Molinar in 1972"; "The author's hands in shackles"; "The memorial service where the monument was lowered into the sea"; "Oswald Sykes and Michael Cottman cleaning the monument"; "The plaque"; "A diver looking at the hull structure of the *Henrietta Marie*"; "The bell from the *Henrietta Marie*, the most significant artifact recovered"; "Glass beads used by Europeans to trade for African people"; "Michael gazes at shackles used on adults and children"; "Part of the nearly one hundred pairs of shackles recovered from the wreck of the *Henrietta Marie*"; "The *Henrietta Marie* interior view of slave storage."

Courtesy of David Moore and the Mel Fisher Maritime Heritage Society: "The *Henrietta Marie* archaeological site plan—south sector"; "The *Henrietta Marie:* A Reconstruction by David Moore."

Courtesy of Josanne Lopez: "Preparing for a dive off Goree Island in West Africa"; "Michael diving near the Door of No Return"; "Diving off the coast of Dakar"; "Working on the book in the United Kingdom"; "Michael and Mr. Joseph Ndiaye in the Door of No Return"; "The Slave House on Goree Island"; "Looking out to sea"; "The author in what was once a holding area for slaves"; "Michael at the Door of No Return with Joseph Ndiaye"; "David and Michael, Bog Walk, Jamaica"; "The opening of the *Henrietta Marie* exhibit in Key West with Oswald Sykes"; "On the last trip to the *Henrietta Marie*, the day they located the box that had held the elephant tusks: Hank J., David M., and Corey Malcolm with the author."

Courtesy of Stuart Cove/Dive South Ocean: "Michael Cottman in the Bahamas."

Courtesy of Sam Saunders: "Returning from a dive in Belize"; "Michael Cottman in Belize."

Courtesy of Haidar Ali, Oceanarium: "A hole in Coral Wall, Goree"; "Underwater at Goree."

Courtesy of Jose Jones: "Shirley Lee, with Dr. Jones standing to her left"; "Dr. Jose Jones and the original Underwater Adventure Seekers (Association of Black Scuba Divers, late 1950s)."

Courtesy of Michael H. Cottman: "The Door of No Return through one of the cells"; "Front Door, Slave House, Goree Island"; "Inside the Slave House"; "Colin Fuller, a probable descendant of slaves aboard the *Henrietta Marie*"; "Workers on the Tulloch Estate, Bog Walk, Jamaica"; "Members of the Association of Black Scuba Divers heading for the site of the wreck of the *Henrietta Marie*"; "Former president of the Association of Black Scuba Divers, Ric Powell, 'calling the spirits' on the way to the plaque."

Courtesy of Mireille Grangenois: "Michael and his daughter, Ariane, age thirteen months, contemplating the sea."

Courtesy of Schomburg Center, Photographs and Prints Division, Schomburg Center for Research in Black Culture, The New York Public Library, Astor, Lenox and Tilden Foundations: "Slaves stowed on a typical slave ship"; title page photograph: *Harper's Weekly,* June 2, 1860, p. 314, wood engraving entitled "Enslaved Africans on the deck of the bark 'Wildfire,' Key West, April 30, 1860."

Courtesy of Pat Klein: "Moe, Michael, and John on his boat, the *Virgalona*"; front cover photograph.

ABOUT THE AUTHOR

Michael H. Cottman is a political writer at the *Washington Post*. He was part of a Pulitzer prize–winning team in 1992 while at *New York Newsday*. He is the author of *Million Man March* and *The Family of Black America*. He lives with his wife and daughter in Washington, D.C.